BREAKING AND ENTERING

A Manual for the Working Actor
in Film, Stage and TV

From Auditions to Agents to a Career

PHILIP CARLSON

BREAKING AND ENTERING:

A Manual for the Working Actor in Film, Stage and TV

From Auditions, to Agents, to a Career

An OPUS Trade Paperback Original.

Copyright © 2017 by Philip Carlson

FIRST EDITION

OPUS ISBN: 978-1-62316-078-4

Audio and E-Book Editions Also Available.

Book Design by Florence Aliesch

A Division of Subtext, Inc. **A Glenn Young Company**
P.O. 725 Tuxedo Park, New York 10987
PUBLICITY: OPUSBOOKPUBPR@AOL.COM
ALL OTHER ENQUIRIES: GY@OPUSBOOKPUBLISHERS.COM

OPUS is distributed to the trade by the Hal Leonard Publishing Group
Toll Free Sales: 1-800-524-4425 • www.halleonard.com

Printed in the United States of America:
10 9 8 7 6 5 4 3 2 1

To: Irene Morse

For: Leslie

"Acting is a brave and wonderful thing to do."
—Kim Stanley

"It's a bum's life."
—Marlon Brando

CONTENTS

INTRODUCTION

A LEAP OF FAITH:
Philip Seymour Hoffman

I was an actors' manager for ten years and a talent agent for twenty-two. I love actors. I love talent. I believe that anyone who has talent has a place in the profession. This book is an attempt to help that person find that place.

I was the first agent to sign Philip Seymour Hoffman (the mere mention of whose name now makes my heart skip a beat), Billy Crudup, Liev Schreiber, Claire Danes, Adrian Grenier, Kyra Sedgwick, Idris Elba and Paul Giamatti. I have worked with Kathy Bates, Lois Smith, Viola Davis, William H. Macy, and Brian Dennehy. I have learned a thing or two about what works and what does not when it comes to getting your foot in the door, walking through the door and being asked back into the room.

Philip Seymour Hoffman's career is a paradigm for this book not only because it was such an admirable career, and not only because I had a part in it. I know the choices he made along the way. Each generation of actors faces the same obstacles, the same ignorance, the same booby-traps as the previous generation. How Phil dealt with those obstacles is still relevant today. The only element that has changed (aside from the addition of social media to the picture) is that Phil no longer has a career or a life. Phil was the actor of his generation and I feel he would be proud to be used as an object lesson in how to conduct a career.

When he died, he had attained a mid-career zenith. He had certainly established himself as a star and as a dazzling and brilliant actor. I would even say a necessary actor. Every profession needs someone who is the best. The career, if not the life, was pretty much indestructible. That may have been what he was thinking in 2012 when he left his longtime agency for ... his attorney.

Who knows what Phil was thinking? I do not. And if you do, put down this book — you'll be late for your table at Nobu. When you make several million dollars a job, does it continue to be worth 10% to negotiate contracts which no longer contain any surprises? Very possibly – but not to Phil in 2012.

You and I came to be knocked out whenever we went to see him work which is why we will continue to revisit his work, possibly forever. He left us so many treasures to love. Which is what stars are supposed to do.

He was an unlikely leader of the pack. Let's go back to the beginning – when he was coming out of NYU undergrad. He got a job at the Williamstown Theatre Festival's Non-Equity company. He was drinking too much, doing too many drugs but he was filled with ambition. He got a bit of a bad reputation – interrupting performances, bad boy stuff. Back in New York, he cleaned up his act. But how to proceed? Then, as always, he was open to anything. He found himself doing a reading for a few nights at the old Circle Rep Company.

A manager with a client who was not Phil had gone to see her client in that Circle Rep reading. She flipped for Phil. (That happens fairly often – go to see someone, fall in love with someone else. Always accompany friends to auditions, if they ask. You might get noticed.) She called me the next day and told me to go to the reading, which I did, that night. I was bowled over.

I'd never seen anything like him. I couldn't sleep until I called her the next morning. Who knew how many others she had told about this genius? The manager's name was Davien Littlefield and she helped guide Phil throughout his early days and, informally, for all his days. At some point she stopped technically being his manager. She looked for projects for him. She set up a company for him. Back then, she was just trying to get him on the map and she had asked me to come on board. So there we were. We had this extraordinary actor who didn't look especially earth shattering but we knew was.

Phil gave off no clues. He built each character from the first molecule and when he wasn't creating a character, well, he just kind of lay there, waiting. I told him people were having that reaction. He asked me what he should do. I said, you're going to have to give them something. So he figured it out. He gave them the few clues he had. They were almost always enough to get him the job. He got better about how to do it and the roles got better, too. The trick in the beginning was getting him into the room. The trick was convincing the people with the jobs that if they would just see him, they wouldn't be sorry. That took a few more phone calls than usual. It took calling in a few more favors than usual. I like to think that I would do anything for a client and certainly for Phil whose genius I did not doubt, I would have done everything.

What did we do? We sent him to everybody with jobs to give away. Back then, that was casting directors, each of the LORT Theatres in New York (we weren't going to send this guy to Cincinnati. I'm not claiming that we knew the giant we had hold of but we suspected), a few TV talent execs looking for projects, a promising movie exec biding time in New York until a promotion appeared, or a stray senior previously-well-thought of line producer relegated to New York until retirement loomed. There used to be such people in New York and they were willing to meet actors who agents and managers thought were special. The few executives in New York now are far too important to meet a beginning actor. Now it's more like: Go get a *Vanity Fair* cover and then we'll see.

The Vineyard Theatre picked up on Phil and cast him in something called "Food and Shelter" in 1991. During rehearsal, the Artistic Director called me about him. He said, yes, he knew Phil was brilliant but "he is going to have to learn to rein it in." He was just so self-indulgent. Maybe I could speak to him? I said I appreciated the Artistic Director making the call. And I did. I didn't understand why the director wasn't telling Phil to rein it in rather than the Artistic Director telling me to tell Phil but maybe the director had tried to no avail. Maybe he didn't have the skill. Or the courage. Not that Phil reacted poorly to criticism but he was fearless and that could strike fear in someone not completely in charge of his own demons. It feels as if ever since Elia Kazan died, directors are not as willing to bring their actors thorny news. In other words – to direct.

I love that Artistic Director. He was afraid of nothing (even if his director was). He gave Billy Crudup his first job in New York, too. Complaining to me was his job. I mentioned the call to Phil. I tried to underplay it but I figured he should know. I said words to the effect of, "Just don't scare them, Phil." He said something like, "What do they want from me, man? I can't control what comes out." But he heard me. Though it is true that the great ones cannot control what comes out. I had another brilliant and volatile client who was left with so much residual feeling at the end of a performance that he put his fist through his dressing room wall. Twice. I got the bill for the re-plastering both times. (I hope you don't think I paid it.)

Phil also did a bunch of movies in '91 and '92. "Szuler" (notable only for being Phil's first film), "Triple Bogey on a Par Five Hole," "My New Gun," and, naturally, a "Law and Order."

Then he did "Leap of Faith" which was a Schedule F job (he was paid for the run of the picture no matter how often or seldom he worked) where everybody fell in love with him and I can only imagine how much he learned. He had a handful of lines in the original script. He wound up with a very nice part. Next he did "Scent of a Woman" which was another small part that he turned into a complete gem. The business noticed. Still, what do you do with him? Was he a star? Well, hardly.

But maybe, well, maybe keep an eye on him. At this point, he was still five years away from "Boogie Nights" – which did make him a star.

In 1992, he also founded – with his friend John Ortiz – The Labyrinth Theatre Company. Labyrinth's mission was (and remains) to push its members' artistic limits and tell new, more inclusive stories that expand the boundaries of mainstream theatre. (That's from their Mission Statement.) Today, there isn't a young actor in town who doesn't want to be a part of Labyrinth.

In 1993, Phil did the movies, "Joey Breaker," "My Boyfriend's Back," and "Money for Nothing".'

In 1994, he shot "The Getaway," "The Yearling," "When a Man Loves a Woman," and "Nobody's Fool," where he got to pal around with Paul Newman, whom he referred to as "a really cool little old man." Ah, youth.

That year he also did "The Merchant of Venice" at the Goodman Theatre in Chicago directed by Peter Sellars. Phil came back and told me whenever Peter Sellars wanted to cast him in anything, he would drop everything and do it. Whatever it was. And that "Othello" Phil did with Peter Sellars in 2009 came under the heading of anything, if you ask me.

In 1995, he did a short film called "The Fifteen Minute Hamlet." That's all he did. His lazy agent must have taken the year off.

In 1996, he did "Hard Eight" and "Twister." Now "Twister" was another run of picture part with maybe five scripted lines. I was hesitant to even mention it to him. He was beginning to be something of a deal. The business had certainly noticed him. Why should he do this (very good) movie on the off chance that he might wind up with a sizeable role? I asked Davien if she thought Phil would be OK with the part which, on the page, was barely there. I didn't want to him to think I didn't know how great he was and that he was destined for greater things. It's just that, at the moment, this was all there was. Davien, with the assurance of a manager who knows her client trusts her, said, "What else is he doing?" Phil, of course, didn't think twice about saying yes. What's the maxim? There are no small parts? Phil believed that and it was for talent like Phil's that that expression came into being.

So he did "Twister" and in 1997, he did "Boogie Nights" and that made him a star. Well, that's a little dash of agent hyperbole. He was six movies away from getting star billing. That same year he also did "Defying Gravity," a play at The American Place Theatre for ten cents a week. And he worked with Lois Smith whom he had met on "Twister." I think they recognized each other's unbelievable gifts. I represented them both and felt enormously proud – for no defensible reason – of the pleasure they took in working with each other.

In 1998, he filmed "Culture," "Montana," "Next Stop Wonderland," "The Big Lebowski," "Happiness" and "Patch Adams."(Well, that ought to make up for 1995.) He also did a play at New York Theatre Workshop called "Shopping and F**king." I couldn't understand how anyone had thought of him in that role and I was completely mesmerized by his performance. I told him he was kind of unexpected casting but he was spellbinding to watch. The second he came onstage, he brought his entire character with him, and I could hardly wait for him to reveal who the guy was, the clues were so tantalizing. And discovering the character's humanity as the evening went along was a profound experience. I said, I hoped Phil never stopped doing theatre because he was so jaw-droppingly inspiring it reaffirmed my faith in what I did for a living. He looked at me and said, "You think I'm unexpected casting?"

In 1999, he starred, with Robert De Niro, in a movie called "Flawless."Star billing. There it was. He got the San Diego Film Critics Society for Best Actor and was nominated for a Screen Actors Guild Award for Outstanding Performance by a Male Actor in a Lead Role, Motion Picture. He also did a play at The Drama Department called "The Author's Voice." A reviewer felt that, "Part of the problem with the production was that Philip Seymour Hoffman who is supposed to be menacing, is, in fact, no more threatening than Truman Capote in a hoodie." This was six years before "Capote" but the insanity of critics is forever. He also tested for a great part in "Man on the Moon" which another client of mine, Paul Giamatti, got. The day we found out it wasn't going to go to Phil, Davien called me, said, "Suck eggs," and hung up.

That year he also did "Magnolia" and "The Talented Mr. Ripley." And the Labyrinth Theatre Company had a hit with "In Arabia We'd All Be Kings" which Phil directed.

In 2000, he did "Titanic 2000," "State and Main" and "Almost Famous."And Labyrinth had another hit with "Jesus Hopped the A Train," with Phil directing again. Plus he did an unbearably low budget movie written by his brother called "Love Liza" (produced by a terrific former assistant of mine) which has to be the most depressing movie ever made (with the possible exception of "The Grey Zone" – brilliant but beyond painful – written and directed by Tim Blake Nelson who was also a client of mine). I cannot think of another actor alive with the balls to go from starring opposite Robert De Niro and practically stealing "The Talented Mr. Ripley" to doing an art house film with zero prospects for commercial success written by his brother. Nor is there an agent in the world who would stand still for his client doing such a thing. Unless it was one of the three agents in the world who understand that the important part of any agent/client relationship is the client part. That would be me and two other agents whose names I forget.

There were six more movies, a sit-com, a mini series and another play at the Labyrinth that he directed before the Academy award for Capote in 2005. And he followed "Capote" with "Mission Impossible III," a big, fat, studio movie – with a big fat paycheck. "The Hunger Games" didn't hurt either. I hope you begin to get the idea.

A map of Phil's career is very much a map of Phil himself. There are many more credits after the Oscar. Look them up. Think about this actor's choices. An actor has choices. You have choices. Phil's career came from his choices. So will yours. What will those choices be?

Let me insert a word here about all the stories I tell in this book. I love show business stories. I love hearing them and telling them. All of the stories in this book are true. I cannot swear they are completely true because where's the fun in that? But their essence is always true and I hope the lessons — if lessons there are — are instructive. I have tried not to be mean — with some exceptions. So let's talk a little bit about how it starts.

BREAKING AND ENTERING

Think Again

First off, is there any way I can talk you out of this mad journey? Wouldn't you rather be a banker or a botanist? There are rolling lawns and two-car garages and country club memberships waiting for you in the suburbs. Are you sure you don't want to go to business school? You really want to bunk in with four other aspiring actors in a fifth-story walk-up? I mean, what is it about show business that's so damn alluring?

Imagine the euphoria of your first day in New York. The culmination of your hard-won dreams, college, and 3 years of MFA training, you bound down the five flights of your New York City walk-up ready to greet your fortune. Your diploma says you know how to act but the people with the jobs don't seem lined up around the block waiting to give you a role. Oh, wait, look. All of your classmates seem to be in the same line with you. Not to mention the class from the year before you. And the year before that. Let alone the ones graduating from the schools you didn't get into.

The showcase of agents and casting directors your school

had promised you was attended by precisely three agents and two casting directors, only two of whom wanted to meet you (but one of whom wanted to meet with everyone). The other one was flattering, but fell through. They didn't call you back after the meeting.

You will have made some connections that will likely turn out to be beneficial to you once you are out of school, just like all the future bankers and botanists will do in their grad schools and so much the better for all of you. But the bankers and the botanists went to school to learn how to be bankers and botanists. Make sure you go to grad school to learn how to act. I have found some wonderful clients – who have gone on to have wonderful careers – at school showcases but, listen to me now, going to a school just so you can be in a showcase three or four years down the road is a horrible reason to go to a school, let alone a grad school.

There you are, in New York City with your BA or your BFA or your MFA and you are looking for work with no help from an agent because none of them were genuinely interested. And you find a job – at a new theatre company in the East Village which pays you $181 a week. Guess what – that's good! (Just don't try living on it.) You're lucky they even pay you. But maybe an agent will come and see the show. One doesn't. Not even one.

So you take an acting class. Never mind that you were in acting classes all day long for the last four years. Maybe in this acting class you will meet other people in your situation who would be helpful or know things you don't know because your former classmates from your former school are as clueless as you are and you don't know anybody else. Two of those former classmates found agents but neither of them are working either. And neither of them came to your show.

Or, let's say you take a different approach to this business of show. Let's say you go to college and get a liberal arts education. I have spoken to and taught armies of young artists and the ones with a liberal arts education are not surprisingly far more interesting, well-rounded and simply better company than the ones who have been locked away in conservatory programs honing their craft.

So you do it. You go to a normal person school. And it's fine even though you know in your bones you're not a normal person; you're an actor. That's what you want, that's what you've always wanted. But you stick it out at the normal person school because you like pretending to be a normal person for a little while longer and your parents really like it when you behave like a normal person. Your family reasons: if you're surrounded by normal people at liberal arts college, you may wind up practicing dentistry in suburbia, after all. It does happen.

So you graduate from your normal person school, and defying all your family's prayers, you move to New York. You find an acting class. Perhaps even a speech class. Dance, too. Couldn't hurt. So now you are in an acting class whose students include two kids from two of the best-known MFA programs – one of them is even your scene partner. Who's better off? Him or you? He knows more about acting. He also has massive student loans to pay back. You are both waiting on tables at the same bistro where you met. The answer to who is better off is ... arguable.

Waiting On Tables

The pay at the restaurant is pretty good. $300 on a good night and you hear you won't even have to claim the whole amount. Then one day in acting class you realize your teacher is not the insightful guru glowingly advertised in *Backstage*. What he said to that poor girl ahead of you was just wrong. You lock eyes with your scene partner and you both realize you have got to get out of there. You do mention this discovery to a fellow waiter at work. "Oh," says your co-worker, "Why are you studying with him? That guy's a jerk. Everybody knows that. Did he make a pass at you yet?"

So a few thousand dollars later, you go in search of a new acting teacher. This time you take recommendations from your new friends. You find a teacher you're crazy about. And you get cast in a Columbia University student movie. There's no pay but you might get some nice footage of yourself on film. That's good, right? Kathryn Bigelow went to Columbia. Maybe the director will turn out to be the next Kathryn Bigelow. That's very good, right? Never mind that on the last day of the film the director decides to shoot all night so you have to miss work which results in the restaurant firing you. But there are always other restaurants, right? Are you still with me?

You came here to act, and you are met not with a welcome mat but with a puzzle called show business which appears to have nothing to do with the art of acting. Well, what do you do with a puzzle? You solve it. You may not feel all that equipped to solve it, but if you come on this journey with me, you may at least consider yourself armed – if not yet dangerous.

Show business has all sorts of rules – few of which have anything to do with acting. That's fine. When you unknowingly break one of the rules and someone yells at you for not knowing what you did not know, one of the comforts to keep in mind is you can simply apologize and never break that rule again. (If they are right and it really is a rule.) Why didn't they teach you these rules in school? The truth is, the rules are so arbitrary and changeable and capricious that they are almost impossible to teach and anyway, the rules of the game are not the responsibility of the schools to teach; they are yours to learn. The schools try. They tell you more than they used to. They invite a few professionals to lay out what the rules are and these people frequently contradict each other. This invaluable lesson demonstrates the truth of William Goldman's maxim: "In the entire motion picture field, nobody knows anything." But I wonder if the schools tell you how it feels on the day after your showcase when only one person wants to meet you — an agent who wanted to meet everybody and, word has it, is kind of a skeeze. Wasn't there another one? Nah. Just kidding. This is not a devastating picture. It's just what happens. And you get through it. And if you hang in there, you will have a career.

Who would willingly choose such a life? Well, hundreds of people make that choice every day, though I would tend to think that the life chooses them rather than the other way around. You don't really have a choice, do you? I could give you reason after reason why you should stay in St. Paul but you will not listen to me. I know that. Ever since you were sitting there at a community theatre production of "Brighton Beach Memoirs" or the National Company of "Wicked" and some actor on stage did some indescribable little thing; some place inside of you was touched in a way you had never been touched before and that was it. You were a goner. You were summoned.

Find out where you belong in this business. You will begin to feel it. This is crucial. This is not some new age nonsense. How can you fit into a profession that does not appear to be holding a place for you? The more you watch other people act, the more you will know where you fit in. You may even begin to believe that you actually do belong. Every novice I have ever known, every hopeful who turned into a working actor, every working actor who became a star can trace the start of their professional career back to the moment when they were watching an actor on stage or on film or even on television and said to themselves, "If that fraud can have a career, I can have a career!" Not necessarily because the actor they were watching was actually a fraud but simply that the actor they were watching was no better than the novice who was watching them. At that moment, the novice became a part of the profession.

Feeling that you belong in the business is a feeling like no other and it is essential in order to make the reality happen. That feeling girds your loins. And your loins need to be girded. Getting into this business is a battle and make no mistake — it's not for sissies. Once you are in, you will be welcomed but proving that you deserve to be there will be your first fight. Doesn't ambition always lead to battle?

Some people are so ambitious they forget to have friends. That isn't healthy. Acting is a collaborative art. If you can't collaborate, you will have trouble. So get to know people. Know the players. Know your peers. How can you be the peer of someone you have never met? Meet everyone. Everyone is either a potential friend or a potential competitor. Should that stop you? Aren't Federer and Nadal friends? Are you in an acting class? Do you go to the theatre? It amazes me the number of young actors who do not go to the theatre. Go. Hang out with the actors after the show. Where do actors go to hang out? Find out. Actors love to bask in each other's presence. If you see small theatre companies whose work you admire, go backstage, ask how you could get to be a part of such a wonderful group.

You found what you wanted to do in life and you didn't even know you were looking. So you make a vow to do it. Because acting is still – even if you end up doing dinner theatre in Denver – a calling. Why else put up with all the nonsense? And it's worth it. You know it will be. When you finally get to do it, it will be worth it. This book exists to tell you how to accelerate the process and improve your odds of finally getting to do it.

Maybe you went to high school and bummed around for a few years and saved up some money and went to New York and decided to study with Bill Esper. Or you just knocked on the door of the Wooster Group and begged them to let you in because that's where Willem Dafoe started and you think Willem Dafoe is the coolest thing in the business. (He's pretty cool.) There's something to be said for just jumping in and trying to get a job but there are enormous advantages to training. Everyone I ever represented who went on to have a career had some sort of training except the exceptional Claire Danes. (I never represented Barbra Streisand.) So get some and then come to New York and act.

You will not receive an engraved invitation to come to New York. You will have to fight for an acting job for which you will likely not be paid. But do so. Fight for it. See if you are any good. If you have difficulty getting cast in something, welcome to the club. Do not whine. If you discover you have specific shortcomings you want to work on, study with someone who can help you with those shortcomings. When you start to get work, find an agent. If that agent leads you to better work, stay with that agent. If not, find another agent.

Improving The Odds

Agents and casting directors and directors and producers all have their own agendas separate from yours but that doesn't make them the enemy. Acting is a collaborative art; the business of acting is also a collaboration. In the same way that costume designers and dialect coaches are your collaborators on stage, agents and casting directors are your collaborators off stage. These professionals are necessary to your goal which is, at the very least, to be a working actor. You may broaden that goal to becoming some sort of reincarnation of the next Marlon Brando or Cate Blanchett but no matter how modest or grandiose your aim, you will nevertheless need to believe that you belong – and you will need to know how to let the gatekeepers realize that you deserve a membership.

I have designed a series of Workshops to let you in on what people in this business with the jobs – or access to the jobs – are really looking for. The answer is simple – they are looking for you.

When an agent meets an actor, the agent's first thought is: What kind of roles will he get? What kind of a career will she build? What kind of a career does he want? How will her career profit my own?

When a casting director meets an actor, her first thought is: What kind of roles is this person right for? How can I use him in a way which will best serve the project and bring the greatest amount of glory and profit to me?

Agents are looking for someone who will make money, someone who will work. Casting directors are looking for someone who will bring the greatest amount of depth, enlightenment, talent to a role. Any role. A nurse with three lines. Cleopatra.

When An Agent Meets An Actor

What are you looking for when you meet an agent or a casting director? Agents and casting directors need you in order to do their jobs. You need them in order to do yours. You are all in this together. No one is an adversary here and it would be a mistake to approach the business as if it were us against them.

The Workshop sections are set up to help you define what you are selling (sorry if that sounds so coarse; it sort of is) – and how best to package and present whatever that is. I want to make you castable, for lack of a better word, though, in truth, that is the perfect word. I don't think it's a real word (my computer certainly doesn't think so), but I trust its meaning is clear: people who have the power to hire you take one look at you and think they have an idea of how to use you. That makes you castable. It doesn't really matter if an agent is right or not about who they think you are. What matters is that she always thinks she is right. And also that she wants to audition you for the role of Ellen Page's sister right now.

If I am meeting with a guy in my office and he cracks wise so I think maybe he could get a sit-com and I say, "Hey, you're funny," it is so predictable (and so boring) that he will almost certainly reply, "No, I think I'm more right for the dark edgy kind of roles, like Jack O'Connell." Well, I think to myself, you aren't as handsome or as interesting as Jack O'Connell and maybe, if you aren't funny, I'm not sure what I could even do for you. So you should probably get out of my office.

Are we clear so far? It is my Socratic plan to lay out the principles necessary that you will need to break into show business. After I have described the principle, I will offer a Workshop to test and illustrate it.

I have met all the actors you will meet in these workshops many times over. I bet I have even met you. So take your place, follow along, and raise your hand when you have a question. I hope in the discussions that follow, you will find your own answers and come to your own conclusions. So let's talk a little bit about how it starts.

A Little Story About Being Special: Matt Damon

Some years ago, I was taking a casting director out to dinner. This guy only worked on A-list movies. He was major. I stopped by his office to pick him up and he was, as usual, watching tapes. And he was freaking out. He was always freaking out. His brow was always moist. It was his thing. It was, shall we say, what made him special. What was today's freak out about? He said he was going out of his mind trying to decide which actors to put in front of his director for this tricky role. Would I mind if he showed me some tapes? I was really looking forward to a drink but I said, of course I wouldn't mind and, of course, I was flattered to be asked. All anybody on my side of the desk has to offer is an opinion and I have so many of them. So he showed me the tapes. There were six of them. There was one actor who stood out.

"Really?" said the casting director. "To me he isn't even in the final three."

"Then what's he doing in this stack?" I asked.

"I don't know. There's something about him. But he's short and he hasn't done much. Do you think he's compelling?"

I did, yes. "How short is he?" I asked. The casting director didn't know. He'd never met the guy. The agent had just submitted the tape. "So how do you know he's short?"

"He looks short," said the casting director. "Why do you like him?"

"I like him," I said, "because he's a really good actor and he pops."

"Do you really think he pops?" This casting director was mental.

"Jesus," I said, "can we go to dinner?"

The actor I liked got the job. It was Matt Damon – who is not short and who is compelling. That job did not make him a star but it did get him some serious attention. It was a turning point. Now I don't tell this story to demonstrate how prescient I am. I tell it because no matter how fantastically special you are (Matt Damon is pretty special), there are going to be people who aren't quite convinced and it is your job to stay in there and convince them. If not on this role, then on the next. Somebody will notice. It's hard to be the first one to say that someone has got it. And that sweaty casting director was particularly adept at getting other people to commit first. It's why he was so successful. Do I expect a thank you note from Matt Damon? Hardly. I was just glad to voice an opinion. The business is filled with people who are dying to help. Really. Let's find them.

Daniel Day Lewis:

"If you have a certain wildness of spirit, a cabinet maker's workshop is not the best place to express it."

HOW IT STARTS

You cannot beat the theatre for going straight to the heart. Parents take their children to the theatre because they think it will be educational. Civilizing. If they only knew the demons they were turning loose! Sometimes those children get hooked. No father takes his son for his first martini in public in the hopes that the boy will turn into an alcoholic. Few parents take their children to the theatre with any idea that the child will some day want to be an actor. If that connection were made, theatre attendance would drop even more dramatically than it has in recent years. The risk of contagion among the uninitiated should not be underestimated.

Most of us working in show business in whatever capacity have been drawn there because we were touched, wounded, moved beyond words, changed forever by a performance given by an actor they saw when they were young. "Beyond words" isn't a bad definition of acting. If words were enough, the world would be reading plays, not watching them. It's what the actor adds beyond the words that creates the craft of the actor.

For me it was Julie Harris in "The Warm Peninsula" by Joe Masteroff. (Not a play for the ages though her performance was). I was twelve. There was a moment near the end. Julie Harris was talking to the audience and she was telling us how happy she was that she was about to be married. She was wearing a wedding dress. She wasn't sure we understood the depth of the happiness she was feeling. And so she gasped; she *behaved* in some way that humans do that communicated to us – me – how truly joyful and fulfilled she felt at that moment. She made us – me – want to cry out at the sight of a fellow creature who was experiencing such happiness. Then she walked off stage and the curtain came down. Wow. Sign me up.

There have been moments since – James Earl Jones entering down the staircase as Othello in Central Park, Peggy Ashcroft listening to Ralph Richardson pour out his heart as fake snow fell on their thick winter coats at The National Theatre in London – but nothing has quite surpassed the surprise and sheer bliss my heart felt when I saw its deepest workings reflected in the behavior of another human being for the very first time on stage. There is still plenty of magic going on. People are scarred for life in theatres all over the country every night and there are young people getting off the bus all alone with a cardboard box at The Port Authority every day and all of them are hell bent on careers in show business.

Your family brought you to New York when you were young and you saw John Malkovitch in "Burn This" or Lois Smith in "Buried Child" or Alfred Molina in "Red" or Christopher Walken in anything and you had your Julie Harris moment. You decided then and there that you wanted to do *that. Be* that. At the very least, be around that. Most of the folks seated around you in the theatre, indeed your own family, were entertained by the play or perhaps even moved. They did not have their lives changed forever. Like you. Poor you. On the other hand, lucky you. You are an artist or long to be.

Did Meryl Do This To You? Or Javier?

Maybe it was a movie that did it for (to) you. Movies are certainly capable of derailing lives. Maybe it was Brando – or anybody – in "On the Waterfront." Maybe it was Jessica Lange in "Sweet Dreams." Or Javier Bardem in "No Country for Old Men." Maybe it was Daniel Day Lewis in "Lincoln." But all those people began in the theatre, right? Including the entire cast of "On the Waterfront." So you suspect the theatre is where you want to start.

It is the job of any adult who loves a child to make sure that that child does not become an actor. Your family discourages you from acting because they love you. And because the history of the theatre from the get-go has been associated with liars and prostitutes. Hard to completely dispute that. Actors sell their bodies and speak somebody else's truth with conviction. And yet, against all their loving counsel, you move to New York. You must act.

Your mama is right. An actor is a very hard thing to be. I am not talking about being a movie star. (Actually, it's not so easy to be a movie star.) I am talking about being an artist and, make no mistake, that is what most young people who fall in love with acting want to be. It is only later, when they discover how little call there is for artistry that they may begin to modify their goals.

Gradually, they give up their dreams of performing Lope de Vega for the crowd-pleasing plays and the horror films and the sit-coms and the tent-pole movies that sustain most of our gifted and highly trained young and then not-so-young people. The possibility of compromise is not something any young person should consider or does consider. The young person who wants to act most probably wants to act in the theatre and that is where you should start.

I am not a snob and I don't want to sound like one of those fanatics who feel that theatre is the only proper forum for any actor who calls himself an artist. (All right. So I am a snob – but not a fanatic.) What's so pure about the theatre? Well, it's the place where an actor has the most control over what he does, where every fiber of his being must be alert and available to him while he works and where his affect upon an audience is the most profound. I suppose that's debatable too. There are some shots of Robert Duvall's face on the screen that will never leave my consciousness. Did you ever see "Tender Mercies" ? How does he *do* that? But extraordinary as he is on screen, he's even better on stage. I will remember every second of his performance off-Broadway as Eddie Carbone in "A View From the Bridge" long after I am dead.

Spencer Tracy, who was trained for the stage, though I never saw him on one, was a brilliant film actor. Brilliant actor period. Second to none. I don't think even the most rabid

35

Actor's Studio zealot would deny Tracy his genius. Still, I'll bet he was better on stage. More powerful. God, I wish I'd seen him. I saw Hume Cronyn on stage and on film and I am here to tell you that Hume Cronyn as Polonius beats the hell out of Hume Cronyn in "The Parallax View."

The actor William Redfield once said "He who has not seen Laurence Olivier on stage has not seen Laurence Olivier." Well, I thought that was the most pretentious thing I had ever heard. But, you know, he might have been onto something. On the other hand, you can sit and watch Philip Seymour Hoffman become a star in "Scent of A Woman" on screen and it just doesn't get any better than that. So let's withhold a final verdict on which is purer.

All actors have an ineluctable longing for the stage. Keanu Reeves had the hunger to play "Hamlet." He did so *after* he was a star, of course. Probably because nobody wanted him to do it until he *became* a star. Even then probably not a lot of people were cheering him on saying, hey, why don't you play Hamlet? No, it was the hunger, the drive inside him. And *they* let him do it because *he* wanted to and people will let stars do whatever they want just to keep them happy. His agents were surely not thrilled. Do you know how much money he could have made on screen while he was pulling down whatever pittance he was being paid for "Hamlet"?

Mr. Reeves also took a bit of a critical drubbing for his trouble. But you know what? I'll bet he doesn't regret doing it for a minute. He played HAMLET, for God's sake. Hell, I'll bet Jennifer Aniston has thoughts of Lady Macbeth. (Do you think?) Julia Roberts came to Broadway. She got massacred but she came. Have I said I *like* Julia Roberts? Crazy for her actually. God bless movie stars. They bring the people in.

Imagine if Streep had been in a play on Broadway every couple of years. There would be a line to Hoboken and back every night. And Dustin Hoffman and Robert De Niro. I saw Mr. De Niro be mesmerizing in "Cuba and His Teddy Bear" at The Public. Indelible. Not a great play. Imagine him in a great play. Do you think people would go? Um, yes. If the business could find a way to keep a slot open for a star in a steadily revolving offering of great plays with great actors in the cast (Pacino's "Merchant of Venice" cast was some treasure trove) people would go. What's more, that production of "Merchant" with Pacino was one of the hottest tickets in town when it was on.

The common wisdom is that audiences are no longer willing to pay for classical theatre. But there they were, paying for it. Well, people say, but that was Al Pacino. The argument may be made that there are not enough actors around practicing their craft at that level to make us shiver in our seats who are also stars. I don't believe that. Tom Hardy? Idris Elba? Cate Blanchett? Viola Davis? Edie Falco? Sean Penn? Al Pacino is a star because he feels things that deeply and he is willing to share the experience with us. Hell, Viola Davis shares her soul with us *on television*. So don't get all cynical on me. There is a hunger for great acting and there always will be.

Three-quarters of the members of the Screen Actors Guild make less than $10,000 a year from acting gigs. The numbers for Actors Equity are actually rather grimmer. Does that figure give you pause? What was your student loan debt? How much is your rent? That these figures, which are widely known, do not deter a young person who has a flame in his or her heart is something of a miracle.

No amount of bad news seems to keep the true believers away. A few dabblers are properly deterred and they may go on to lead productive, normal lives – don't forget botany – but they should count themselves lucky to be out of acting. An artist, almost by definition, is incapable of listening to reason. This does not mean that those who remain are all brilliant actors. Their gifts may range on a scale anywhere from the barely adequate to Daniel Day Lewis but they will belong in the community of actors. Or in the art form which is now conducted as a business.

Developing your craft as an actor is vital, but, alas, it is not enough. This book is about a parallel craft. The craft of getting an acting job and building a career.

Not, perhaps, a comparable skill but a very palpable skill nonetheless. It is my own belief that nothing compares to being able to act. (Have I said how much I love actors?) Being able to get the chance to do so can be another matter. Let's go back to your talent and what to do with it for a moment.

As a very young person who has identified a longing to act, should you study? Possibly, but not necessarily. There are programs all over the place for teen and pre-teenaged actors. Rather than throw yourself upon their mercy, I think you should just act. Act in front of an audience. An audience is the best teacher you will ever have. Ever. I mean that. Yes, there are skills to be learned. Do you want to sing? A teacher is a good idea. Do you want to dance? A teacher is essential.

Do you want to act? Act. Sandy Meisner, one of the best acting teachers in the history of the world, used to say he didn't want to even talk to young actors until they were twenty-one . If a young person has no idea who they are, how on earth are they going to imagine they are someone else (i.e., act)? Meanwhile, if you are not yet eighteen find a theatre and work there.

Every town in America has loads of theatres from school to community to professional varieties. You may have to dig for them but they are there. Maybe not as many as in Chicago or St. Louis but they exist. There are fourteen in Buffalo. They are there in your hometown, too. Find them. Go to them. Present yourself. They might let you act in all sorts of stuff you are right for and even some stuff that you aren't. They're not union? So what? They put on plays, don't they? The LORT Theatres (League of Regional Theatres) are union and you might even get your Equity card if you work in one of them, if you have your heart set on an Equity card.

I represented a superior actor named Robert Prosky who worked at The Arena Stage in D.C. for twenty years and raised a family while doing so before he moved to Los Angeles and sold himself on a very profitable television series called "Hill Street Blues" like my brother D. B. in Hollywood. Bob had twenty years in the theatre before he ever even thought about show business. The Artistic Director of the Arena Stage, the legendary Zelda Fichandler, said to him one day, "You just tell me when you're ready to play Willy Loman and we'll mount it for you." And they did. No wonder he stayed there for so long. Bob's kids were ready for college by the time he was ready for LA. And Bob Prosky wasn't the only genius at that regional theatre. Dianne Wiest came out of the Arena. So did … . Hell,

Google Arena stage. It was and is an amazing place.

I know regional theatres are called not-for-profit theatres. Why is that? I will tell you this: in the 1980's, The Guthrie Theatre had a resident company of actors each making $1,000 a week all year long and the Artistic Director made $100,000 a year. Presently, The Guthrie has *no* resident company, actors are jobbed in for that *same* $1,000 a week they were paid thirty years ago – but only for the weeks they work, of course. And the recently departed Artistic Director made $682,000 a year, until, in an attempt to lower the annual budget, he took a 10 percent pay cut – bringing him down to just over half a million dollars. So some people can still afford to raise a family.

Who's In Charge Of Your Destiny?

Never turn over the reins of your career decisions to someone else. No, not even me. The need to plot your own path doesn't stop when you become famous (if you do). Daniel Radcliffe was starring on Broadway when he was asked by a reporter what other theatrical roles he'd like to tackle. He promptly replied, "Rosenkrantz and Guildenstern Are Dead" which had never been revived on Broadway (he knew that) and "Company." Both brilliant choices for him. There speaks an actor who thinks about his choices. He doesn't leave it to others to steer the ship and he easily could because I am sure there are no end of others involved in his decisions. (There's a lot of money there.) But my money is on Daniel Radcliffe still being famous in fifty years because *he* is in charge of his career.

The actor is always in charge of his career. Any other reading of the situation is an all-too-understandable but deluded flight from responsibility, which will lead to unemployment and obscurity.

But let's get you a career before we worry about how you are going to stay on top. Fun to think about being Daniel Radcliffe, though, isn't it?

When Should You Start To Study?

There's no right answer that applies to everyone. If you are inclined to take a theatre class when you are an undergrad, go for it. If you're turned on by the program and want to major in theatre, try it out. Brown has a superior undergrad program. Why don't you go to Brown? If you want to go to graduate school for acting, study all your options carefully. If you don't feel you need training, try yourself out on the boards. If you decide later that you want training, get it. Whichever choice you make, do it because it feels right, not because you think graduate school will help you get an agent. That's just wrong. How do you know what feels right? You're an actor, for God's sake. Feel.

Should you study at all? Yeah, I think so. Naturally, there are exceptions but Geraldine Page studied until the day she died and a greater actor never lived. However, not unlike students who take a year or two off from college and then return, perhaps a year or two of pursuing being an actor might be an appropriate prelude to study because you will discover what you need to know. If after five or ten years of acting you feel the desire to return to the classroom, do so.

A return to acting class is not a defeat. It's an awakening. I don't know what happened to the model of life-long learning,

41

but I vote we bring it back. Piper Perabo studies and she works all the time. (She is also gorgeous.) Peter Gerety studies and he works all the time. (He is not gorgeous but he is supremely gifted.) There are people not quite in the profession yet who are studying until they feel *ready*, whatever they may mean by that. (I suspect they mean perfect.) Frankly, I don't get that. My feeling is that if you want to act, then act at your first opportunity. Why not do both? If you feel like you need help acting, then study. No blame to the superior man.

I Want Total Acting Immersion

Undergraduate conservatories (North Carolina School of the Arts and the ubiquitous Juilliard come to mind) are a different species from straightforward undergraduate training. They usually only admit twenty or so students (a few more at North Carolina, a few less at Juilliard) and are completely dedicated to recognizing and nurturing artists. Something in the training at these schools seems to instill students with the idea that they are God's gift which will have to be knocked out of them before they start to get work in the real world but then again that burden appears to be attached to graduates of any institution the world deems to be of note. (What is the difference in attitude between a graduate of Harvard Medical School and The Juilliard Theatre School? Not much.)

Juilliard also now offers an MFA program so you can add Juilliard to your resume no matter how many lesser undergrad degrees you have spent your time acquiring. I am sure the folks at Juilliard do not intend to instill this superior attitude but the pedigree of entitlement can actually stand in the way. Still it is impossible to quarrel with the caliber of talent they attract – Viola Davis, Tim Blake Nelson, Michael Stuhlbarg, Andre Braugher, Robin Williams and Jessica Chastain come immediately to mind. I've worked for many of them, by the way. (I gotta crow.)

Let's say you are hell bent on conservatory training but Juilliard and North Carolina are a little daunting. Or expensive. Where else could you go? Have you considered checking out where some of your favorite actors got their training? I mean, it's a question. It worked for them, right? And what is known to have worked once might well work again. The odds are even good. And part of why this is important is that you don't really need the best school – what is that anyway? – you need the school that is best for you. And maybe someone who traveled this road before you did and who you admire managed to scope out a program that would work for you.

Start with your five or six favorite actors and where they trained. They won't all be colleges and universities. (Johnny Depp never studied acting. He has a career. Did I say there are exceptions to everything I am saying?) Chris Noth went to Yale. Sam Rockwell went to Bill Esper, a superior private acting studio in New York. (We will get to private acting studios in a section called "Which Coast?" shortly.) Michael C. Hall went to NYU. Edie Falco went to SUNY Purchase. Gabriel Macht went to Carnegie-Mellon. So did Matt Bomer. (Want to work on USA Network? Go to Carnegie-Mellon.)

You will have to audition for these schools. How they treat you when you audition and what your experience is with their whole admission process will be a pretty fair harbinger of what your experience will be like if you go there (if you get in). If you do not get in, do not collapse. Or collapse for a day and then get over it. What do they know anyway? Really, what do they know?

Michael Caine was told by the gatekeepers that there was no place in the theatre for him and he should pack his bags and go home. His hair was weird. He wasn't a leading man; he looked gay; basically no one would want to hire him. And that was in England. Don't they know everything over there? Guess not.

Every successful actor alive has been told by the best producers, the best directors, the best casting directors, agents and the best schools that they should give it up and go home. If you listen to them, then they are right – there is no place for you in this business. I don't care who they are or how important they are.

All that matters in the end is your desire to be there. If you make a list of your top five or six schools and you don't get into *any* of them, it's only normal to collapse a little. But if after all that rejection you still think you belong in the business, then forget school and start auditioning. Rejection is part of every actor's life. Get used to it.

I Know I'm Great But I Need Some Basics — What Do I Do?

Let's say you're a natural genius but you're still curious about what these schools have to offer. A chance to learn about the profession? Don't bet on it. A chance to discover the great plays of the past? I was stunned to hear that there is very little reading of plays going on at even the best MFA programs. A professor at Yale said to me, "Why bother assigning them plays? They won't read them." Can't they be made to read them? What? Put pressure on students? That's so last century. So what else? A chance to study with Master Teachers? Well, maybe. What is a Master Teacher? It's a term thrown around for which there are no quantifiable requirements. Was Sigmund Freud a Master Therapist? I guess. Are there Master Teachers at some of these schools? Sure. I don't think there are Master Teachers at all the schools that advertise them but I think there may be excellent teachers there. Master Teacher is a term which has come to be part of the hype. Who decides these things? Was Stanley Kubrick a Master Director? He never won an Academy Award.

So what's so great about these schools that offer actor training anyway? What's so great is the chance to be in play after play after play. This is golden. If you move to New York, you will be lucky in your first year to get two lines on "Elementary," five lines on "Law and Order: Criminal Intent," carry a spear in the Park, do an independent movie (one good scene) and do a nice supporting part at the Huntington in Boston. That may be a decent first year but it is hardly a chance to act. The schools give you a chance to act. Go for it!

Is that all? Actually, there is more. These schools offer the chance to develop what they never tire of referring to as a technique. Now I've never really been sure what technique is but I suspect it has something to do with all the things that Kevin Kline can do. So fine. Develop that. Who would deny that Kevin Kline is talented? And who would deny that he is handsome, has a beautiful wife and can sing? Quite apart from my discourteous tone, I wish to make it very clear that I think Kevin Kline has exquisite technique and that an actor with technique possesses considerable advantage over one who does not.

Casting directors and directors and producers and even agents are comforted to see that you have taken the time and spent the money necessary to acquire a technique which will enable you to handle a sizeable role were they to offer one to you. However, be aware that before they offer you a sizable role, they will first offer you two lines to see how you do. Do those two lines well, graciously and with all the technique you can muster.

I had a client, who had no training but whom I had seen in a play and I felt was dripping with talent. He just felt like a star. He got his first job through me in a studio film. He only worked for a few days. He had a very nice moment in the film but it was only a moment. Still, enough to get noticed. At the end of his first day, I asked the casting director if he had made any friends on set. (What I meant was: How did he do?) She said that if he didn't stop telling everyone what a big star he was going to be, by the end of the week he wouldn't have any friends left. Ah. Good to know. Now if that kid had gone to one of the better schools, chances are sooner or later one of his classmates or one of his teachers would probably have told him what a jerk he was and he would have avoided turning an entire movie set against him in one day on his first SAG job. Being surrounded by peers in search of a common goal and being guided by compassionate people who have your best interests at heart (in other words, being in school) tends to lead to knowledge, maturity and a degree of humility. (Possible exception for Juilliard. Sorry. Can't help myself.) Of course, that guy might also have gone through three years of grad school with everybody kissing his ass because they wanted his approval or his body and he only got more entrenched in his own awesomeness.

If everybody at your school from your friends to the faculty thinks you are going to be a big star, they are probably so busy cultivating you as a source for future fundraising, they wouldn't dream of offending you by telling you to stop behaving like a jerk. (But they will still help you with your technique.)

It is not the fault of show business and it is not the fault of the schools that people tend to defer to people who have a great deal of charisma. If you happen to be one of those people with the charisma, it is your job to make sure that you keep it real. In school if you act like a jerk, sooner or later someone will point that out to you. In show business, you will just stop getting jobs. So that's a good reason to train in a school, right? You bet your ass.

The definition of technique will vary from school to school and some techniques are better than others – or, like the schools themselves, better for *you* than others – but at the end of the day, all the schools offer some sort of a technique and, let us not forget, a degree. You're going to be in a business, remember?

It's Gonna Cost You

And like any business, it's gonna cost you. Professional actor training programs at the schools costs on average $35,000 per student per year. (Check all these figures I am about to quote. They rise at an alarming rate every year.) NYU undergrad is $68,000 a year. SUNY Purchase (state school) is $32,000. Yale grad charges you for the first year and after that it's virtually free. They are on their way to being fully endowed. The Stella Adler Studio has a three-year conservatory program for $7,750 per semester. And no degree at the end. The disparity in these figures is a source of never ending amazement to me.

In England there are three or four schools worth mentioning. It is assumed that if you graduate from one of them, you may reasonably expect to have some sort of career as an actor. No such expectations apply – at even the top schools – on this side of the pond. I know actors from all the schools, *including* the top three, who after two, three, five years of knocking on doors have folded their tents and gone back home. Many of them were gifted. At least two of them were brilliant. Last year, a casting director friend told me he was invited to 125 showcases.

Before we try and answer it, let's join a Workshop. Let's try and feel like an actor. That's our goal here, right? For the First Workshop, please bring in two monologues for which you feel you are perfectly suited.

WORKSHOP ONE:
Monologues

Welcome to my studio. We are on the sixth floor of a colorfully run-down office building somewhere in New York City's West 30's. Perhaps the last affordable neighborhood in the city for Workshops like this one. Though if I were to tell you my rent, I doubt you would agree it was reasonable.

Gathered here are twelve aspiring actors who have come to learn how to get into show business. You are one of them.

Today the elevator in the building is not working but most of you are young and six flights isn't going to kill any of you. Neither will what I have to say. In fact, it is my hope that what I have to say may enlighten you about how to get into show business.

Choosing a monologue will be in the service of determining who you are, who you think you are and how well those two play together. All our classes will be an exercise in letting you in on how an agent thinks. At any rate, how I think. Not all agents think alike and many of them would likely disagree with some of the things I say to you. But there are some things, some ways of thinking, that all agents have in common. Casting directors, too. Even directors and producers.

How Can We Use You?

All your business collaborators want to know how we can use you. Some might say how we can *help* you. That would be a more positive way of saying the same thing and I strive, not always successfully, to be positive. We want to know who you are and what you can do for us. We also deeply hope you can help us do whatever it is we are doing. In other words, we are on your side. So the question is, what do you want from us?

Do not answer: You want us to sign you. Do not answer: you want us to hire you. Do not answer: you want us to like you. What do you specifically want? Do you want to do Shakespeare in the Park before you die? Do you want to work in a Coen brothers film? That is information about you which would be very useful to us. So fork it over.

Mostly, and I know this is a lot to ask, tell us who you are. Do you know?

The only way you will discover the answer to that question and your own productive way of sharing it with people who can help you is for us to work together. So let us begin.

A word: This is not an acting class. I wouldn't pretend to

know how to teach acting. If I sometimes seem to forget that and sneak in some advice about actual acting, please forgive me.

When I first started sending Liev Schreiber out, people would meet him and they would say, "Well, yeah, I liked him. He didn't have much to say for himself but he read pretty well. I can't tell what he's right for. What do you think he's right for?" Of course, I think to myself: You're the casting director, you tell me what he's right for. I do not say this. Since Liev is a great actor, the correct response to that idiotic question would be that he is right for whatever you've got. I do not say this either. What I say is, "He would have been perfect for that guest star you had last week." "He's not going to get a guest star. He's just out of school, for God's sake. What guest star?" "The mob guy." "He's not right for that. We needed a name for that." "I know you needed a name but you asked me what he's right for and he would have been right for that." "No, he wouldn't. That guy needed to be kind of sexy." "You're kidding me, right? Liev is totally sexy. Ask a woman. Do your job."

Well, I think today we can say today that Liev Schreiber is plenty sexy. But when he first got here, he didn't look like Paul Newman so people were reluctant to be the first to say that he could be a leading man.

In my first meeting with Liev, I asked him what his goals were. He thought about it and told me he wanted to be on the cover of *Tiger Beat*. Well, I thought about *that*. What was this Yale graduate whom I had seen do Shakespeare and didn't exactly look like Shaun Cassidy doing telling me he wanted to be on the cover of *Tiger Beat*?

He was telling me he thought he was a sexy guy and could play leading men. Frankly, that had not been my assessment but clearly it was his and I wanted to represent him so I was happy to go along with what he wanted. He was also pulling my leg – big time – but behind that, he was in deadly earnest. So I said, "How often do you go to the gym?" He loved it. And he signed with me.

I started introducing him to people and those people started telling me what they thought of him. Remember that comment that he didn't have much to say for himself? I told him that. "So what should I do?' he asked me. "You should have something to say for yourself," I said. "Like what?" "I don't know. Just talk. Let them know what you're like. Let them know you're a leading man while you're at it." "Should I tell them I'm a great actor?" (Did I say Liev was not shy?) "No, that's my job," I say. "Do you tell them?" "Do I do my job? Yes." But, and here's the thing, no one cares if you're a great actor. I did not tell this to Liev. I am telling this to you. But I think Liev figured it out. If you are a good actor, if you can *do* the job and do it well, everyone is happy. Great actors are always appreciated but they are not really necessary. Great actors are freaks. Divine freaks, I grant you, but freaks. I adore them. They are life to me but if every project that got produced needed a great actor to get made, not many projects would get made.

So I sent Liev to meet everyone – in those days there was still time to do that – and word started getting around. He started getting the hang of this meeting thing, too. Sometimes people thought he was an axe murderer. Mostly they thought he was what they were looking for. He saw to that.

I asked you to come to this first class prepared to do two monologues for which you think you are perfect. (Monologue rules: No screaming, no props, and no Shakespeare – I'm an agent, for God's sake.) It is always fascinating to me the monologues that people choose to reflect themselves. Is that really who you think you are? In what universe would anyone ever cast you in that role? What about that role attracts you? What monologues you pick tells me reams about you and how you think of yourself. Not infrequently, actors have a very good sense of what they are right for. But just as often, they don't want to be seen as types and so they hedge their bets – if not in the material itself, then in how they perform the material. They want me to know they could do it differently than the way they are doing it and so it becomes tentative.

If you have something that represents you to your core, go for it! If it is not quite 100% you, give it everything you've got anyway. If you are auditioning for a part, do you imagine you will be cast in the role if you hold back even a little what you are capable of bringing to it? Do you think the person auditioning just before or just after you will be holding back who they are? Don't bet on it.

Types

What's wrong with being a type? Well, you're special, you say, you are not a type. This, of course, is true. Stars are types – archetypes, really – who have never been seen before in just that way. They are unexpected. Thus the business is frequently flummoxed about what to do with them.

When Humphrey Bogart did "The Petrified Forest" by Robert Sherwood on Broadway, Leslie Howard, who starred in the film, wanted Bogart to repeat his role for the movie. The studio did not. They did not like Humphrey Bogart. He looked odd, they felt, and he talked funny. What was that thing he had, a lisp? Not really but it was ... something. But Leslie Howard insisted and when he showed up for the first day of shooting and discovered that Humphrey Bogart had not been hired, Leslie Howard got back in his car and went home. He said he would return when Humphrey Bogart was on the set. Today, naturally, there is such a thing as a Humphrey Bogart type. If you happen to be such an original, you'd better go out and find yourself a champion like Leslie Howard. Not saying it can't be done. Am saying: Do it.

How do you choose a monologue? You might start off by asking your friends, teachers, even family (and I say *even* because family members almost never see you objectively) what roles come to mind when they think of you acting in something. Maybe one of them will have a great idea for you. Go through reputedly good but little performed plays. How about William Inge's "The Dark at the Top of the Stairs"? Or James Baldwin's "Blues for Mr. Charlie" or Lanford Wilson's "The Fifth of July"? Why 'little performed'? Because that way, no one, neither you nor the people you will be auditioning for, has a pre-formed picture of how these characters *ought* to be portrayed. They can be acted however you want to act them.

There is no right way. There never is. There is only your way. True, Ken Talley was originated by a young William Hurt but who remembers what Bill Hurt was like when he was young? (Except Bill Hurt.) For the same reason, I do not recommend doing monologues or even scenes (especially scenes) from films because casting people tend to think that the way it was done in the film is the right way to do it. And why volunteer to be compared to Al Pacino? Plus the writing is never as good, never as rich in movies as it is in plays. It's not supposed to be.

Choose contrasting monologues. Not polar opposites but different. You are not two different people – but you have different aspects (and certainly more than two). Sandy Meisner used to say you can never judge an actor based on one performance. You must see him create two different characters. (Sandy was so smart – and so mean.) Your first monologue should be as close to what feels as authentically you as possible. As if it were written just for you.

A very successful casting director once told me that when she is interviewing an actor and she turns on the camera, if the actor's voice changes *in any way* for the audition, "I promise you," she said, "that actor will not get the part." Because the actor will be acting and they do not want you to act. They want you to *be* it. So *be* it.

Imaginary Circumstances

What else did Meisner say? Acting is living truthfully in imaginary circumstances. So do that. And make some interesting choices while you're at it. This is not an acting class and I am not an acting teacher but, for God's sake, make choices which will benefit you in the marketplace. By which I mean? Make yourself look decisive, caring, funny, sexy, whatever you see as likeable. You don't care about being likeable? Give me a break.

The second monologue can show some range. Don't go crazy here. Don't become Russian. Don't age thirty years. Don't turn into a screaming queen. (Never do that.) Just be someone a little different. Someone else. And have fun.

A monologue should be something you look forward to doing. Like wearing your favorite shirt. It should be comfortable. I once told a client he had to do a monologue for an English director. (They tend to like monologues.) I told him I knew it was a drag but buck up, he was perfect for what they were looking for. "I don't mind doing monologues at all," he said. "Really?" said I. "It's my chance to act for the day," he said with great glee. Now that's a good attitude. He works all the time, that guy.

So let's see some monologues. Who's first? Ah, Mr. Davis, you have wormed your way into my heart forever by volunteering to go first. What will you be doing for us?

"Stanley Kowalski in 'A Streetcar Named Desire' and Phil in 'Hurlyburly' by David Rabe."

Does Stanley Kowalski have a monologue?

"I've actually put a couple of speeches together."

Normally, I am not a fan of that practice. Especially with great writers like Mr. Williams. With such writers – Miller and Albee are others – every syllable, every pause is there for a reason. When you stitch two speeches together, you are forcing yourself to make emotional connections which the writer never intended. But there was no way you could have known that little bias of mine so knock yourself out, Mr. Davis. Let us see your "Streetcar."

And he performs it.

What is the class's reaction is to Mr. Davis' choice of monologue? You'd be amazed at how much better complete strangers are at picking up on what you radiate than you are. Even when I teach at a school where everyone has known each other for several years and half of them have slept together – students are shocked by their friends' choice of monologues. *That's* who you think you are?

Mr. Davis, what on earth possessed you to do one of the most iconic characters in all of dramatic literature and made you think you might have something to add to our knowledge of him?

"You mean why do I like it?"

Something like that. Start there.

"Well, you know, it's Brando. He's the best. That's what I want to be."

And he's hot and steamy and sexy?

"Well, yeah."

And so are you?

"Just look at me."

You are being funny?

"I'm trying."

Humor is always appreciated, Mr. Davis. I would suggest to you that it is possible to evoke Marlon Brando without actually begging to be compared to him. If you consider yourself hot and steamy and sexy, I would suggest that you are not far off the mark but if you simply wear a tee shirt and blue jeans we will get the message. You don't need to go all the way to a motorcycle jacket. It is enough for us to realize you might be right for Marlon Brando's roles without asking us to compare your talent to his. The Rabe play, which I will ask you for in a moment, is a better choice. I like that it's funny because you are. Your hero Mr. Brando was many things but funny was not at the top of the list.

"I never said he was my hero."

But he is, is he not?

"Yeah."

Definite points to you, Mr. Davis for knowing you are a leading man. Leading men with a sense of humor are rare. You would do well to capitalize on that. And I would urge you to always be defining in what *way* you are a leading man. Do not volunteer to have us compare your nascent offerings to one of the greatest performances of all time. Introduce us to Sam Davis. I have no idea who that is but you do. Keep me informed. I once represented a great actor and received an inquiry about his interest in actually playing Stanley Kowalski in a Broadway revival. When I relayed the interest to him his reaction was, "Do they think I'm crazy?" You see, Brando was his hero, too.

"I've got a question."

Yes?

"What's nascent?"

Look it up. One final point. Stanley Kowalski is a grown man. He is thirty years old. He has a wife and a job. How old are you, Mr. Davis?

"Twenty-one."

Precisely. I believe the assignment was a part you are perfect for. The business will never cast you outside your age range. Never. Unless you are Dustin Hoffman. And you are not. I do not mean you are without talent. I mean you are not Dustin Hoffman. We await your rendition of "Hurlyburly" with bated breath.

"Should I go?"

Yes, bated breath means go.

And he does.

That was rather good, Mr. Davis. Very modest of you not to choose the lead.

"Well, I want to show I'm versatile, you know?"

Who played Phil in the original production?

"Um, I don't know. Bobby Cannavale played him in the revival."

Yes, he did and Harvey Keitel played him in the original. And Chazz Palminteri played him in the movie. Who was Eddie in the movie?

"Don't know."

The correct answer is Sean Penn. You should know the history of the work you perform – if it has a history. Not because we want you to imitate somebody else's performance. But to know the range of takes on the role. Obviously, if you are auditioning for a new play on Broadway, it will have no history. But the writer might. The director might. Be aware of ... history. It adds to what you bring.

That is a very funny monologue, Mr. Davis and you were very funny performing it. I think I saw you going for the laughs more than I might have liked but I am not an acting teacher. As the sort of teacher I am, I would suggest that Phil is a little bit too close to Stanley and you could demonstrate a wider range for yourself with another choice.

"Such as?"

Oh, no, Mr. Davis. That's your job. I wouldn't pretend to know what you felt suited you. Though I would be prepared to disagree with what you felt did.

"But I mean, like what kinda thing?"

Something with a bit more grace, perhaps.

"Is grace what you think I'm selling?

I think you would be very interesting selling grace. I think Christopher Walken, no matter how twisted and psychotic the character he is playing, is always selling grace along with it.

"You got me."

If that means you see my point, I am glad. Who's next? Ms. Hamer? How about you? Let's get the class beauties out of the way right off the bat. What are you doing for us, Ms. Hamer? Madge in "Picnic" by William Inge and Augustus and Ruth Goetz's "The Heiress"? I sense some canny choices at work.

And do you have any objections to being called a beauty, Ms. Hamer?

"None at all."

Good. Please proceed with "Picnic".

And she does.

Very nice, Ms. Hamer. And why did you choose Madge, may I ask?

"Because she's..."

Ms. Hamer and I say this together: "The prettiest girl in town."

Exactly right and you yourself, Ms. Hamer, are exceptionally pretty.

"Thank you."

It was an observation. No thanks are necessary. Why don't you go right into "The Heiress" and we can compare and contrast.

She does precisely that.

Thank you, Ms. Hamer. Let's for a moment go back to how pretty you are. I would point out to you that a role which was created by Janice Rule and played in the film by Kim Novak and in a major revival by Ashley Judd and in a minor revival by Maggie Grace, such a role would seem to have no particular requirements other than the actress must be pretty. Who she actually *is* is up to the actress playing her. You seem to have decided that she is a mass of insecurities.

Which would be a good deal more interesting if you hadn't also decided that Catherine Sloper was also a mass of insecurities. I had thought you might be going for the pretty one being an emotional wreck and the repressed one being serene. That would have been notable. But such was not your choice. Which leads me to believe that you are under the impression that your insecurities, Ms. Hamer, are the most interesting thing about you. I shall consider our work together successful if I can disabuse you of that notion. A pretty girl who has no idea why she is unhappy is so much more interesting, not to mention sympathetic, than a pretty girl who embraces her neuroses. And a girl who adores the father who terrifies her finding some unexpected steel in herself would be a wonder to behold.

Next we shall hear from the remaining ten people in the class. However, as this is not a novel and I am not Charles Dickens, let us say we have heard from you all and move on.

Quarterbacking The First Workshop

How was that for you? Was that good for you? I hope it moves us, moves you, from this raw desire to *become* this thing – this actor – to where you might consider yourself to actually *be* that thing. Wanting is such a powerful feeling that it's possible to forget that wanting alone doesn't get us there. What will get us there is clarity.

I once interviewed a young actress (who had gone to a very good school and who was very beautiful) who told me, when I asked her what kind of things she wanted to do, "Well, I certainly don't want to do a stupid movie." When I asked what she meant by a stupid movie, she said, "Oh, you know, something with Julia Roberts." Now in what universe did that young woman think that trashing Julia Roberts was something I would join in on? (I am on record as liking Julia Roberts and whether or not she is Sarah Bernhardt's equal has nothing to do with anything.) I passed on that young woman. Her sense of entitlement might have been laughable had it not been so self-destructive. Five years later, she moved back to her hometown – having turned the entire business off. An accomplishment of sorts, I suppose.

But what about that question of mine? What kind of things does the young actor want to do? What kind of roles do you want to play? "Obviously, " shrugged one young Julliard beauty, "young women." Wrong answer, sweetheart. *Which* young women? Have any of you considered, even for a moment, where you belong in the casting universe? What *kind* of young woman are you? Which "Mystic Pizza" sister would you be? Maybe Meryl Streep can play anything that is put in front of her but it took a while and she was a pretty big star before they let her play blue collar ("Silkwood").

Range

If you have range, fine. Great even. But you are going to be defined, at least initially, by your type. Do not shrink away from this category. I am right about this. I am not some shyster trying to put you in a box. Of *course* you don't want to be type cast. Nobody does. But now hear this: You should be so lucky as to be type cast because that would mean you are getting cast. After that, it's your agent's job (with your talent helping every step of the way) to get you past that type and into another one and, if necessary, another one until you are finally recognized as your own type. So you don't want to play a bad guy? Do you think George C. Scott started out playing Patton? George C. Scott started out playing Shylock. Then he played a *really* bad guy in "Anatomy of a Murder." You're afraid you're not as great an actor as George C. Scott? That's really out of your control. Play what you get cast in and play it as well and as fully as you can. If it's a string of bad guys, so be it. If you are any good, sooner or later somebody will let you be the hero. If it takes a while, do not be discouraged. Hey, they're paying you for all those bad guys, right?

Of course, every young actor thinks it will be different for them and thank God young people feel that. Because, even when they are extraordinarily gifted (like Philip Seymour Hoffman) or extraordinarily beautiful (like Cameron Diaz), or both (like Billy Crudup), it still takes the business some time (though not much in Billy's case), to discover where this great talent or great beauty is going to belong. Sometimes somebody comes along, makes a splash and, boom, they're a star. Next time you look, they're gone. (Where *is* Wes Bentley, anyway?) (Oh, no, wait. He's back.) But let's say you are not a flash-in-the-pan. Let's say you are a good person and you want to *deserve* a career. In fact, you think you do deserve a career. How are you going to convince the gatekeepers of that? Why should you be allowed in? It is the actor's job, his work, his task, to assist the business in answering that question. And the ones who know the answer themselves will be first through the door.

So is that how it happens? Know thyself and it shall be given unto you? Well, not completely, but knowing yourself is a very good first step. Think long and hard about those two defining monologues for yourself. They will say the world about you. Even if you never perform them in public, they will help define you to yourself and thus to everybody else. Will they communicate how special you are? Maybe but I would suggest that's your job on top of choosing the monologues. If you know you are special, you have to let everyone else know it, too. Not in some loud-mouthed, annoying kind of way. Thrust yourself into the arena, stand there and be special. I have a niece who, when she was a little girl, used to go up to perfect strangers and announce, "Hi, I'm Kristan and I'm great." She was, too. (Still is, for that matter.) Well, that's what you have to do – only when you're a grownup, the "I'm great" should be silent. Think you can handle that?

You may be spotted right away. Or it may take a while. More likely, it will take a while. Where do they come from? Did Ryan Gosling just come along and, since he was so self-evidently brilliant and he had those eyes, they cast him in "The Notebook"? Hardly. He had been around for *nine years* by then and he was a Mouseketeer before that. Did Josh Hartnett waltz into the room, looking like he looks and did the powers that be decided to make him a star? Not that Josh Hartnett has any exemplary kind of career or even that he is an exemplary actor but he did not just come out of nowhere. He did a goddamn TV series. Did everyone just fall down and die the first time they saw Philip Seymour Hoffman act? (No – but they did the second time.) Bradley Cooper is one of the most coveted stars today — he spent over a decade in Hollywood doing nothing but TV shows (does anyone remember him alongside Jennifer

Garner on "Alias"?) and playing the bad guy in movies like "The Hangover" before he finally got taken seriously.

It's a process. It took Philip Seymour Hoffman a while to break in, though most folks think it happened pretty quickly for him. The first time I saw him was in that reading at Circle Rep and I fell down and died. I offered to sign him because my heart had been in my throat the entire time I watched him work. And he got a few jobs. The good jobs, the "Scent of a Woman" type jobs, took a while. In the beginning, as people were getting to know him, when I would suggest him, casting directors would tell me they actually felt he was a little over the top, maybe not *quite* right for whatever part they happened to be casting especially if it happened to be a good part. They could see his talent, of course, but, you know, did they have to really pay attention to him? They were perfectly happy to give him a few lines here and there – but a role? They didn't know how to cast him in a big role. What would the producer say when he walked into the audition? What would the studio say when they saw the tape?

Was he sexy? Hardly. He was kind of schlubby-looking. Whenever I pushed for him to be seen for a larger role, I got resistance. I started to worry. Phil didn't. He just kept working. He'd do *anything*. And he had a wonderfully supportive manager who said it was fine that he did anything so long as he worked. There was none of that attitude: This part has to be worthy of Phil stuff. Who, after all, was Phil? But those small parts were starting to get to him. For one audition, he actually asked about a larger part that I had pushed him for and they hadn't wanted to see him for. "Do they think I couldn't handle

it?" he asked me. I assured him it wasn't that. "Then what is it?"
"I don't know," I told him honestly. "Maybe they want a star."
"They're going to have to see me for bigger parts," he said. He
looked at me to make sure I agreed. Of course I agreed. And
we both got to work.

And they started seeing him for bigger parts. I don't know
how it happened but it did. In small but effective ways, he let
it be known to people he met that he was something special.
And I went into overdrive about how great he was and people
should not miss out on him. Phil had thought the work would
speak for itself. But it hadn't. What spoke the loudest in the very
beginning was the quiet, unassuming way he padded into the
room. His body language said, you don't need to pay attention
to me. And so they didn't. When he opened his mouth and
started to act – brilliantly – they had already stopped listening.
He stopped doing that. He took his specialness out of the bag
and started wearing it before he walked into the audition.
People noticed. The casting director of "Scent of a Woman"
noticed. She wanted him for that part the first time she read
the script. And so she danced the dance she had to do to make
the studio open to casting a newcomer in such a star-making
role (and a far from traditionally handsome newcomer at that).

Phil got the role. And everyone saw the movie and said, oh,
I get it, he's a great actor. Well then, that's a different story. Of
course, Phil had known that all along. I don't generally believe in
using brilliant actors as an example of anything because I think
that generally brilliance makes its own rules but Phil is a terrific
example because he never broke the cardinal rule: he never gave
up. Until he gave up on life itself and that is tragic beyond words.

67

Your Daily Monologue Routine

A Fox TV executive told me, "Nobody uses monologues anymore." Well, I am not surprised they have no use for monologues at Fox TV. But you still have to do monologues to get into an acting school. You have to do them for regional theatres. Some of the LORT Theatres in New York (The Public, Lincoln Center) ask for monologues. British directors love monologues as a way of getting to know an actor quickly.

Working on a monologue is like going to the gym. It's a workout. And it uses you. And you get to act. Larry Moss, acting teacher to the stars, recommends changing your monologues every few months. That's a swell idea. You get to keep looking for new material in addition to not going stale. Maybe you should study with Larry Moss.

Before you pick a monologue, sit down and have a serious talk with yourself. Who are you? Who do other people think you are? Who do *you* think you are? Try to narrow any difference in your answers. Other people have a pretty fair idea of who you are and they get that idea fairly quickly. And contrary to popular opinion, other people are not stupid. If you are going to be an actor, you are going to be in a business and you will need to know what that business is. In the language of the day, you will need to be a brand. It doesn't matter so much what that brand is. What matters is that it be clear and that it be accurate. In the early days of your career, you will need to call attention to yourself and once you have gained that attention, you will need to make the person or persons who have turned their gaze to you glad that they have taken the trouble.

Barbra Streisand's very first bio in a Broadway Playbill read that she had been "reared in Rangoon." Well, she had not been reared in Rangoon but anyone who had taken the time to read their program before the curtain went up was probably going to be on the lookout for this girl from Rangoon. Because it's interesting. When Tom Berenger read for his very first casting director, that casting director thought, this guy is not a very strong actor but I would pay money to see him act because he's so gorgeous. Now if you cannot raise the roof of a Broadway theatre with your talent like Barbra Streisand or blow people away with your looks like Tom Berenger (could), what can you do that is equally memorable? Nothing? Get out of the business.

Come on, you can do something. You have something to say. Something that is unique to you. Find out what that is and say it. Don't actually *say* it, you nincompoop, but say it with your body, your bearing, your being. More on this later. But in the back of your mind, consider why we should pay any attention to you whatsoever. Tom Berenger grew to be quite a decent actor but what really launched his career was: that face – and the body didn't hurt, either. Find your own propeller.

Mae West:

"Do you get me?"

THE PROTOTYPE

A friend and I were leading a workshop for one of the Big Three Schools when she said to a student, "I'm sorry, I'm having a hard time getting a handle on you. What's your prototype?"

Before you think that "Prototype" is casting director lingo for putting people in a box, think again. Choosing a prototype, in fact, asks you to create your own box. And why? So that people will not only know quickly how to cast you but also they will have recognized what's special about you. What you decide is your prototype is not something you necessarily have to actually say out loud very often. But it is something you should know. It is helpful. It is so helpful.

I was Kyra Sedgwick's first agent when she was sixteen. I was wild about her then and now, but in my early days of representing her, I was having a hell of a time trying to describe her to casting directors on the phone. I thought she was so pretty but there was something scrappy about her, too. Plus she was very funny and, even though she was only sixteen, she was sexy as all get out. And she was smart. It sounded too good to be true but it wasn't. Kyra was all those things. I just couldn't put them all in a sentence. "You've got to see this girl," I would say. "She's... well, she's great." Not exactly the most articulate pitch I ever made. So I called a big deal casting director who I had introduced to Kyra and who I knew liked her. "Help me out," I pleaded, "how would you describe Kyra to a director?" "Oh, that's easy," the casting director replied, "She's a Jewish Julie Christie." Perfect. That became Kyra Sedgwick's prototype – in my mind, at least. Probably not in Kyra's. Though I can't help but think it might have helped her if I had shared that little nugget with her.

Cast Me!

Come up with a prototype for yourself. This is not to limit you, not to make you fit into some existing way of thinking. I want you to create a whole new category that is custom-made just for you. At the same time, your prototype gives casting people a ready-made concept of how to cast you. This, after all, is what you want to communicate: Cast Me! Cast me in this part! The people who have the power to cast you need to be told. *How* should they cast you? You need to tell them. Not necessarily in words but in everything about you. Your demeanor, your manner of speaking, what you choose to speak about, how you put yourself together, every piece of clothing and jewelry (or lack thereof) on your body lets people know who you think you are.

You may think it is cheap and beneath you. It is cheap but

it should not be beneath you. I know all the objections. Can't they use their imaginations? I'm an artist – not a loaf of bread. What are you supposed to do – limit yourself by picking a single image?

Stars, you think, never had to suffer this indignity. Stars are their own prototype. Stars are unique personalities (that's why they are stars) who often had trouble getting people to pay attention at the beginning of their careers precisely because there had never been anyone quite like them before.

You Are So Many Things — How Can You Pick Just One?

It's easy to swallow that people didn't know what to do with Philip Seymour Hoffman but listen up – Julia Roberts and Meryl Streep were both thought too odd, too tall, too awkward, too *galumphing* to be leading ladies. Now, of course, they are considered – certainly by me – to be two of the world's great beauties. If there is nothing odd or quirky about you, if you are just plain beautiful, that's not such a blessing either. People will write you off as unfunny or untalented and probably an entitled pain in the neck. Before you've even opened your mouth. It doesn't matter if you are gorgeous or off-center or just plain weird. What matters is that you are *something* and what that something is is very, very clear. But, you protest, you are so many things. How can you pick just one? Because you have to. Because stars do. Could you describe Sandra Bullock in a single sentence? I can. She's Maya Rudolph – beautiful. If that's too much trouble, get that first class ticket back to Bloomfield Hills.

Here are some examples of prototypes suggested to me by casting directors:

- Matthew Modine is a contemporary Jimmy Stewart

- Will Patton is a Southern Robert De Niro

- Paul Giamatti is a cross between Charles Laughton and Bruce Dern

- Bill Macy is a mix of Howdy Doody and Robert Duval

- Viola Davis is a cross between a younger Alfre Woodard and Allison Janney.

I once represented Allison Janney and couldn't get her arrested. No one knew what to do with her. Wish I had thought to sell her as a whiter, taller Viola Davis. She might have been famous a lot sooner. But then, when I represented Ms. Janney, no one had ever heard of Viola Davis. And try selling Viola Davis when she first started. Surely, one of our finest living actresses and no one knew what to do with her. Mark Schlegel, her first agent knew what to do – he signed her.

What's your prototype? Not only is it worth thinking about — it is worth obsessing about. I am not asking you to alter your behavior to come up with some fake personality. I am asking you to discover your behavior and what it says about you.

Don't change a thing. If you are not happy with who you are, that is not my department. Just don't deny it. Get over being unhappy about it. Don't worry about the special little sparkly parts of you that you feel are essential to your being. If there really are special little parts of you vital to who you are, they will shine through no matter what you do. If they don't, they weren't there in the first place and you were deluded. Do not be deluded.

Define Your Spine

Locate and define the spine of your identity. Do not muddy it up with all the things you *might* be if you were given half a chance. Do I really care that Brad Pitt can play a bozo? He can do "Burn After Reading" *after* he becomes a star. (And he did.) Is it essential that I know Vera Farmiga could make an interesting love interest for George Clooney? Not at the beginning of her career it's not because that's not the first thing that comes to mind when I go to cast her. Brad Pitt is a hunk. It is a bonus for his career that he can play a clueless dork. Vera Farmiga is a complex creature with a lovely sense of humor. She is Irene Dunne updated. It is icing on the cake that she is also a very sensual woman who has great chemistry with male stars.

Will they see how special you are? That's your job: walk into the audition room and, in the most compelling way possible, say, hi, here I am. This is me. This is my deal. All before you open your mouth. Whatever that deal of yours happens to be you must discover and hone to a fare-thee-well. When someone you have never seen before walks out on Fallon, you know by the time she sits down if you like her or not. When some twerp on "American Idol" opens his mouth to sing, you are ready to put him in the top ten or send him packing by the time he has sung the first line of his song. This is how people respond to each other. Get used to it.

If the people you meet think you are a star – or capable of being one – they will know within the first 30 seconds. But remember, they spend most of their time casting non-stars who will make their stars look good.

Everybody in show business thinks they have a corner on being able to see a future star. Everybody in show business is mostly wrong. You have no control over whether or not you seem like a star. OK? You do have some control over *how you project your identity.*

Once you have defined yourself as a castable entity, put whatever elements make you desirable at the front of your behavior. Wait a minute. Should anyone really have to think about actually behaving that way? Isn't that just wrong?

Lead with the desirable parts. If you're a big fan of the casting director, say so. Say why. Do not gush. If you tell good stories, have one or two ready. If you have a good body, do not hide it. Do NOT flaunt it. If you are particularly skilled in some field that is germane to what you are auditioning for – soccer, clowning, speaking French – say so. Just work it into the conversation. If you graduated summa cum laude and it applies to this project, say so. If you dropped out of high school, say that, too. Anything that makes you right for this role is a desirable part of you. The rest of you will not go away. The rest of you is and always will be you. You just don't need to present every part of you all of the time. In fact, if you do, it will confuse the hell out of the people with the jobs. Not to mention it will be exhausting to you and anyone near you.

This is an exercise, not a way of life. This is meant to be a tool after all, not to turn you into one. Pick a day or an hour and put the distilled version of you on display. Make it how you show up in your life – the way you dress, the way you walk into a room, the way you eat a meal, behave at a party, act in a restaurant. I think you will discover that, while it sounds limiting at first, it is, in fact, life enhancing. So long as who you are is at the core of everything you do, you will be able to do everything you do in a much clearer, cleaner way. And people will not only know *how* to cast you, they will *want* to cast you.

Some other descriptions of various young actors which have proven helpful have been:

A younger Julia Roberts.

Keanu Reeves with a sense of humor.

A cross between Jonah Hill and John Cusack.

The love child of Derek Jeter and Bjork.

A mix of Jennifer Lopez and Mo'Nique.

A combination of Rod Steiger and Wally Cox.

Ellen Page and Kat Dennings had a baby.

Ben Affleck with a hint of Jane Lynch.

All three Marx Brothers.

Idris Elba is a black Steve McQueen, because he is the epitome of cool, he is great looking and he is a superior actor.

We are concerned with careers. Yours! So let's brainstorm, shall we? Surely, as I have been speaking, you have been considering possibilities for yourselves. If not, please start now and continue while I digress for a moment.

One exception to the prototype rule: it does not apply to the greatest among us. There are no rules for those who sit in the pantheon. In my experience, the greatest actors – Laurence Olivier, Maureen Stapleton, Meryl Streep, Sada Thompson, Dustin Hoffman, Mary Alice, Alan Arkin, Philip Seymour Hoffman – are almost indescribable when you meet them. They seem to be blank slates. They are forms of humanity (as opposed to castable entities) waiting to discover what is required of them. It cannot be easy to be someone like that. But these are the priests of the temple.

The real truth about the greatest among us is maybe that they don't know *how* to lie. The rest of us would benefit from having a prototype. When Stephen Dorff comes alive for a photographer's still camera in "Somewhere," he instantly becomes a complete personality which might as well have a sign on it saying: I am a movie star. It is a *great* piece of acting. Am I suggesting Stephen Dorff belongs in the Pantheon? Why do you bother me with that question? You think you're a better actor than Stephen Dorff? Show me.

In the meantime, let's hear and see and feel your prototype. That will be the subject of our next Workshop.

WORKSHOP TWO:
Prototypes

*You have come armed with your prototype. I see no
problems ahead for any of you. And I'm just going to
pretend I do not feel the tension rising in the room.
There is no need for tension. This a chance for us all
to be brilliant. And that's always fun.*

Who wants to start?

Bless you, Ms. Logan. Describe yourself to
me. Ah. A combination of Janeane Garafalo and
Cate Blanchette with a touch of Carrie Washington. Well. Ms.
Logan, I must say I agree with the Janeane Garafolo part of the
equation but why Ms. Blanchette? Choosing Cate Blanchette is
a bit like choosing Meryl Streep. They can do anything which
tells us nothing and does not serve you in this exercise. And
Carrie Washington?

"For a touch of soul?"

Ms. Logan, I would encourage you to come up with your

own soul rather than borrow Carrie Washington's. There is little enough work for actors of color without Caucasians co-opting their inner turmoil.

"I didn't, I don't, I didn't mean to – what you said. Take her inner turmoil."

Do you have another definition for soul?

"I was just trying to make myself more interesting."

I think we can leave behind the romantic notion that Black Americans are more interesting because of all they have suffered. Frequently, Black people are more interesting than Caucasians but I do not know why that should be so. It frequently is so. Is "soul" the reason? I am not so sure. And I am all for Black actors having white prototypes for themselves, if only to encourage more color blind casting. Let's get back to Cate Blanchette. What were you hoping to imply with her?

"Skill."

Good. A very straightforward answer. How about: A classically trained Janeane Garafolo?

"I like that."

You are welcome to it. Keep in mind that none of these descriptions we come up with are meant necessarily to be voiced or talked about in any way. They are meant to give you a clear picture of what you have to offer, who you are, how other people may think of you. Do not, in the middle of an interview confide to a casting director that you are kind of like a classically trained Janeane Garafolo. She will think you are crazy and I will deny all knowledge of you.

Mr. Fitz-William, how about you? The love child of Barbara Stanwyck and Michael Urie? I love that. I love that you have even heard of Barbara Stanwyck. It's also inventive as hell. And it's not a bad description of you. Nice work.

Who's next — Mr. Younger? A cross between Matt Bomer and Stephen Amell? Are you kidding me, Mr. Younger?

"Yeah, I am."

You are a wise guy, Mr. Younger. I generally like wise guys. Especially when they are smart. Can you follow that up with something which accurately describes you?

A straight Jim Parsons.

Not bad. Would you elaborate?

"I'm kind of weird looking but there's something sexy about me. Something appealing. And I'm smart. Probably won't be playing too many high school dropouts."

I think we may say that Mr. Younger has an unbiased and an accurate picture of himself. Very nice, Mr. Younger. Ms. Andrews?

"This was really hard. I couldn't come up with anything."

Surely you must have had some ideas.

"I feel silly. Maybe Mary Lynn Rajskub?"

Mary Lynn Rajskub is a first class talent and you may be as well but you are mad if you think you are like her in any way. Perhaps her co-worker Ms. Cuthbert?

"Oh, gosh, no."

And why not?

"She's so pretty."

As are you, Ms. Andrews. In fact, I would say that you are the simplest person in the class to come up with a description for. You, Ms. Andrews, are the girl next door.

"But that's so boring."

Yes, frequently it is. And it's up to you to make it interesting. Thank you all for your efforts.

Rose Schulman, acting teacher, Boston University:

"An actor must first have an instrument. We are prone to believe that if we can imagine and pretend, we can act. If as children we could make something of "three little kittens lost their mittens," could mimic others well; then as we reached the adolescent stage, work ourselves into a good crying or laughing scene because of our emotional experiences, like falling in love for the first time and being jilted in love for the first time, we are inclined to believe we can act. All of this may at some time bear fruit, but as the study of acting begins it is as good as useless."

THE SCHOOLS

W ell, every school has a football team, why shouldn't every school have a theatre department? I applaud all these theatre departments. My only beef is that some don't tell you how hard it is out there in the real world. Some encourage the perceived advantage of having a graduate showcase. That showcase, many schools imply, is going to give you a leg up in the business. It *may* – it's possible – but it is certainly no reason to go to school for three years. Getting an agent, carving out a career, sustaining that career, prevailing in your profession and being successful are all very hard things to do and they may not even happen. You might fall considerably short of your goal. Applications don't seem to be down at USC for Trojan hopefuls as a result of young people and their parents knowing not only how hard it is to work in pro-ball but also being fully aware that the chances of sustaining a life threatening injury along the way are pretty high. Both the actors and the athletes are driven. They're both crazy. The difference between them, I would suggest, is that the jocks marginally are better informed.

Surely not everybody playing college football imagines there will be a place for him in the NFL when he gets out of school. What if the kid just likes playing football? And if he wants to play while he's in college, there's a team he can play on. If it's a good team, then great. If it's the Trojans, the kid is probably a gifted athlete. Does that mean he's going to be guaranteed a place in the draft? Same goes with acting, right? There's a theatre department and there are plays to act in. Go for it! Just don't expect the keys to the kingdom with your diploma. Maybe you won't even want show business at the end of three years. Maybe you'll just go on to be a more compassionate doctor than you would have been without the drama classes. Or you might become an architect who wants to create dramatic low-income housing when all you thought you wanted was design beach homes in the Caribbean.

Diplomas Are Not Keys To The Kingdom

When we invite young people into our theatre departments, let us do so with open arms but let them know we are offering them a skill and not a career. They will be paying us money. We will be training them to be worthy of other people paying *them* money.

Our primary concern here is the student who does want the business. It's not going to be a walk in the park. It's not going to always be fair. No one should feel discriminated against because of looks, talent, drive, originality and whatever else is currently considered desirable. Why should this be? Does this reflect reality? Let me tell you, the business will discriminate plenty when the time comes to handing our jobs. There is nothing democratic or fair about the business.

A great actor or a great movie star, even a great talk show host (hello, James Corden) can come from anywhere. This is good news for anyone who is too intimidated or too broke or too timid to try for one of the top schools. That's what makes the business so exciting. Ever since Abe Lincoln walked five hundred miles a day to that little one room school house, it has been held possible in America to come from utter obscurity and wind up at the top of whatever field of you aim for. We all know stories of now famous people who were turned down by every single one of those famous acting programs. You don't know those stories? Give you an example? What do you think this is – gossip? Maybe you don't even want to be a great actor. Maybe you just want to be the Sexiest Man Alive. And if you don't give a crap about art, if you are just pure ambition from head to toe, well, that's fine, too, but you can skip this part about the schools.

When I was starting out as an agent, I would comb the off-off-Broadway theatres and basements of New York's West Village and Lower East Side looking for driven, gifted performers. That's where the good ones were then. And I was driven to find them – being young and hungry myself. And the chances of finding someone quirky and exciting were much higher at a theatre (no matter how ramshackle and out of the way it was) than they were in the halls of academe. That is not so much the case anymore. More and more these days, even the passionate youngsters, the holy ones, are choosing to go to the BFA or MFA or conservatory programs of our nation's colleges and universities.

Know Your Guru

Maybe you just want to go to a good school and that good school happens to be in New York. Maybe you will find you love to study and, for now, that is all you want to do. A few years ago I met an African American actress who took the excellent four year undergrad conservatory program at SUNY Purchase – and she decided after she graduated there to take the three year MFA program at NYU. What was she waiting for, I asked her. Why not just get to it and go out and get work? She told me she didn't feel ready for the business. Not the first time I've heard that and I always admired a young person who knew they were not fully cooked. (Actors who have been studying for a decade and still don't feel 'ready' are a different story. They're just deluded.) But there was more.

This young woman, in addition to being gifted, was overweight. She said she wanted to take three years and become thin because she did not want a career as 'the fat one'. Now there is a motivated person. So she went to NYU and she lost the weight. I just saw her in one of her final shows.

She's still not ready. She's still three quarters-baked. And it breaks my heart – because she is talented. She just needs to work. She needs to get out of the classroom. Maybe she picked the wrong school, maybe she needs therapy and not an acting class, maybe she just hasn't found the right teacher. I think she picked the wrong school and, after talking with her, I think she knows it. Don't pick the wrong school. And if you do, change.

How do you know which grad school is right for you? I had a client who chose his school for their alleged devotion to Shakespeare. He didn't get to do Shakespeare until his third year. You can't really say to your potential school choice: what plays will you be doing while I am there and what roles will I have? They don't know what plays they'll be doing. Can't they at least promise you a major role, two major supporting roles? Doesn't work that way.

Actually, it works all sorts of ways. Some schools, you are simply assigned a part. Other schools, you must audition – either for the faculty or for a jobbed in director. Or both. Other schools you have to audition for the director *who is also a student!* The blind leading the blind, if you ask me. But in almost none of the schools do they have the least notion of what plays they will be doing the following year, let alone during your entire tenure while there. This is fine. Just be aware.

I used to think that being in school in New York City was an advantage because there is all this theatre to go to but those kids at NYU and Juilliard, and even Fordham, Marymount, the New School and Pace barely have time to brush their teeth, let alone go to the theatre. In New York, however, the theatre can come to you – agents and managers and casting people can come to see you in your shows and maybe they will love you. Grad school or conservatory training should be like Chicago – all about you and your growth as an artist. If that makes you want to throw up, skip grad school.

How do you know you will be happy with your choice of schools? You don't. Are you capable of being happy? (Not my department.) You hope. Do your research, visit the school, pick somewhere that feels good and pray.

The Showcase

All of these programs, *all* of them, put on showcases for agents and managers and casting directors in New York and Los Angeles – many schools do both coasts – where these young aspirants expect to find an agent. It's not outside the realm of possibility. If you go for the training, you may leave with a terrific experience – if you go for the benefit of the showcase, you may well be disappointed. More often than not, it turns out to be a hysterical, misguided, not terribly relevant offering of your gifts to a questionable number of people who may or may not be able to help you find work. Never mind that you might have an off day doing your scene or scenes at your showcase. Never mind that the scene might have been ineptly chosen for or by you. Never mind what a nervous wreck you will certainly be. The pressure and the palpable air of desperation are suffocating. Never mind that the kids have no idea how to dress – young men in un-ironed oxford shirts or, more opportunistically, *no* shirts (if they have logged time at the gym), young women in silk dresses (which look terrible under lights). Never mind that there are not that many agents or managers or casting directors in the audience anymore. Unless we're talking one of the top ten or eleven schools and then there will be a smattering.

You do not need to go to one of the so-called top schools in order to learn how to act. By showcase time, you ought to have learned how to act. And if you think the showcase is going to get you a career, well, you haven't been listening to me. If we are talking about the top three schools, there will be people from the industry in attendance – actually quite a few – most of whom have come so that they can tell their bosses the next day that they were there and to text their peers that there was no one of interest on view – was there? – and what a phenomenal waste of time it all was. Do I mean the agents don't just love going to the showcases? Yes, I mean that.

Agents texting each other is an important part of what I just said. Everyone is afraid of missing someone. Was there a star? What if there was? What if the agents missed him – or her? Agents usually like to sign somebody – all while they are claiming there was no one worth signing, just to cover their ass. Maybe somebody had a spark or two. Maybe the agent will sign them. (They can always be dropped if it doesn't work out.) Obviously, if someone looks like a star, they will get signed. But stars don't always look like stars. At a showcase, they look like beginners which, at a showcase, they are. People were not lined up around the block to sign Wendell Pierce. They should have been but they were not. (You don't think Wendell Pierce is a star? Get his career and then tell me that.)

Beautiful people, however, do tend to look like stars

because many stars are beautiful. But a beautiful person is not necessarily a star. Not by a long shot. Nevertheless, beautiful people tend to get signed at showcases. So if you're beautiful, you will have an easier time at the beginning. You will go into the beautiful people line. Which is shorter than the other lines. But still, not short.

You would think that outsize talent would just leap off people like Fran McDormand and Jane Kaczmarek and J. Smith Cameron and Joan Allen. Well, there was no line outside the dressing room door for any of those women all of whom were first signed by an agent named Susan Smith. She was a superb agent with a near infallible eye for talent. She was also rather a nightmare to work for. I worked for her. What she taught me – other than how to survive ignominious put-downs all day long – was that when you see a talented person, sign them. Most agents go through this tortured process of: How hard would it be to sell that person? Is that kind of look in style these days? Is that guy going to be a royal pain? These are questions that have nothing to do with talent. Dan Hedeya and Glynnis Johns were two of the most unpleasant people I have ever represented. Neither of them were beauties and neither of them ever stopped working – in other words they made money. Did Susan care that they gave me shit all day long? Of course not. *She* gave me shit all day long. She cared if the clients were working or not. The point of the office was to make money and we did. You know who else Susan had on her list? David Paymer. One of the best actors and nicest guys alive who you wouldn't look at twice if you passed him on the street. One of the best actors alive? Yes. A star? See: Wendell Pierce.

Most of the schools are descendants of the dozen or so programs created to supply actors to the regional repertory theatres that sprang up across America in the '60s to present classic theatre and discover new American playwrights. There were so few classically trained actors in America back then so these university programs were devised to make some. Since all of those repertory theatres had companies, these schools were training actors for actual jobs that would be waiting for them.

Today there are few companies waiting for the newbies, there is only show business and The Oregon Shakespeare Festival. Well, kidding. Or exaggerating. There remains, however, a vast number of training programs training actors for jobs which no longer exist and large numbers of buildings called theatres with large staffs and no resident companies. It is up to you, the student, and soon to be graduate, to map out your path when you get out in the world. Why not start your own company? This is an increasingly popular choice. But it's a helluva lot of work; most companies don't make it. You were trained to act, not to run a company.

Why not write a one-man show for yourself? Camryn Manheim and Linda Hunt, neither of whom is what anyone I know would call highly marketable, both of whom could be described as artists with excellent careers, were languishing in New York (we're talking different decades here) without agents or careers. Each of them wrote a one-person play, put it on, got an agent and got a career. They knew that would happen. That's why they wrote the damn plays. ("Wake Up, I'm Fat" and "Elizabeth I" respectively.) It helps that they are both wildly talented. I saw "Elizabeth I" and wanted to sign Ms.

Hunt but my boss at the time wouldn't let me. That's another story, though really part of the same story.

If an agent wants to sign you, make sure the agency is behind the agent who wants to sign you. That same boss wouldn't let me sign Bruce Willis, either (said he was balding and over the hill – well, he was balding). I should have left and started my own agency. That's another thing. Make sure your agent has some balls – mine dropped a few years later.

Summing Up

Learning how to act at a university can be a fantastic experience. Some of the teachers at those schools are excellent, inspiring even. And doing nothing but acting all day long can get into your bones and you really will become an artist, which is what you want, right? So, if you choose a school that feels right to you because you have visited there and talked to students who said things that made sense to you and felt good about the faculty you met, you are likely to have a glorious time. You will come through your three or four years there knowing how to act. You can learn how to act anywhere. It is your passion that counts, not the school's reputation.

Do not choose a school for its showcase. Do not spend years of your life based on the imagined results of a one hour dog and pony show put together to show off your most marketable self by people whose field of expertise does not include knowing what your most marketable self is, let alone how to market it. Half the time *agents* don't even know what's marketable and that's their *job*. I vote for talent. That's always marketable. Is

Peter Dinklage marketable? He seems to have a career. Maybe he's just GOOD.

Naming Names

Yale, NYU and Juilliard. Those are the top three schools. Because of their first-rate training, yes, but also because they are in or close to New York. And because they attract the most talented young people thanks to their reputations. Where did they get those reputations? They have the largest number of graduates who have become famous. Simple as that. An actor who becomes famous is pure gold for whatever institution can lay claim to having trained them. If you've got the best and the brightest clamoring to get in, naturally you'll be able to claim credit for the successes you turn out. Naturally, top teachers are attracted to top talent. They bask in the glory of their students' future successes. Stella Adler and Lee Strasberg were each fabulously brilliant acting teachers. There are books written about their methods. But what do most of us know about them? Stella Adler taught Marlon Brando, and Lee Strasberg taught Marilyn Monroe.

If you are gifted as all get out and you can only afford to go to Podunk U. which happens to be near your hometown, then go there and become famous and they will name a building after you. But will you really learn how to act? Don't you need some genius to take you by the hand? Before Marlon Brando studied at the feet of Stella Adler, he studied with his mother first. (Who might have been a genius, not sure.) Podunk U. could be fine.

The schools just below the top three but still considered

outstanding are University of California at San Diego, Rutgers, Brown/Trinity Rep, North Carolina School of the Arts, University of Tennessee (fully endowed, by the way), SUNY Purchase, University of Texas at Austin, Carnegie-Mellon, ACT in San Francisco – and, I guess, the University of Michigan which is particularly good for musical theatre. Hey, musical theatre performers are actors, too. If you prick them, do they not bleed?

There are loads of programs that do not make up the top tier which are excellent. (There are even more which are not.) Do your research. Contact graduates. Find somebody who knows somebody who went where you think you want to go. Make sure the reason you want to go somewhere still applies to that school. Northwestern lived for years on the legacy of a great acting teacher named Alvina Krause who had been dead for decades while they were still promoting her name. It's still a very fine program but for different reasons. There is an extraordinary acting teacher named Robin Lynn-Smith at Cornish College of the Arts in Seattle. Ever hear of it? Worth hearing about.

What are the schools themselves looking for? I asked the heads of the programs at several of these places what turned them on. An answer I liked greatly was: "First we look for people we want to spend three years of our lives with." That was North Carolina. I can tell you for a fact that that also applies to producers and directors who are looking to cast a role – someone they want to spend three months with or three weeks with or three days with. Someone who is a joy to have around. Be pleasant, for God's sake. It won't kill you.

A thoughtful answer from Yale: "What I'm looking for is talent but that is such a vague word. It means a lot of different things to different people. I think talent has something to do with an actor's depth of imagination. A talented actor has a vital imagination and can make me believe in something that isn't actually real but seems so real to them that I buy into it. It's a childlike quality that most of us shed rather early on in our lives. If you can imagine deeply enough that you can transform into another person, and that act of transformation is both the artistry of acting as well as the greatest source of pleasure to the actor, then I think we are talking of a person with talent." That guy should write his own book. (His name is Ron Van Lieu.) NYU said, "a unique voice." Tennessee said: "I am seeking actors with the ability and drive to succeed at a high level." So he's looking for stars. I like that. Most actors are looking to *be* stars. Most people don't start out wanting to be the maid in the second act. Linda Hunt wanted to be a star. All four feet nine inches of her. And she is!

So that's a little window into the inner workings of how decisions at some of the schools are made. It's safe to say that all of the schools would offer similar versions of those answers. If you decide that some form of academic training is what you want, above all, make sure your motives are clear. Make sure that your reason or reasons have something to do with acting and not with getting an agent. Once you've got that figured out, enjoy the ride.

One professor I know was told by her Dean that her log entry of 200 hours to direct a play was surely a typo. Directing a play couldn't possibly take more than 20 hours. In what universe? With tone deaf Deans like these in charge of the teachers, we must be extremely grateful for the lion's share of teachers who continue to care so very deeply.

In very large part, getting a job has not much to do with acting. Acting is what you get to do once you get the job. Does being a good actor matter? What do you think I am, a complete philistine? I'm just saying that there are skills which have nothing to do with acting but that have everything to do with getting an acting job that are essential to know. There are actors, sometimes wonderful actors, who are one, two, or even five years out of school wandering around wondering why they can't get work. They *know* they can act. But acting is simply not enough.

MARTHA GRAHAM on a creative life:

"There is a vitality, a life-force, an energy, a quickening that is translated through you into action and because there is only one of you in all of time, this expression is unique. And if you block it, it will never exist through any other medium and be lost."

FROM THE SCHOOLS TO THE BUSINESS

The schools do not comprehensively address how to get into the business. That's not their mandate. Nor should it be. Let's face it. What does the business have to do with the art? Years ago, I saw a wonderful teacher at one of the schools act in a play with her students. I was enchanted by her and asked if I might send her on some auditions. She told me she had no ambition other than to teach. I insisted and she said OK. So I suggested her for quite a nice part in a film that had just been announced and the casting director said she would see her as a favor to me. Immediately after the audition, the casting director called me and said, you cannot send that woman out; she's terrible. I said that first of all, she is not terrible. She might have had a different idea of the role than the casting director had, or she might have had a hideous taxi driver on her way to the audition or....No, the casting director insisted, cutting me off, she's terrible, she's too big, she's too loud, she doesn't look at the camera, she has no idea how to audition. Oh. Well, that's different. She doesn't know how to audition. So I thanked the casting director for seeing the actress/teacher in the first place and for the (actually helpful) feedback and then I called the woman. As gently and diplomatically as I could, I explained that there were perhaps some audition skills that might be helpful for her to think about. The woman laughed. Loudly. She said that of course she had no idea how to audition and no interest in learning. She thanked me for the experience – reminding me that the whole sad saga had been my idea. She added that she had probably been terrible. Oh, said I. I was sure she hadn't been terrible.

Many schools have classes in how to audition. The ones that are most helpful are taught by casting directors or former casting directors who tell you to never audition like *this* and then the following week by a different casting director who tells you to always do it like *that*. In other words, classes which will reveal to you that nobody has a corner on the right way to audition and the final path is up to you. There are certain things all casting directors will agree are essential and these things you must treat as gospel. Everything else is personal preference and you should know that. There is nothing wrong with personal preference. Just don't mistake it for gospel.

Talk to these casting directors. Engage with people who do it for a living. Are you not destined to be one of them? And maybe those *former* casting directors shouldn't have been out of the business too long because there are styles in auditioning and what works today did not work five years ago. Unless you're auditioning for "Hamlet." And even then, who's to say? Did you ever see Michael Almereyda's film of "Hamlet" with Ethan Hawke and my old clients Liev Schreiber, Karl Geary and Tim Blake Nelson? It's fantastic and it's got nothing to do with how we traditionally look at Shakespeare. Mr. Almereyda, who is brilliant, is a child of film, not theatre. I promise you none of those boys auditioned for him by bellowing out "Oh what a rogue and peasant slave." Though Mr. Hawke probably did not have to audition.

Sometimes the schools will invite individual agents and managers to talk to their students – take advantage of the exposure. The agents and managers get a first look at who will be coming on the scene from this school next year and, not incidentally, a first chance to offer representation. This, of course, is the hope behind the invitation. Not likely to really happen, however. And ethically questionable if you ask me. Though, in general, ethics and agenting have very little to do with each other.

A year ago, I led a workshop which had a wonderful kid in it. He was fat and obviously quite gay and extremely gifted. Even though the stage and screen are both populated with many fantastic gay actors who play straight roles surpassingly well, a casting director may have a hard time believing that this kid could when he walked in the room. He had no idea what he brought to the table and suspected he would probably wind up working in a box office somewhere. But before he started a career with Ticketmaster, he wanted to give acting a whirl because he loved it so. He met a bunch of agents through his school when they came to talk to the kids and none of them were interested which surprised no one, least of all him. After a year of auditioning and meeting people and discovering what works and what doesn't, he recently signed with an excellent agency – which had passed on him when he was still in school because he was fat and too obviously gay. That's all he knew how to show them when he was in school. They signed him because he was a complete pleasure and a superior actor and right for a lot of roles which a cursory glance at him wouldn't immediately tell you. He learned in his year out of school that being helpful, talented, and right for stuff was what people were looking for. (I just saved you a year in the trenches.)

The doyenne of New York casting directors is held in such reverence because she was consistently the first person to hire a truly impressive number of people who went on to have important careers. Plus she recognizes talent when she sees it. The minimum requirement for being a casting director, you would think. An agent, too. You would think. The difficulty here is that these days agents, and to a lesser degree casting directors, are no longer looking for talent.

What they are looking for now are stars. Remember the dark ages when it used to be fun to go see a Dustin Hoffman picture to see who he was going to be this time? You don't? Well, remember recently wondering if the new Focker movie was going to be as funny as the last Focker movie? It was more fun in the dark ages. Do I seem obsessed with having fun? Is that bad?

Acting in Classical Theatre — A Word

If you want to do classical theatre, you absolutely have to get training. It is necessary. Shakespeare requires a degree of technical expertise – speech, voice, movement – that you don't possess when you wake up in the morning, no matter who you are. Speaking that language is something no amount of talent is going to give you the ability to handle without training. Speaking Shakespeare is a skill and skills must be acquired. Unless you are Marlon Brando whose Mark Antony was brilliant and he never studied Shakespeare a day in his life. Marlon Brando will be an exception to every single pronouncement I make in these pages. Therefore, he doesn't count. Genius makes its own rules. What's that? You think you may be a genius? Well, then, put down this book immediately.

It is a never-ending source of wonder to me, the number of young people who want to do classical theatre. Shakespeare, Ibsen, Chekhov, Congreve, for God's sake – people, *young* people continue to be moved by the power of these great ones and how fortunate for the human race that this is so. But someone should be jumping up and down pointing out that there are very few venues left which put on classic plays and they don't pay very well. There is the Oregon Shakespeare Festival, which has a year-round performance schedule. I had a client who was classically trained, made a lot of money in show business, moved to Oregon, became a member of the company there and thought he had died and gone to heaven. But he had made his money and raised his family while working in show business. So there is Oregon. They may even pay a living wage.

Nothing to make an agent's blood rush to his heart (if he had one) but enough for an artist.

Then there is everywhere else. That means a few dozen Shakespeare festivals scattered around the country, which have seasons of a few months, mostly in the summer. There is The New York Shakespeare Festival, run by The Public Theatre, that does a couple of classic plays (usually Shakespeare – when they are not doing musicals they hope to move to Broadway) in Central Park each summer and always at least intend to do one at their downtown theatre during the regular season and frequently they do. The Central Park season has become a playground for stars and, sometimes, some very good Shakespeare. The salary? Forget about it. It's charity work (which stars can afford to do). There is a wonderful organization in New York called Theatre for a New Audience. They do classic plays. Sometimes as many as three a year. (I can't get the irony out of that sentence. Three is actually a large number.) The salary is somewhere around $800 a week (same as the New York Shakespeare Festival). Classic Stage Company in New York also, as advertised, does classics. The salary there is around $700 a week. Sometimes one of the regional theatres in this country, which were originally built for the express purpose of presenting classic theatre across America, will decide to do a classic play. The Guthrie frequently does classic theatre for which actors are paid $900 or $1000 per week, a figure that has been constant for the last twenty years. (Bears repeating.) So work – for the classical actor in regional theatre – is... spotty. And it's no longer a world in which to make a living.

The actors' salaries at all regional theatres haven't really budged in the last few decades. It hovers around $800. The Long Wharf Theatre and Yale Rep are both in New Haven. Long Wharf pays $700 And Yale Rep pays $1000, (and all these numbers are, of course, if you're in the union). As an agent, I used to feel, what's the difference? Then a client, who was working at Long Wharf, suggested I compare his commission to me with the commission a friend of his working at Yale was paying his agent. Ah. I saw the difference. Anyway, no one expects actors to live on the money they make in the theatre because who could? They think the actor will be subsidized by commercials or voice over work or family money. And many of them are. Are you? (How dare they think that, if you ask me.)

In the early days of The Actors Theatre of Louisville, there were twenty actors in the company (year round), five people in the office and 85% of the seats were sold. Currently, there is *no* acting company, there are 40 people in the office (year round) and the attendance is still around 85%. What is wrong with this picture? When did the theatre become about the *support staff*? I'm sorry but there's something seriously out of whack. How is The Actors Theatre of Louisville relevant? Well, they occasionally do something by Shakespeare. That's nice.

Acting In The Real World

If you want to work in classical theatre, God bless you but make sure the trust fund is intact. If I haven't discouraged you yet, God bless you again. Of course there are other acting possibilities for classically trained actors beside classical theatre. There are all the regional theatres which now present whatever was the hot show in New York two years ago and however many one- and two-person shows their subscribers can tolerate. This will pay about that same $700, $800 or $900 a week. And at least the hot show in New York a few years ago was probably a serious play. Maybe even "The History Boys." Or "Dancing at Lughnasa." You don't really need to be classically trained to do "Dancing at Lughnasa" but these theatres and their casting directors like to give the jobs they have to people who have taken the trouble to learn how to act (and then pay them not even enough to pay off their student loans) because the good thing is, people at these places really do care about talent.

Then there is Mecca – New York City. Most of the really good theatre in New York is done at the non-profits. (Even though both "History Boys" and "Dancing at Lughnasa" were commercial productions. Both British, as well.) You could work at Second Stage (one of the absolute best of the non-profits) for $700 a week. (The Artistic Director makes $380,000 a year or approximately $7,000 a week.) And what of the theatre's holy grail – Broadway? Yes, Broadway pays a living wage (and employs, on average, 400-some actors a year). Equity minimum on Broadway is $1861 a week. It will be your second or your third time out on the Great White way before you will make more. And it will be a while before you make the $100,000 a week (each) reputed to be paid to Nathan Lane and Matthew Broderick. The generosity of individual producers varies but, unless you are a star, it is unlikely you will make more than $3,000 a week on Broadway. This sounds like and is decent money but, keep in mind, most Broadway shows have a life expectancy of just a few months.

Lincoln Center prides itself on paying actors well and they do. Everyone in the cast of "War Horse," all thirty-six of them, made $100,000 a year. (God, no wonder ticket prices are so high.) But I'll bet the theatre was still raking it in.

What about television? There are currently more than fifty television shows shooting in New York. If you do good roles on three of them in a year (and a very good year that would be), you may make close to $10,000. For the year. Sure, there are movies, as well. A studio film could pay good money (though not above scale – $2800 for the week and you are not likely to work more than a week), an independent as little as $75 a day. I had a client who made over $250,000 on his second movie a decade or so ago and currently can't get arrested for scale. I had another client who made scale for his first ten movies and then won an Academy Award and stopped complaining about money. (He found other things.) Maybe one of the more gratifying perks of an Academy Award is that it shames people into stop offering you scale. At least for a while.

If you are a character actor, it serves the casting director to keep you from getting larger roles. Let me illustrate the truth behind this rather shocking statement. I represented Paul Giamatti. There was a time, early in Paul's career, where he was offered a role in a film which was going to be tricky to work out with the dates of a play to which he was already committed. The casting director of the film gave me no end of grief about the problematic dates and he kept using that difficulty as leverage to make Paul's deal less and less attractive – money, billing, dressing room – anything he could take away, he threatened to take away. Many years later, at some gathering, in the spirit of reminiscing about old times, I reminded that casting director of the problems we had with that deal. Funny to look back on now, no? Especially now that Paul was so successful. The guy didn't think so. He snarled at me, "Well, who knew the little creep was going to become a star?" As if Paul's success were some sort of betrayal and this guy could no longer use him for small parts. So petty, yes? But helpful to know.

Summing Up

One of the finest acting teachers in the country told me he felt the word *Professional* should be taken out of Professional Actor Training on a school's curriculum. Learning how to act has nothing to do with professionalism. Acting is acting. Beware of the school that implies they know what the business is looking for. Have I mentioned the business is looking for you?

For our next Workshop, I would like you to bring in a more perfect monologue, by which I mean: more perfect for *you*. I would ask you to choose a monologue as if your life in show business depended on it. If you liked (and I liked) what you chose the first time, find something we will like even more. If there is no more perfect monologue for you than what you chose originally, then do it more brilliantly. Do it better than it has ever been done in the history of the world. No pressure. Relax. Just do it.

WORKSHOP THREE:
Perfect Monologues

I'm beginning to like this dump. Especially now that the elevator is working. I am definitely beginning to like my students, which includes you. It's fun when you see it dawn on someone's face that wanting the business is not enough. No matter how much you want it, you have to know why. And to know that you have to discover what it is you want to do and to say and to offer and to be. These are not things you will necessarily learn in acting school. Nor are they things you should learn in acting school. But they are things you will need to know. Why not start learning who you are while you are learning how to be someone else?

W hat perfect monologues have you brought us today, having had time to consider how the business will consider you? What defining words will we be hearing? Who's to go first? I still haven't got your names into the front of my brain. You who look like Karl Malden. Who are you?

"Carl Donnelly, Mr. Carlson."

Has anyone ever told you that you look like Karl Malden?

"Yeah, one of my teachers."

And how did that sit with you?

"Tell you the truth, I had to look him up."

I wish you had not told me the truth, Mr. Donnelly. Karl Malden was a great actor. You should know his work.

"He had a pretty big nose."

And so do you, Mr. Donnelly.

"Yeah."

What will you be doing for us today?

"'A Loss of Roses' by William Inge, the role of Kenny."

And why would someone who is a dead ringer for one of our greatest character actors choose to play a role created by one of our handsomest leading men? Does anyone know who that was? Not you, Mr. Donnelly? You would do well to know who created the role by which you are about to define yourself. Ah. Ms. Harris. And who is the actor to whom I refer?

"Warren Beatty, Mr. Carlson."

Yes indeed. Warren Beatty. And will you be going next after Mr. Donnelly, Ms. Harris?

"I would prefer not to."

Mr. Donnelly, why this choice?

"I just want people to think of me for big parts."

Succinctly put. Canny. Smart. I like it. The stage is yours, Mr. Donnelly.

And the barrel-chested Carl Donnelly proceeds to do a very credible job with a role that was written for a sensitive mama's boy. Sensitive but not a sissy – Warren Beatty, remember.

That was nice work, Mr. Donnelly. I would suggest you might look for a little humor in your approach. I realize "A Loss of Roses" is not a laugh riot but humor is always welcome. Even a glimmer. You do realize that you are completely wrong for the role.

"I figure most people don't know the play."

And you would be right. But how does that help you? You want people to recognize you as capable of leads, correct?

"It feels like a lead."

You feel correctly. I think you are a smart cookie, Mr. Donnelly. Could you name me an actor whose career you covet?

"Gene Hackman."

Yes, a very smart cookie. And how many pounds would you like to lose, Mr. Donnelly? You cannot become Gene Hackman at your bulk.

"Fifteen."

Sounds right. See that you do so. In the meantime, look for a role to more accurately define you. Take a look at "I Never Sang for My Father."

"Mr. Carlson?"

And who might you be?

"Lucie Alvarez."

And how may I help you, Ms. Alvarez?

"Can I go next?"

Please do. What do you have for us?

"'Master Class.' Terrence McNally."

Sharon, of course. Does everyone know this play? Does anyone know this play? The original star of this play, Zoe Caldwell and the actress who created the role you are about to see Ms. Alvarez take on, Audra McDonald, both received TONYs for their efforts. Please proceed, Ms. Alvarez.

And Lucie Alvarez proceeds to tear the place up.

Thank you, Ms. Alvarez. May I ask what attracts you to this role?

"It's just so rich. There is so much going on with her. It's crazy."

It is. Perhaps it need not be quite so crazy as you make it. I can tell that you went up to Lincoln Center and watched Ms. McDonald's performance on tape.

"I did. How did you know? Was that bad?"

On the contrary, I'm impressed. If you are going to steal, steal from the best and Audra McDonald is the best. What did you want from the woman playing Maria in this scene? And what just happened?

"I want her to tell me she loves me. I want her to tell me I'm her favorite student. I want her to tell me she thinks I'm as gifted as she is. And I just heard she has terminal cancer and I want her to know how sorry I am."

My goodness, that is a lot going on there. What about, you just found out she has cancer and you need her to know how much you love her? Do it again. Right now.

And she does. And it is so much better, cleaner and clearer. And your need for her approval is evident in the intensity of your concern. Can you feel that? The more specific your choices, people, the richer your work stands a chance of being. Thank you, Ms. Alvarez. I think you need to decide if you are Emma Thompson or Whoopi Goldberg.

"I was going for Queen Latifah but that's cool."

Well, no, that's instructive. Queen Latifah, at the beginning of her career, was going for Whoopi Goldberg. She was a clown. She was funny. Then she became a funny actress. Then she became an actress. She was probably an actress all along but she went for the clown and earned the right to the rest.

Choosing a monologue for yourself is a process. The monologue you choose says the world about you and how well you do it flows from that. Change them every once in a while. Working on a monologue each day is a chance to act each day. Plus it centers you, allows you to focus and, hopefully, teaches you something about who you really are.

Never let up in your quest to be the most perfect version of yourself that you can be – but first you must know what and who that is.

LIFE AFTER THE SHOWCASE

S howcases were a good idea when they first started. Hell, when they first started they were a *great* idea. Not least because only the top twelve schools had one. Who determined which were the top twelve schools? Well, there was a blue ribbon panel, then there was a board, then there was a committee, then there was infighting and now any school who can cover the cost of a studio rental can hold a showcase and well over a hundred do.

How Did Showcases Become Such A Big Deal?

Everybody who could be of help to a young actor used to go to them. Even Artistic Directors used to go. Who goes to them now? At most of them, there will be the usual assortment of people who care about the graduates – their teachers, surely, and as many friends and family who can physically get to New York or Los Angeles as possible. Some alumni of the school will be there. Maybe some success stories. These onlookers and family can offer all the good feelings in the world but have zero ability to help the newly-minted thespian get to the next step. Which is? Do you know? Do they? These earnest actors in waiting have just spent three or four years of their young lives and somewhere between sixty and one hundred thousand dollars learning how to act. You'd think they would know what the next step was.

Well, many of them would probably say that the next step is signing with an agent. And several of them will do that. But many, many more of them will not be so lucky. (Not that the ones who signed with an agent were lucky – some of those experiences are destined to fail miserably or just fail and hurt for a while.) And even the ones who signed with an agent have no idea what happens after that. Most of them think it's now all up to the agent. Oh, my friends and oh, my foes – no, no, no.

I will get to what the next step is in a minute after I have done with my rant about showcases. So maybe some kids got signed at the showcase. Maybe you were one of them. Maybe you went with a mid-size office. Maybe the agent is happy he signed you but in a half-hearted sort of way. Not exactly jumping up and down. Even if he is excited about you, there is a lot of work ahead and he is thinking of that work. Even a suspected great actor, even a self-evident great beauty is still, let's face it, a novice coming out of school and it will be at least a couple of years before that agent will see any money from that possibly great actor – if the actor stays with the agency once he starts to make money, which he probably won't do.

But first, the actor will have to prove he has the heart. How do you do that? By showing up. Doesn't sound hard? Try it. I am always shocked at the number of people who come out of the schools and then take a step back. Even the ones who get agents. They want to take a rest. Huh?

If you're chosen in the first-round draft, that's no guarantee you will have what it takes to play pro ball. Stick around. Stand there. In the spotlight. Many don't. They find it daunting. It is. Your agent hopes you won't be one of those. I had a client fresh out of school who I was reasonably excited about and who decided to give himself a graduation present of six months in Greece. On the beach. Everybody forgot about him by the time he came back. Don't do that. As I said, not jumping up and down.

Geeze. No money for a couple of years? Is that all agents think about? Really? Sigourney Weaver was five years out of school before she got "Alien." And she's gorgeous. Sometimes it happens more quickly. Billy Crudup was less than a year out of NYU when he got the lead in "Arcadia." He's gorgeous, too. Alexander Sharp was still at Juilliard when he got the lead in "The Curious Incident of the Dog in the Night-time." Not gorgeous but definitely gifted. They are all three of them immensely gifted. They all three of them went to one of the top three schools. Two of them are beautiful. The one who wasn't got his break in the shortest amount of time. (So much for looks.) What about their classmates who never even got an interview from their showcase? At those schools? Yes. Rest assured, there were some such poor souls at those schools who were not invited to the dance. Many of them, though, perhaps most of them, will start to work. If they continue to show up. One or two may even become stars. Let's not forget they got into those schools. They may have been exceptional in the first place. You know who else was exceptional? Many, many people who auditioned and did not get into those schools.

Which might include you. Let's say you went to a school that is never even mentioned in those random lists of best acting schools on the internet. Should you despair about your showcase? Hardly, the experience of the showcase – the pressure, the choosing of a right scene, the taking of a moment in the sun, all of this will stand you in good stead when you are sitting in your seat waiting to accept your TONY.

I went to showcases every year. Maybe I saw two hundred hopefuls. Maybe I signed two. Maybe there was another one I wanted to sign who elected to go with another agent. Maybe there were ten people with talent whom I just didn't respond to. What about the other hundred and ninety I didn't even like? Well, some of them got agents. What about the ones who didn't? Do they have a place in the business? Some of them do, yes. Even some of the ones I didn't like. What about all that work and all those hopes and dreams they had invested in their showcase? And what about the other hundred and some schools and their five thousand students who were seen by precious few, if any, industry professionals?

You just graduated from a senior training program. That's huge. Give yourself a moment to feel very, very good about yourself. You are one step, a very big step, closer to being a working actor. Enjoy it. But do not step back. (Do not go to Greece.) Your showcase, which had seemed like such a gigantic deal, was a moment in time and it has passed. Just because you didn't get an agent doesn't mean you are not closer to getting a job. You know, your friends who got agents did not get jobs. (Can you guess what your next step is? Yes, a job.) Frankly, I don't think about showcases very much. Except when I think about how crazy they make young actors.

I am grateful that so many reputed-to-be-talented young people are showing their wares under one roof. Going to a few showcases is a lot simpler for me than running around the fleabag theatres of New York looking for the stars of tomorrow. But the truth is, I am just as likely to find somebody wonderful in a storefront theatre on Ludlow Street as I am at some hot shit school's MFA presentation. I think Paul Giamatti would still have the career he has if he'd studied with some broken down drunk who taught out of an illegal loft in TriBeca instead of The Yale School of Drama. Actually, I think he'd have a better career if he'd stayed with me but that's water under the bridge. And I don't think Ashton Kutcher would have a bigger career if he had gone to Juilliard rather than the University of Iowa (though he might get more respect).

What was our original question before I lost control and mentioned Paul Giamatti? Oh. Agents will go to the showcases, especially the better-known schools, because they like to see each other on their cell phones and complain about missing a day at the beach and, incidentally, check out this year's crop of actors but nobody is really looking to sign new clients. Well then WTF? If they see someone is blatantly a star, they will sign him or her. Chances are they have already signed that person. Chances are you will come out of your showcase without an agent. But you will come out ahead of the pack if you have gleaned something about what the agent is looking for.

Moving On

Most actors are not as gifted Paul Giamatti – though many actors may think they are. And why shouldn't they? Why shouldn't you? Actually, *how* gifted you are or are not is none of your business. Your business is that there is a career – even a sizable career – to be had for the taking if you believe in yourself and if you know what you bring to the table. But you will not only have to bring it, you will have to tell everyone that you have brought it and you will have to define for them what it is you have brought. There is a very long line of people who want a piece of the same pie that you want.

Not every artist has that assertive gene which allows him to barrel in and take what he feels he deserves. Let's say you are one of those people. You don't know how to really put yourself out there. What if you have this enormous ambition and you just can't speak up because all you can think to say is: "I am so brilliant you just have to give me this part or I will kill you." Well, you know that isn't going to work so you say nothing. And that isn't going to work, either. How do you get around that? Let's break it down.

First of all, you have to believe that you belong in the business before you can believe you deserve any specific role. When you meet agents and casting directors you have to believe they are curious about you – because they are. They don't want to miss out on something special. (That would be you.) Agents and casting directors are always looking for new actors no matter what they say because the business feeds on new actors. Actually, they are looking for the next big thing, not just an actor, but every actor who comes to New York or

LA (via Greyhound or Yale) is looking to *be* that next big thing so we can still say and mean: they are looking for you.

An agent or casting director hears about you and wants to meet you. They don't want you to audition or anything, they just want to meet. How did that happen? I don't know. Maybe you waited on their sister at the local diner. What do you care? They heard about you. And you're thrilled but you're freaked. Get over it. Treat it as an acting exercise. Treat it as a date. What's the best outcome to a date? Sex! What's the best outcome to a meeting with an agent or a casting director? A contract or a job! Don't let this person interviewing you miss out on you.

If you are fabulous, you don't have to behave in some clichéd fabulous way. "I'm the Greatest Star" worked for Barbra Streisand (because she was) so find something that works for you – a story, an anecdote. Some truth that reveals how great you are. Jane Kaczmarek doesn't have a career comparable to Susan Sarandon's but she has worked since the day she got out of school. She is a wonderful actress and, most importantly (and she knows this), she is fabulous. And you feel it the minute you meet her. She got out of school, started meeting people and everyone she met just fell in love with her. She has a personality that reflects how great she is.

Not everyone radiates greatness. Let's assume that you do not. Let us say you are reticent. Putting yourself out there gives you the willies. OK, as Hedwig tells us, that is what we have to work with. Every time you act, you are asking a room full of strangers to pay attention to you. But when you are acting, a writer has given you words. So it would appear that words can get you out of your shell. We can say that words are what you need to assert yourself. Is that fair?

Let's look at that non-assertiveness gene of yours for a minute. The ranks of actors are (surprisingly) filled with people who have such a gene. But let's look for those moments in your life when you have felt empowered. What allowed that to happen? Feed yourself those circumstances before a meeting, before an audition. Imagine you are your favorite actor – who is perhaps an odd duck like yourself – and is about to have the same meeting you are about to have. What would he do? What kind of stories would he want to tell in the meeting? What would he want to reveal about himself?

You don't have to go into a trance and become another person. Just channel this favorite actor of yours for a minute. Then try and think of moments, or one moment, when you felt assertive, when you felt in charge, or like taking charge. Sit with that moment. Burnish it. Not in some bogus, self-help kind of way but really imagine it. Imagine it is really OK to be whoever you happen to be. And then, I realize this is the hard part, imagine yourself putting it out there. Even a little. Is this a little too touch-feely for you? Is it too weird? It's a little weird. Am I saying you should psych yourself into behaving like a different person than the one you really are? Would I do that to you?

I am suggesting you behave like the person you really are and the key word here is *behave*. The people you will be meeting want to want you. Let them know who you are. If you are hard to know, well, that's interesting, but do some of the heavy lifting for them. You are a great actor, are you not?

The first time I saw Will Patton act I was blown away. I called him into my office and gushed about how great I thought he was. He just sort of smiled and – this is the important part – agreed with me. But he had nothing else to say. Will was terrible at meetings. I can only assume he has gotten better because he goes from job to job and is never out of work. Though these days he mostly gets offers instead of having to take a meeting, let alone audition. Early in his career, a director called him back five times for what turned out to be his breakout role. When they called after the fourth audition to tell me they needed to see him yet again, I lost it. I said, what can you possibly be looking for that you haven't seen? Unless somebody gives me some direction here, Will isn't going to another callback. The director called me and told me what he was looking for. I told Will. Will said, well, don't they have to give me the job to get to see that? Talk about a Eureka moment. No, said I, you have to show them that in order to get the job. He showed them his soul and he got the job.

How many great actors have we got? Ten? Twenty? Thirty? (I don't think so.) How many of them are young? So there is room for *you*. How can you most effectively tell the business that you have arrived and are available for work? Let's say someone shuts the door in your face. You have to look for another door. That's what Philip Seymour Hoffman did. He knew he didn't come over as an especially assured person. So he thought, if I *were* such a person, how would I go about letting people know who I am – given my natural reticence, given *me*? (Isn't it remarkable how I know what went on in Phil's mind?) Phil once asked me to submit him for a part I thought he was all wrong for. I mean, I really thought he didn't have a prayer. I took a moment and said, "Do you think you're right for it?" He took a moment himself and then he asked, "You don't?" Something in his tone, maybe just that he said, "You don't?" rather than, "Don't you?" Something. He changed my mind in that second and I submitted him. Well, I probably would have submitted him anyway because I always did what he asked but I submitted him with gusto and got the appointment. In those days, submitting Phil was hardly a guarantee of getting him seen. He did not get the part. (He wasn't right for it.) But he was seen. And the casting director was blown away by his brilliance and had him in for everything after that.

So are we clear? No more shrinking violet. Agreed?

Where Do You Fit?

Your assignment every day is to study the business. Who has your career? Who has a career you admire? Oh, come on. You can say those names in your sleep. Then what will your career look like? How will you be cast? What property will you option after you have had your first big break? Who do you want to work with? What actors? (Don't say De Niro or Streep.) What directors? (Don't say Scorcese or Spielberg.) What parts do you want to play? Who *are* you? (Don't say whatever the role requires you to be – unless you *are* Meryl Streep.)

Do you do plays for no money? Why not? What kind of parts will you do in these plays you do for no money? Is there a thread? Does everybody see you differently? (Not good if they are not casting you. Good if they are. Do you know why? Sure you do.) Do they only see you for one kind of part? (Not good if you are a star but if you are doing plays for no money you are not a star and at least you are doing plays. Worry about getting typed after you start to become visible.)

Do you have an agent? You will need an agent. Why else are you doing plays for no money? Unless the answer to that is you just want to be the best you can be. In which case, God bless you. But if you want to make any money, you will need an agent. I once interviewed an actor who told me he had gotten all his jobs without the help of an agent. Why then, I asked, did he need me? Well, he said, it was time to start making some money. Oh. The jobs he'd had gotten himself were jobs for no money. Oh. In what other profession are there jobs for no money? Is there a field today that doesn't have its interns? I think it's the actors' payback for all those years they have been expected to put in for free while their friends were working on getting that corner office at Morgan Stanley (and being paid rather well while they were going about it). Is making money acting comparable to a corner office at Morgan Stanley? So much better!

Don't Be Clueless

I have watched people, in most cases talented people, build careers. I have *helped* them build those careers but in the best of those careers, I got my clues on how to proceed from the actor. And I have seen actors harm their careers, in some cases irreparably, because they gave me the wrong clues or no clues because they had no idea what it was they really wanted.

I have been most effective to the clients who knew what they needed and quite correctly led me to help them get it. This profession is not rocket science. I have learned you have to put into words what it is you want. And being able to define what you want is pretty basic stuff no matter what the profession. Didn't anyone ever tell you that?

It's not that people are keeping the truth from you. Most people don't know the truth. (Or they can't handle it?) Or they only know their piece of it. The truth comes from sharing information. If I don't know your priorities, I have no real way of knowing if I can help you. Think about it: the huge number of clients that agencies have, the ever smaller number of roles available on television, the fact that there's only 400 actors on Broadway each year and many of them not even Americans.

All this is necessary information to process. You've got to know the odds to beat the odds. The truth about how grueling restaurant kitchens are didn't seem to discourage young people from wanting to work in them when a career in the restaurant business started sounding glamorous in the nineties. In fact, that just encouraged a spate of very expensive cooking schools which started popping up all over the place. Even colleges offering degrees. (Sound familiar?) Like the acting schools that can teach you how to act, the culinary schools can teach you how to cook. But working in restaurants? A different story. My wife was a chef and I used to hear her rail about how ill-equipped the graduates of even the best cooking schools were to work in a real restaurant kitchen. Does The Culinary Institute tell you what do on a Saturday night when your dishwasher's parole officer comes into the kitchen and takes him away in handcuffs? Through the dining room?

Dress For The Part

Do they teach you what to wear at Yale when you go to read for a movie about a motorcycle gang? I had a client, a Yale graduate, who wore a suit and tie to such an audition. Did I know that? No. Would I have told him to wear jeans and a leather jacket if he had asked? Yes. Was he surprised when he didn't get a callback? He was shocked. Me, too, because he was perfect for the part. I called the casting director to ask why no callback and she told me that my brilliant client had walked into the audition looking like a business management major and that he wouldn't shut up about Yale – which has not produced a large number of people who subsequently became members of motorcycle gangs so far as she knew. I talked the casting director into calling him back. Wish I could say he got the job, but at least the casting director did wind up a fan of his. She started calling him in for lots of things and he started to get work. He's a big deal now. And, thanks to that experience, I always offer my opinion on what actors should wear to auditions – whether I'm asked or not.

I'm not suggesting you gain fifty pounds and wear a crown when you audition for "Victoria Regina" but maybe wear a skirt and not cut-offs. Some actors get perverse pleasure out of walking into the audition room and astounding the people there with their transformative powers. Gee, you looked like Little Bo Peep when you came in and all of a sudden you turn into Lady Macbeth. Isn't that fantastic? I've got news for you – no, it's not.

Those people in the audition room do not want to see you transform. They want the character they are looking for to walk into the room. Now, if the character they are looking for is an axe murderer, obviously do not go in acting like an axe murderer. (However axe murderers act.) But give them *something*, some indication that you can go there. Do not belabor them with what a good person you are. Unless that's what they are looking for – a good person who is also an axe murderer. Nobody cares what a good person you are. Except your mother. If you're auditioning for a football player, you don't need to wear shoulder pads but a jersey wouldn't hurt.

Street Smarts

What newly minted actors looking for work need more than anything (aside from a really good 8 x 10) is street smarts. That's what this book is for. Nothing in these pages is meant to supplant your knowledge of acting, your craft as you have come to understand it – your, God help me, technique. This is different stuff. If the best looking guy I ever represented needed to be told that guys tend to look good in black jeans, then I tend to think that much of what would seem to be innate in the actor's psyche is not innate at all but can be learned by anyone who is even mildly driven to succeed. And if you are not at least mildly driven, what are you doing even near the profession?

If, as Aristotle would have it, the unexamined life is not worth living, I would suggest that unexamined ambition stands an excellent chance of not getting out of the gate. Let's say you know why you want to act. Let's say acting makes you happy. Is there a better reason? Assuming I haven't discouraged you so far, let us proceed. And if I have discouraged you, you are well out of it, I promise you.

Catching Your Drift

When I was a nipper growing up in Buffalo (how bleak was my puberty!), I used to long for the monthly arrival of a magazine called *Theatre Arts*. It was filled with the most tantalizing articles about what actors in the New York theatre were doing, what the theatres themselves were doing and what was going on in the newly established regional theatres around the country. I remember reading about that first season at The Guthrie with Jessica Tandy, Hume Cronyn and George Grizzard doing a modern dress "Hamlet" directed by Guthrie himself. I didn't know Tyrone Guthrie from Tyrone Power but he looked like a god in the magazine's photographs. (Tyrone Power looked like a movie star. There is a difference.) I remember the planes in his face. I remember that nose! I didn't know what a modern dress "Hamlet" was either. (Everybody in a dress?) Each issue of *Theatre Arts* always contained the complete text of some new play. "Stalag 17" made a particular impression for some reason. I loved Robert Strauss who played Animal. Somehow I thought he was from Buffalo. (He wasn't.) They also wrote about something called off-Broadway where Geraldine Page lived on peanut butter sandwiches while she made $45 a week doing "Summer and Smoke."

There were the most wondrous and evocative photographs of actors in shows or living their lives and they always seemed to be in various stages of undress (in shows or out of shows) and appeared to be thinking about sex every minute of every day and during everything they did, from smoking a cigarette to walking down the street. And they were always in the theatre district or near the theatre district or near or in a theatre. The theatre was everywhere. You could *feel* the theatre. And its importance.

American Theatre is the only game in town for theatre news these days. Young people across the country are likely lapping it up with the same lust and longing that I did *Theatre Arts.* It also holds the theatre in high esteem and still has pictures of people in various stages of undress. So you should check it out.

You may have discovered Broadwayworld.com or *Variety.* You are not quite sure what to make of those weekly Broadway box office grosses but you track them anyway. You memorize them. You may care more about movie grosses. You may just spend your life at the movies. Maybe you rent Bette Davis and Spencer Tracy movies from Netflix. Maybe you saw "Star Wars: The Force Awakens" twice in its opening weekend, despite the fact that you weren't even alive when the first three movies came out. We have established that you are hooked. What do you do now? Stay in Buffalo? No, you should probably get out of there eventually. But don't run away from home. Finish your education. Continue living among civilians. Live your life and know that one day you will be an actor. But until you can begin your life in art in earnest, find places where people are putting on plays and get involved. We've discussed this. Have you already forgotten about those fourteen theatre companies in Buffalo?

Which Coast?

I moved to New York when I was twenty-one because I wanted to study acting and I wanted to act in the theatre. It wasn't so much that I thought the theatre was superior to movies and television. (That came later. And it wasn't that I looked down on movie stars or television stars – who could look down on James Stewart and June Allyson? – I just didn't relate. Hell, I was from Buffalo. The theatre seemed much more possible. And there had been that Julie Harris moment at the Erlanger.

Today young people grow up wanting to be in movies and television from the start. It's a possible profession now and that's a very good thing. Movie and television stars may be better looking than most of us but really, there is a case to be made that they just spend more time in the gym. (Though Angelina Jolie didn't get that face from any gym.) Aspiring to be a movie star is not such an outrageous stretch anymore. If you want to act, of course you want to be a star. Nobody grows up wanting to be a featured player. So where do you go? Go to New York even if the movies are your ultimate goal. (The movies are everybody's ultimate goal.)

Los Angeles, the headquarters of film and television (though New York is still a financial hub to both) is a very tough town to crack. It is also an unforgiving town. If you get a nice role and blow it, the town will write you off. Really? How will anyone even notice? All those casting assistants watch *everything*. They have to. That's their job. When their boss says, "Who's this new girl from NYU who just got this thing at The Taper?" The assistant is going to have to be able to say, "I saw her do three lines on 'The Good Wife' and she's pretty good." Then the boss will say, "And you didn't show me her scenes? What the heck is wrong with you? Don't you like your job?" To which the really good assistant might say, "I saw her a few years ago on

'Parenthood' and she stunk up the place but I heard she went to NYU and she must have learned how to act because when I saw her on 'The Good Wife' a few weeks ago she was good. I mentioned it to you and I put the disc on your desk. I guess you haven't gotten to it yet." So they aren't just looking for who's new and good, in Los Angeles they're looking for who's new and who's to be avoided. But they are always looking. Even Steven Spielberg, for God's sake, watches soaps. (That's what I heard.)

By the time you move to Los Angeles, you should know your, oh Lord, I hate to say it, *craft*, but you should know your craft. You should know your power over an audience, you should know what works in front of a camera and what does not. You should be *ready*. For anything. Because if you get something good and do not do well, no one is going to shrug and say, come back in a year. You will be written off. Summarily. Sounds harsh. Is.

If the worst happens in Los Angeles, you can always go back East and study. Like that poor girl who stunk up the place on "Parenthood." Hell, Piper Laurie moved back East and studied and became a serious actress after having been a starlet and been written off. (Piper who?)

Go to New York and study acting. Harder but less harsh. There are all sorts of schools and conservatories and individual teachers who are aching to help you learn how to act. Meet them. Watch a class, if they will let you. Some do. Deborah Hedwall does. William Esper does not.

William Esper has the reputation of being the best acting

teacher in New York. That does not mean that he will be the best teacher for you but he is a superior teacher. And he has taught some of the best actors around. Google him. The American Academy of Dramatic Art has a hell of an alumni roster. Kirk Douglas, Spencer Tracy. Grace Kelly. Anyone still living, you may ask? Well, Paul Rudd, Adrien Brody, Dennis Haysbert. Hm. I like Adrien Brody. Anyone under 40, you may legitimately wonder? Well, if the next James Dean wandered in to AADA, would he emerge a star? He's James Dean, ferchrisake.

Is great training so important? A very smart casting director told me that Viola Davis was going to be huge but it would take her a couple of years for her to lose the training. It took Viola a few years to integrate her own natural gifts, which are gigantic, with the conservatory training she received which I frankly find a bit rigid with no allowances made for genius. A too full of himself teacher can intimidate an unformed actor but not forever and not for long. And Viola had good teachers. I am not suggesting they were bad.   Just, if you ask me (and no one has), not quite right for her. Pretty cheeky of me, I grant you, but anyone who has the gall to make Viola Davis question herself makes my blood boil. If you find yourself at an inappropriate institution, find another institution. Or grin and bear it. Do not worry about your gifts being dismantled by some inept instructor. Bad teachers do not prevail in the end. Talent does. If you are gifted, you can learn from most anyone.

There is The Neighborhood Playhouse, where Sanford Meisner taught some of the finest actors alive (who are now mostly dead). Sanford Meisner himself has been dead for some time now. There is The Stella Adler Conservatory. Ms. Adler has also departed the premises. There is a wonderful teacher named Caymichael Patten who has her own studio. There is HB Studios. They have some excellent teachers. Maybe it's better now. The Scott Freeman Studio is excellent, too. There are so many and many of them are good.

Go meet these people. Even if you can't audit the class, you can meet the teacher. See what you think. You are going to be putting yourself in these people's hands (do not be afraid to do so). Pick a good pair of hands. If you are wrong, if you thought someone would be helpful and they aren't, like that guy who was so cruel to that girl, leave. Wait a minute. You will notice that you are now in the exact same position as your scene partner in that class with that horrible teacher and your scene partner had an MFA. Call him up. See what he's up to. Don't lose touch with people.

Sandy Meisner used to say, "I can teach you how to act but I can't make you interesting." Right and right. He – and his brilliant technique – can teach you how to act. (Yes, there are techniques of which I approve.) I think most good teachers out there today would agree and teach some version of what Sandy put together. Anyone who has been teaching for longer than ten years, of course, has developed his or her own system. That is good news. It means they have something to impart. So go get it. And then get a dose of what someone else has to offer. Soon you will act the way *you* act.

The Creepy Guys In The Black Suits

Get a job. Get cast in a play. I am serious. Do I really think you can get cast in a play when you have just moved to town and know no one? Yes, I do. You will get a job or at any rate a role. It probably won't pay you anything but do it. How do you get cast in a play without an agent? Holy cow. Go to the theatre. Go to off-off Broadway plays. Go to off-off-off Broadway plays. Go to plays in Brooklyn and the Bronx and Staten Island and Hoboken. No danger of running into an agent there (do you think agents work on plays where there is no money involved?) but you might make a connection or perhaps a friend.

If you see a play that even approaches being good, go backstage and find out how to get involved with that company. Backstage, there will be young, devoted people, much like yourself, who care about the theatre. Much like yourself. There will be no creepy people in black suits. Working around these caring people will eventually get you to the creepy people in the black suits. Are you sure that's where you want to get to? It's a lot more fun down there on Ludlow Street with the cockroaches and the toilets that don't work. Actually, it's not that much fun once you're not so young. Someone asked Michael Caine why he no longer worked in the theatre. His response was, "May I show you my art collection?" The creepy people in the black suits are the cockroaches of the well heeled.

I know an agent who says to actors: "Just do something – we will find you." There is wisdom there. There are low- to no-paying theatres all over town – all over New York and Chicago anyway – don't bother in Los Angeles because nobody in the business will bother to go. They might not go in New York, either, but then again they just *might.* In Chicago, the actors do it for love, not because they hope Ben Brantley or Michael Feingold will walk in some night. But in New York there are theatres with reputations for using good young actors. They are usually run by those same good young actors. Find them. The particular theatres change every few years. The players change. People go back to Kansas. People get cast on TV shows. But passion is always around. Seek it out. Be a part of the scene. It's expensive? Nonsense. You are a student. Don't you have a student discount? Can't you offer to usher in exchange for seeing the show? Don't you have a friend in the cast? Don't you know somebody in the box office? Well, meet some new people, damn it.

Backstage, the trade newspaper, lists every theatre in the city that is looking for actors with descriptions of the roles they are looking for. You can also get an online subscription, and Playbill.com also lists most casting calls. Get something called *Up To Date Theatricals* or *The Theatrical Index* which is released monthly and lists contact information for agents, casting directors and theatres. Find out the names of people who work in those offices. Maybe you know someone. Or someone who knows someone. Six degrees of separation? Get *The Call Sheet,* also monthly, also lists agents and casting directors – and TV shows.

Variety, Hollywood Reporter and *Billboard* are mostly aimed at movers and shakers but they sure have a lot of information. And feeling like you know stuff is an invaluable feeling.

What can you do in Los Angeles? Less. You can write

individual casting directors and offer to be a reader for them. You can hang around The Mark Taper. You can go to open calls at the Geffen or audition for South Coast Rep. You can crash parties looking fetching. You can move to New York and frankly I wish you would. You should find a good barber wherever you are.

TV

Do you watch television? It always shocks me how many young actors don't watch television and yet they expect to work on it. If you tell me you don't want to work on TV, I will wring your neck. Do not make me drag out the list of wildly successful actors who started in television beginning with Steve McQueen. (And for those who do not know Mr. McQueen, how about George Clooney?) It's money, it's experience, it's exposure, and sometimes, especially these days, it is even very good. How can you be on television if you don't know what they are looking for on television? Who do they hire? Whom do they hire a lot (in other words, who is doing it right and how do they do it)? Get familiar with each show's taste in actors. As you immerse yourself in the work of other actors a feeling deep inside begins to well up. When you see someone your age and vaguely your type, you think to yourself: if that fraud can have a career, *I* can have a career. It leads to the best kind of entitlement because it's based on real belief in yourself.

Have I convinced you to consider television (I hope so)? Would you consider a soap? Rethink that *no*. Tommy Lee Jones, Meg Ryan, Judith Light, Ryan Phillippe, Timothy Busfield, Kathy Bates, Josh Duhamel (well, he was a soap waiting to happen), Parker Posey, Julianne Moore, Kevin Bacon, Will Patton all did soaps. (I love Will Patton. He is incapable of not telling the truth when be acts.) These days, all the soaps are in Los Angeles, so if you are there, maybe try for a soap. People will tell you not to. Screw 'em.

Even more to the point, did you ever research who was the first agent for your favorite actors? That's not so easy to do but you can learn a lot by trying. And then, when you get a name, go after them. Oh, they are no longer developing actors? They are fielding offers? Then go after them for *advice*.

There are places where actors pay to meet an agent or a casting director (frequently the casting director's assistant). You meet the agent or the casting director (or the assistant) and have an interview. At some of these places, you audition for them. Sometimes they give you feedback. The agents and the casting directors are reimbursed for their presence – they do not do this out of the goodness in their hearts.

I met an actor in LA at some fund raising event. He was maybe 40 years old and charactery (funny looking). He told me that four years ago he had moved to LA from Seattle and had budgeted $5,000 a year to pay for those things where you meet agents and casting directors. I started to launch into what a rip-off I thought those places were. The guy stopped me. He said, "No, wait a minute. These people I met liked me. They started calling me in. I started booking jobs. I'm a good actor and they noticed and now I know everybody in town." "And what did it get you?" I asked. "I'm on 'Star Trek," he said. "I'm a regular." Well, screw me.

No Coast?

Chicago is a great place to start. There are tons of theatre companies there and you can go from play to play to play. You probably will not make much money. The Goodman and Steppenwolf are about the only paying gigs in town, and they import a good chunk of their actors from New York and LA. But, it's entirely possible for you to get an ensemble or understudy role there, especially if you're Equity. If you get cast at one of those, you can expect that there might be someone important in the audience at some point. Other than that, though, no one is in Chicago to get picked up by a Broadway producer.

Which is probably a good thing. That way, you can spend your time in Chicago honing your – here's that word again – craft, and saving money on rent while you do it. (Don't ever tell your New York City friends what your Chicago rent is.) Chicago is also a hotbed of improv troupes and comedy clubs, which is definitely a useful skill for you to gain so that you don't become one of those actors we've talked about that just isn't funny.

With all due deference to the hardworking actors who do theatre in LA, the level of the work in Chicago is simply better. Deeper, stronger, more committed. No one is hoping that a representative from show business will sweep in and take note. There are some other cities where passion prevails. D.C. Seattle. Minneapolis. And, well, you already know about Buffalo. The friends you make there will be with you in the business your whole life. Because you are all doing it for the love of it, not for Scott Rudin's possible presence in the audience.

You could go study in England but you will not be able to work there once you graduate. I do not understand the appeal of living where you will not be able to work. Oh, for the sheer quality of the training, I suppose. Well, OK, sure. That's valid. I mean, I love the Brits as much as anyone. Just be aware that when you get back home, you will be in the same boat as everyone who studied here – without the connections you missed out on while you were away.

Summing Up

Every single choice you make, you must follow your heart. Do what makes the most sense to you. Not what you think someone else – with more experience – would do but what *you* would do. Choosing an acting teacher is an important and complicated process. But it is not life and death. Choose what feels right. If you come to feel it was not the right choice, make another one. The most famous acting teachers in the last century were Sanford Meisner, Stella Adler and Lee Strasberg and they didn't even talk to each other. Was it possible to learn how to act from each of them? Of course it was. But one of them might have been more right for you than the others. What does "right for you" mean? Well, make a choice and you'll find out.

Let's consider these three giants of the profession for a moment. Was it true they didn't talk to each other? Yes, it was true. Lee believed in the importance of sense memory, Stella (the only one of them to work with Stanislavski personally), believed more in the actor's own imagination, Sandy put his emphasis on moment-to-moment truth telling. So fine.

Why couldn't they just get along and agree to disagree? Well, they were artists as much as the people they taught. They had passionate convictions and they were looking to create allegiances from their students so that they might rightfully claim a degree of credit for their student's ultimate successes. They were, to use a term none of them had ever heard of, *branding* themselves. And while they were the most prominent in their newly formed profession, they were not alone. There were many others in their wake: Bobby Lewis, Paul Mann, Uta Hagen, to name but a few. And while the list of wildly gifted actors at that time in the world was long, it was finite. Lines had to be drawn. I will give Al Pacino but you must grant me Robert Duval. Brando never tired of giving credit to Stella Adler. I would simply suggest that you find someone you feel that good about and commit to that teacher.

Step back, do some research, get some perspective, and research an actor's career which you find to be admirable. Start as far back in his or her life as you are able and list for us the choices they made. What schools, what teachers, what agents – if you can find such information – and what roles. I will be transparent about my motives. I want you to become aware that actors do indeed have choices and the choices they make impact their careers. Sometimes for good, sometimes for ill. But you are not all branches in the wind, subject to the whims of fate. You are in charge. You are in control.

Laura Linney, actor:

"The greatest thing about what I do is that I am always a student, every single time."

GOT A DEGREE, NOW WHAT?

What a relief! You have decided on a particular office and your work is over! Now the agent's work begins. WRONG! First of all, your work is never over. What happens next is crucial.

I once signed a young NYU grad who had 87 people wanting to meet him after his showcase. His girlfriend had none. The reason I know 87 people wanted to meet him is because he told me so. Several times. I was one of the 87. I'm available for bandwagons. If everybody wanted him, I wanted him more. I went after him like mad. And he picked me and my agency, hooray! But we had a difficult time with him. We sent him to meet everybody. Hell, we sent him to meet *producers.* We thought we had lightning in a bottle. Trouble was, nobody much liked him. He was turning people off right and left with his 87-people-wanted-to-meet-me act and we weren't paying close enough attention.

We thought people would be throwing jobs at him. So did he. That was the trouble. Little too fond of himself. Maybe a manager might have gotten him to modify some of that raging egotism when he walked into a room. Maybe a manager would have *noticed* how he was doing himself in. We did not. We should have. It never occurred to us that the narcissism we had taken note of in his initial meetings with us, and had ignored because we wanted to sign him so much, was something he couldn't shut off when he went out to actually get work. No, it was part of his DNA. We didn't actually get bad feedback on this guy. People were reluctant to say *anything*.

Nobody wanted to be the first to say they didn't like him because he had made such a great first impression on the entire business at the showcase. (He had gone to one of the top three schools so the entire business was there.) So I don't blame us for not telling him to tone it down. (And you shouldn't blame us either, dear reader.) Frankly, it is mostly up to the actor to be aware how he is going over with the people he meets. Feedback is fine in its place but no one really likes giving it and few agents pass it on (unless it suits their purpose of the moment), let alone pass it on accurately. If you sense a meeting isn't going well, I never have a problem when an actor says to me, "This isn't going so well, is it?" because maybe then we can fix it.

Now wait a minute, I hear you thinking. What's wrong with a little vanity? You've got to toot your own horn, right? You can't be all self-effacing. Haven't I been saying that? Yes, I have. You have got to put yourself out there but you don't want to be, well, a jerk, either. It's a fine line. And you've got to learn to walk it. When I finally became aware of what was going on with that guy and the extent of the damage he was inflicting on himself, I suggested, gently at first, that maybe he was turning people off. I tried to do it diplomatically because clearly underneath all that braggadocio, he was one fragile dude. Plus I didn't want him to leave me. Still I thought he was a winner, after all. He just...wasn't getting any callbacks. But I kept after him as he kept losing jobs and finally I became too forceful and he left me. Then he left the agency he left me for. Then his next agency dropped him. Today, he is out of the business and his then girlfriend (who got zero meetings) is on her second television series and happily married to boot. (Truth is, I can't help you with happily married.)

So how do you pick the right agent? The answer is easy: you pick the one who makes the most sense to you, who *gets* you (or seems to) and spouts the least amount of bullshit. And you stay in very close touch with him while you are spending your first year in his care. Perhaps not "friends" close because most agents are not all that receptive to being friends (nor should they be) but you can let him know how deeply your career matters to you and, of course you are in this (your career) together. And then you stay with him until you have a damn good reason to leave – if you ever do. (And if you don't, God bless you.) And if you made the wrong choice, change agents. It's not life or death here.

Nobody Wanted To Meet Me — What Do I Do?

All right. Let's move away from that rosy scenario and go back to the most common outcome: no one is outside the stage door waiting to meet you. Is it the end of the world? It is not.

You put yourself out there and nobody cared. You feel a little bit like Johnny Depp must have felt after the opening of "The Lone Ranger." Actually, I feel sorrier for Johnny Depp than I do for you. I mean, his grandchildren are going to be able to see that movie. Your grandchildren will never hear about no agents wanting to meet you after your showcase. But what do you do now? The answer is: you pick yourself up, dust yourself off, etc. Yes, but what do you actually do?

Maybe you'll realize that you just have to hurl yourself into the heart of the business (a business with a heart?), preferably in New York and not Los Angeles (where hearts are harder to come by) and not come up for air until you are a working actor. If that sounds hard, it is hard. And you have to do it. But you have to know what to do. That's why you're listening to me.

It may sound like small comfort but, in truth, how you will fare in show business has absolutely nothing to do with how well you performed at the fair. People who tank at the showcases go on to have splendid careers and people who kill at the showcases frequently find themselves back home five years later – like Mr. 87 People Want To Meet Me. The truth is, many a conservatory graduate has a bad day at the showcase. Most young actors are not used to the kind of pressure that comes with these showcases and it takes a toll. But, you may reasonably ask, isn't there even more pressure on Broadway on opening night or in front of a camera with Steven Spielberg watching your every move and millions of dollars flying out the window every time you blow a line? Well, yes – but no, because by the time you open on Broadway or work for Steven Spielberg, you will have a little of what they call *experience* under your belt and you will know something about performing under pressure.

You know what experience is. It's that thing it takes time to get. When people tell you that you need more seasoning, this is what they will mean. So go out and get some seasoning. Succeed at something. Better yet, fail at something.

I sometimes can tell from the way a young actor walks into my office how long it will take for them to actually start to get work. And I am usually right. What was it that I saw or didn't see? Getting work as an actor has very little to do with acting.   But the naiveté that just drips off these young people as they sweetly saunter, tentatively stumble or determinedly stride into my office speaks volumes about their hireability. I have to consider how embedded that naiveté is. Is it some endearing surface humility that comes from being new to the game and will disappear after a few appointments? Or does it point to some pathological fear of failure? How entrenched is that bravado? In the case of Mr. 87 People Want to Meet Me, the swagger began in his soul. And it was fatal.

It is one thing to appear young and eager. It is another to look like a hapless beginner. How much confidence you are able to instill in me may be a legitimate harbinger of how much confidence you may be able to instill in a producer who has the ability to give you a job. Or not.

Step 1: Know Thyself

Be clear about *who you are and what you want*. It is comforting to me that a young actor has considered the kind of roles he or she might be right for, the kind of career they envision for themselves. Once you know who you are, you can offer to share your discovery with everyone you meet. How can I help you if you do not know the kind of help you want? And how can I know what that is if you do not tell me? Of *course*, I will have my own ideas of who you are the minute I lay eyes on you. But bring your own considered history, hopes and dreams into the room. There will be so much more to work with. So much more to talk about. Not to mention how reassuring it is to me that you have bothered to think about your place in the business.

I believe I said to hurl yourself into the business. How do you do that? Have you been paying attention? Get a job. It's exactly the same routine I would urge you to pursue in your hometown before you ever even got to New York. Now that you are there, go to the theatre and tell the theatres you go to that you exist. Not Broadway, obviously. They will laugh in your face. (Which will be good for you – toughen you up – make a man or a woman out of you – get you seasoned.) But you won't do that so you will have to get your seasoning another way. Go to the small theatres, the tiny theatres, the rat traps, the "what I did for love" lofts.

There's a new company in town getting lots of attention every other month. There are three separate companies begun in the last couple of years by graduates of The Atlantic Theatre School. Two companies begun by alums of SUNY Purchase. The Araca Group was started by a few Syracuse alumni, and now they've got "Wicked" under their belt. Hang out at The Public. Everyone hangs out at The Public? So you aren't everyone? Whose work speaks to you? Does The Mint Theatre Company speak to you? Does Elevator Repair Service? Does The Transport Group?

And just as, back in your hometown, when you started working at all those little theatres, word started to get out that you were pretty good and maybe people ought to cast you, the same thing will happen in New York but in New York when you get cast and word is you are pretty good, maybe Scott Rudin (or someone from his office) will come and see your show and *move* it to Broadway and he may even give you a part in one of his movies. In Chicago, the point is to just do a show. In New York, it's to get Scott Rudin to come see it. You're not good enough yet for Scott Rudin? Stay in Chicago.

Step 2: Attract An Agent

Agents always say they don't want new clients, they have too many clients as it is and what they really want is to drop some people. Fine. They do, however, want new clients. Always. They want *better* clients. What they want is a new client who is great. Well, who wouldn't ? The hope that the next one is going to be Jennifer Lawrence never goes away. Hell, Chris Pine wouldn't be bad, either. Is he the next Harrison Ford? Well, the clock is ticking on that one but, yeah. He could be. He really wants it or seems to and that goes a long way. Actually, Harrison Ford himself never seemed to give a crap. That was a large part of his appeal. But he did. Give a crap. He must have. Look at all he's done. And he's still doing it, for God's sake. Somewhere underneath all that cool is a *furnace*.

So why shouldn't the agent you have targeted as the perfect agent for you want to be your agent? There is no reason on earth. Make it happen. (You do have a wish list, right?)

Actors need to take responsibility for their careers. Has anyone ever told you that? It's a requirement. Most people don't even know what an acting career consists of, much less how to get one so how can they go about taking charge? Take charge of what? A young actress from the heartland recently wrote to me, "We are taught that the next obvious step for an actor after undergrad is an MFA program. Because in order to get anywhere you have to be seen, and the only way to be seen is in a showcase, and the only way to be in a showcase is to attend a graduate school which offers one." When I read that letter, I went berserk. There is more misinformation in those words about how to become an actor than in any statement I have ever read about any subject ever. So I wrote this book.

The Headshot

And before you do absolutely anything else, you will get an absolutely phenomenal headshot of your gorgeous face. This is annoying but essential and annoying *how* essential but it must be done. This is a heartbreaking, expensive, maddening but – yes – impossibly crucial requirement to be let into show business.

Back in the early 90's, I was head of the New York legit department at Writers and Artists. One day, my assistant, David, brought the mail into me and there was an 8x10 glossy of a young girl on top. I did not know this young girl and I routinely asked David to throw out all unsolicited pictures and resumes. I asked David who this young girl was. He said he didn't know but wasn't she adorable and didn't I want to meet her? I agreed she was adorable. As for wanting to meet her, I put the picture in the wastebasket and said that would be all.

The next morning, David came into my office with the mail and that same picture was on top of the stack. I asked if she had sent in a second picture. David confessed that no, he had retrieved the picture from my trash and didn't I just want to meet this girl for five minutes? I said the girl was a child and I, this agency, did not represent children and did he, David, have any idea what a nightmare the parents of child actors were? That was reason enough to never represent a child. The following morning David delivered the mail with that girl's haunting picture on top. The day after that, I met with her.

She was 13. She came in with her mother (of course). She was a radiant young girl. And I was totally charmed. I don't think I have been so completely taken by a human (whom I didn't marry) before or since. The mother was pretty delightful as well. I kept trying to include her in the conversation and she kept saying very politely that this was Claire's meeting and Claire's career and she was not there to get in the way. (Well, how much did I love her for that?).

I asked Claire why she wanted to act. She just shrugged and said something along the lines of "that's what I do." It was, I gathered, like breathing to her. I asked her why she wanted an agent. She said that a casting director had recently come to her school looking for children for a movie of the week and had passed over Claire deeming her not worthy. Claire did not want that to happen again. Good instincts. It was either the first or second time that Claire came into the office (everyone has a callback) that I asked my co-worker Karen Friedman to sit in on the meeting. Karen was as blown away as I was. In the coming months she and Claire actually bonded like a house afire. We told Claire and her mom that we would be in touch. Her father may have been at that second meeting as well. He was a doll, too. It was a love fest. And then the Danes left.

I think we counted to ten, then called them to say we wanted her. This was before cell phones, so they didn't call back till a few hours later. They said they were thrilled and would be in touch. In touch? What did that mean? Turns out, Claire had sent out nine pictures to nine agencies and had gotten nine meetings. Not to worry. She chose us. A very, very happy story with a very happy ending. Except for poor David. I fired him a few months later. He had a good eye but he was a terrible assistant. But I owe him for Claire.

Will you be the next Claire Danes? You'll never know unless you have a headshot that can survive being thrown in the trash twice. You must do this before your showcase – if you go to a school that has a showcase – because there is nothing worse than an 8x10 of an actor who has never worked professionally and *looks* like a picture of someone who has never worked professionally. And with this excellent headshot, you are now ready for your showcase. Hell, you are ready for anything. Let's talk about how you get that headshot. Bring yours in next workshop, along with your resume.

WORKSHOP FOUR:
The Window Into Your Soul:
The 8x10

So let's talk about your pictures and resumes.

Resumes are easy. Film, television, theatre. In that order. It is helpful to include as much work as possible. Do not include the church pageant when you were ten. But work you have done in school is helpful. It lets me know the kind of roles you have played – leads, nerds, old women (Lady Bracknell? Really? Not necessary because confusing – no one will cast you as Lady Bracknell for several more decades – I know it's a lead and that's good but it's an old lady so throw it out), "Kiss Me, Kate"? Oh you sing? Excellent news. You sing but you have no musical credits? Put it under special skills – alto, or what you will. Student films are good to know. Tells me you are industrious. You may even have film of yourself. Do not be discouraged if you do not have many credits. Everybody must begin at the beginning. Any work you have done or classes you have taken with people who are known in the industry should be on the resume.

Never pad your resume. Never lie. Not only will you risk losing the job you're up for, you may well lose a career.

Ms. Andrews, it is fascinating to me to see that you, who look like Rebecca of Sunnybrook Farm both in your picture and in person, played Sister Woman in your school production of "Cat on a Hot Tin Roof".

"Why is that fascinating?" asks Ms. Harris.

Ah, Ms. Harris, I would think Ms. Andrews would be asking that question though perhaps Ms. Andrews already knows the answer?"

"Because," says Ms. Andrews, "I look like the girl next door and Sister Woman is a complete bitch."

Perhaps your director just made an adventurous choice?

"Or maybe I just have no trouble playing a complete bitch."

And somehow, Ms. Andrews, I believe you.

I am not a fan of listing your height, weight and hair color. That information ought to be obvious in your picture. Short people look short – even in a headshot. If your headshot makes you look short and you are not, get another headshot. Some casting people like height, weight and hair color (which I never understand – do they not have eyes? How many minutes does it take to change an actor's hair color?) I feel it gives them three excuses to not have to see you. If they don't need tall women this week, the tall actress is going to the bottom of the pile. My feeling is that if they want to know your height and weight, they can damn well call you into their office.

Vital statistics smack a little bit too much of a meat market for me. Of course, it *is* a meat market but I am for as much civility as possible. If you are working with an agency or meeting a casting director who would prefer such information to be readily available, by all means offer it up as soon as they ask. And if your agent wants it on the resume, put it there. I personally just don't like it.

A Great Headshot

It is impossible to overstate the importance of a good headshot. And not just a good headshot. You will require a great headshot. Once you have it, you will be ready to embark on your acting career. Let's talk about how you get that headshot.

A great picture of you looks exactly like you on a good day. Not a great day. It is not flattering. It is accurate. It is filled with energy and it is specific. You are thinking something the second the picture was taken. Not a second before and not a second afterward. Ask people in the business for their opinion of your picture. Do not ask family members. Particularly not your mother. Your mother will say the picture doesn't capture how sweet you are. Screw how sweet you are. Nobody is sweet at their core. Not even Mother Theresa. Perhaps especially not Mother Theresa. And your core is what is called for in your picture.

A headshot is a head shot, it is not a body shot. Sometimes ¾ body shots come in and out of fashion. I would go with a head shot. Color, of course.

Choosing A Photographer

Choose a photographer with whom you feel comfortable. If he or she is a world famous photographer but they strike you as a jerk, go to someone else. If you feel he is doing you a favor by taking your money, go to someone else. Do not be concerned with how well-thought of they are in the profession. Annie Liebowitz is not required. Someone you feel good about is ten times more important than someone who has photographed ten famous actors. This photographer you are seeking should be someone you enjoy being around, who gets you, or at least who you feel gets you. Whatever you feel about the photographer is going to be in the photo so make sure what you feel is good. The best first photo I ever saw (besides Claire's, of course) was Matthew Modine's. I don't know who took Claire's photo, but Matthew Modine's was taken by his college roommate.

When someone on the other side of the desk sees you walk in the door, you must be exactly the person they first met in your photo. I have seen headshots of people who are not physically imposing but whose headshot makes them look physically imposing and the result, when that actor walks into the audition room, is instant disappointment. Do not let this happen to you. Do not disappoint. A person's stature can be conveyed in a photo. A person's aura, too. Make sure your headshot has as much (accurate) information about you as it is possible to put there. If you're kind of a sissy, do not strive for a head shot which makes you look like David Beckham.

I once sent a picture and resume of a new client to a West Coast casting director who was coming to New York for one day to cast one part. A few days later, I called her in LA to schedule the appointment and her assistant informed me that her boss would not be seeing my client. I expressed some appropriate indignation and demanded the casting director get on the phone. She did. "What's the problem?" she began and I told her. She replied, "I don't want to see her. She's not what I'm looking for." "How can you tell?" "I have her picture right in front of me. She is not what I'm looking for." "But," I protested, "the picture doesn't really look like her." And it didn't. "Oh, really," the casting director came back at me, "who does it look like, then, if not herself?" There was no right answer to that one.

The picture is a quick MRI, a shot of where you might belong in this business. It's also your best shot at success. Because where you belong is crucial. What kind of roles? What size roles? Can you carry a movie, a play or a television show? Might you one day be the reason a project sees the light of day? (Are you a star?)

Back to the 8x10. It is not a prom shot. And ladies, do not let the photographer talk you into using someone for hair and makeup. Unless you walk around in your normal life perfectly coiffed and in full makeup. Actors loathe the idea that who they are in their heart of hearts can be captured in a single image. And who could blame them? It is an extremely difficult feat to accomplish but it can be done and it must be done.

And wear something neutral. The headshot is not a chance to show off what great taste you have in shirts. This is about your face, not your wardrobe.

It is also expensive – more than you may think at first. Because aside from the initial cost, in the likely event you will want to reshoot (because you hate the shots that were taken or your agent does), reshoots cost money, too – though you should pre-negotiate how much. Discovering you have picked the wrong photographer and need to start from scratch with someone else will cost even more. The whole process is annoying and frustrating beyond words but it is essential.

This does not mean that when you walk into the room, there are no surprises to come. On the contrary, it means that when you walk into the room, the people waiting to meet you will be relieved to discover you and your 8x10 are one in the same. And you will tell them more, by the way you come into the room (more or less in character), say hello (kind of in character), sit (in character), and chat (in character). The truth is, at that point, the job will be yours to lose.

They want you to be right for it. They want to give you the damn job. They want you to be what they are looking for so they can get this whole difficult-for-everyone process over with. They hate auditions almost as much as you do. Sometimes more. Actors scare the hell out of most producers. The good news is, if the way you walked into the room and said hi allowed them to imagine that you are what they are looking for, there is a very good chance that they will fall in love with what you are about to do which is act.

God, there is so much to say about this silly little thing but, well, I guess I've repeated how important it is as much as I've repeated the reasons why.

When you get the contacts from the photographer, his or her own choices will be marked. Do not choose any shots the photographer did not choose. You may disagree with something he feels does not work but he will be right, I promise you. Next, show the contacts to any agents or casting people you have met. Not all 200 shots. Pick your top five. Listen to the pros. These people look at 8x10s for a living. Do not show them to (or at least do not listen to the opinions of) parents, boyfriends, girlfriends or favorite bartenders.

Most parents hate most good headshots. There is nothing clean and well-behaved about a good headshot. (And we all know how clean and well behaved you are — at least around Mummy and Daddy). Nor should there be anything nasty. (Unless you are nasty.) It is simply that a good headshot has nothing to do with the little angel that most parents hold their children to be.

In the end, choose the picture that stands out to the most professionals. You must not see your picture on a casting director's desk as you walk into the room and cringe. You have to feel: that's me, that's my headshot and they want me. There will be people who do not like your headshot and they will not hesitate to tell you so. Thank them for their wisdom and move on. If there are *many* such people, get another headshot. Because aside from your own talent and your agent's hard work (fingers crossed), there is nothing more essential to breaking into this business than having a superior picture. So let's talk about yours.

Ms. Hamer, your 8x10 looks as if you might have been thinking something a minute ago and you may be thinking something a second from now but when the camera clicked you weren't thinking anything at all. It's lifeless. Your eyes are dead. You are an extremely pretty girl and there is nothing going on here.

Ms. Logan, I'll bet you like this picture. I would if I were you but this picture looks better than you do. You are an extremely castable young woman. I can think of ten million parts you would be right for but not one of them is going to come to mind if I am disappointed that you are not as pretty as your picture.

Your Picture Needs to Look Like You — Now — Today

Mr. Zawadski, this isn't bad but you have a beard in the photo and you do not have a beard in real life. This is bad and wrong. Women are fond of getting a headshot and then going out and getting a new hairstyle or, even worse, changing the color. Do not do that. Men are no better where their facial hair is concerned. Your picture needs to look like you look now. Today. I am not surprised that you can grow a beard, Mr. Zawadski. If I want to hire you and I wonder what you would look like with a beard, I will ask you not to shave before the call back. Or I will draw a beard on your picture. (I once drew bolts on an actor's neck and got him an audition for Frankenstein.) Or I will do a makeup test. Do not dazzle me with your ability to grow an unasked-for beard. I am not a big fan of facial hair anyway. It's limiting.

Ms. Paley, this is almost a good picture. There's nothing wrong with it. I just want more. More of you. Oh, Ms. Paley, are you going to get your teeth fixed? Yes, you need to. Good. Do it soon. It's obscenely expensive, I know. Will it become less expensive in five years? How much less will you earn between now and then because it's obscenely expensive today?

Sydney Pollack to Dustin Hoffman in "Tootsie":

"You're a wonderful actor but you're too much trouble."

ENTER: THE AGENT
(AND THE CASTING DIRECTOR)

We can use some good news. Let's pump up the optimism quotient. Let's say you do your showcase and several agents want you. (Let's make it a very rosy picture.) What then? How do you choose which one? Pick the place with the nicest waiting room? We're being serious now. Ask your teachers which agency is best? Well, a teacher might be able to help you sort through your feelings but it's a rare teacher who has an informed opinion about agencies. Not their field, after all.

A bunch of agents want you. Isn't that great? Can be.

Some little part of my heart gets all excited when I connect with young talent. Talent is the reason I am doing what I am doing. I have to hope the actor wants me, of course. I am fairly well-known for having a discerning eye and for going after not just good but superior young talent. No reason for modesty here. But I am hardly the only agent in New York with a decent reputation and, while I always bear the imprimatur of whatever prestigious agency I am working for, that agency may not always be seen as the most powerful office by youngsters getting out of school. So I may have to hustle. But I usually get my man – or woman.

In any given showcase there are at most two or three students who speak to the entire audience because they are gorgeous, because they are brilliant or because the have a famous parent and these students will probably go to one of the large agencies. That never used to happen. Never. It happens now but, of course, if at the end of a year this young person has not fulfilled his or her promise, they will be dropped. Famous parent or not. (Well, depends on how famous.)

The Advent Of The Agency

Agents are necessary. It was not ever thus. Did Edwin Booth have an agent? Did John Wilkes Booth have an agent? Actually, John Wilkes Booth might be very good casting for the way people think of agents today – soulless, ruthless people who would kill their mothers (or the President) without thinking twice. But stars, or major players as they were called back then, did not have agents because agencies did not exist. Major players had what was called management and it is likely that that management was themselves. In olden times, I'm talking the nineteenth century now, stars managed their own careers, or paid someone or married someone to do it for them – while they orchestrated every move – much as agents do today. The supporting players in the star's companies were friends or simply people they knew or people who had wormed their way into the star's good graces or people the stars had stolen from another star's company of actors with the promise of better roles or more money – much as agents do today.

William Gillette, James O'Neill (father of Eugene O'Neill), Minnie Maddern Fiske – these were the actor/managers who had most of the jobs to give away. Then the impresarios came along, people like David Belasco and John Golden. They were bigger than the actor managers. They *hired* the actor managers. Then people who built and bought entire chains of theatres came along – people like B. F. Keith and Edward Franklin Albee (grandfather of our greatest playwright – arguably, OK, OK), though the Keith-Albee circuit was more vaudeville than theatre, they still hired actors and actors will go wherever anyone who will hire them chooses to send them. Then individual producers came along and they put on shows they liked because they were out to validate their own taste (a running thread on the other side of the table) *and* make money. Soon there was more work than any one actor (who was not a star) could keep track of and that's where agents came in. Hard to say when agents became *necessary* but they did and they are.

Talent agencies as they exist today were spun around a concept created by Jules Stein and refined to a fare-thee-well by his lieutenant and eventual successor, Lew Wasserman. That concept is quite simply: "I am an agent and you need me to get a job. You will pay me for leading you to that job. The terms under which you will be paid for that job will be defined by me and, as the years go by, my demands for a bigger piece of the pie for you will increase and you will become very rich. So will I." Lew Wasserman created the idea of first dollar participation for his star James Stewart whereby Stewart was paid a percentage of a movie's gross earnings from the first dollar ever made by that picture, which happened to be "Winchester 73" (1967), not a memorable movie. But the deal was memorable because the deal was unheard of. Until then.

Jump to Arnold Rifkin, Bruce Willis's agent, who was the first to demand and get five million dollars for his client for a movie which happened to be "Die Hard" (1988) which was more memorable than "Winchester 73." You would have thought the world had ended as far as folks in the business were concerned. Five million dollars! To an actor! And, actually, the world did end – just a little. That was the beginning of there being less money for actors whose names are not above the title. These days there are stars making five to twenty-five million (to fifty million, yes you, Mr. Neeson) dollars a movie while everybody else in the movie makes scale (with some exceptions). This is a shame. You think I'm trying to guilt trip poor Bruce Willis on the chasm between his salary and everybody else's salary? I'm actually not but it's still a shame. Sandy Meisner used to say, "That's your soul up there and it is worth any amount of money." I have no doubt that Bruce Willis has a soul, ergo, he is worth the twenty-five million dollars he is now getting (and bless him for coming back to the theatre).

While I am not suggesting Sandy Meisner was wrong, I might point out that something is out of whack when a star makes twenty-five million dollars for a film and a veteran co-star is lucky to go home with fifty thousand. If an agent says to a star, I can get you twenty-five million dollars, I don't think it is in human nature for the star – any star – to say, oh I don't need that much, just give me half of that and give the rest to some deserving person below the title.

So what are agents, anyway? What do they really do? They are licensed by the state (of New York or California or – name your state) as Employment Agencies. Their charge is literally to find and negotiate work for actors. It is not a part of their mandate to nurture and develop young talent. If an individual agency has half a brain they will realize that developing young talent is a smart and self-serving thing to do. So, yes, that is something that agencies ought to do and most of them used to do routinely. The sad fact is that over time, that part of agency work has been put out to pasture or turned over to the smaller agencies who have what is dismissively referred to as very little clout.

Clout is a concept worth discussing. Clout as in, "My agent doesn't have enough clout to get me in for film and TV." Clout is simply being able to get people you need on the phone and have them believe you can help them solve their problem which today might be to find someone to play Elvis Presley in yet another television movie about his life. If I am producing that movie about Elvis and I believe you might have someone who can play Elvis of whom the network will approve then I will take your call. So you have clout.

Clout is leverage and it is fair to say that small agencies have less of it than large agencies. Nevertheless, small agencies are where most young actors start out and will stay – until they tell themselves, or an agent at a large agency tells them, they now require the clout they will get from being with a larger agency. The truth is that if a few actors would stay with their small agents as they began to move up the ladder, the small agencies would start to have more clout. Because power resides in the actor.

Power begins with the actor. This is not a chicken or the egg situation. There were actors long before there were agents. The actor, however, thinks power resides in the agent (or perhaps he would prefer to think so since it takes responsibility off his shoulders) and so he signs with a big agency and makes that agency a gift of his burgeoning power. Thus do actors, even when they wind up making 25 million dollars a movie, remain basically powerless. Oh, they may have a 50-foot trailer with a perpetually restocked mini bar and a car and driver and even co-star approval but in exchange for all these feel-good little perks, they will have to deliver the toned anatomy and the flawless skin that the studio is paying for. Not to mention act in the developed-to-death tent pole scripts that the studios churn out and stars are expected to do. This is because the studios have decided these scripts are what the public wants to see and are, therefore, the scripts that are available to stars. And the star's agent may even represent the writer of that tent pole script so the agent is not going to say, my client needs a better script and he'd like to do something where he can keep his shirt on for a change. In fact, the small agencies are in a much better position to stand up for their clients but they don't because ... they don't have any clout.

Now wait a minute, you say. Ryan Gosling is not some toned pretty boy, who makes disposable movies. No, Ryan

Gosling, while he is toned and he is pretty, is what you call a prestige client. He's good to have because he gives credibility to all the more famous pretty boys on the agency's list who are not great actors and who make more money than he does. Ryan Gosling does not make 25 million dollars a movie. I am not suggesting he is worrying about his next meal. Just that his quirky desire to make good movies keeps him out of the mega bucks enjoyed by the very top tier of stars. That could change. Robert Downey Jr. used to be thought of as a prestige client and then along came "Iron Man." It used to be felt Johnny Depp was only interested in small movies and then, hello "Pirates of the Caribbean."

Big offices have big rents to pay and agents with big salaries to support and they don't really have a lot of time to spend bringing along beginning actors who are not going to make a dime for their first couple of years in the business and will be ripe for poaching after their first big break anyway. Although keep in mind, large offices don't just steal from small offices; they steal from each other as well. So the large offices don't really have the time to develop talent – they are too busy trying to keep their mitts on the income producing commodities (actors) they already have. There aren't enough hours in the day to make sure stars are happy, return phone calls and try to convince some exec to take a chance on this great young kid for this breakout part that Zac Efron will wind up doing anyway.

Much simpler and more cost-effective to let the smaller agencies do the developing. And then, when one of them starts to make money, swoop down. It was said of Mike Ovitz that he had no idea how to develop an actor's career. But he could steal a career faster than a speeding bullet. Word was he was also a good negotiator. I do think he may be responsible for the idea that you need a large agency behind you because large agencies package.

Packaging

Oh, I hate this part. Packaging is bullshit. Large agencies package for their large-earning actors. They do not say: You can have Sylvester Stallone but you have to take Betty Boop who just got out of Yale. They don't say that. They say they say that. They don't. Period. What they say is that Sylvester Stallone is busy, why not take Bruce Willis (who makes more money and Sylvester Stallone is not busy at all). I am talking about how these offices operate in principle; I am not really talking about Sylvester Stallone or Bruce Willis so please call off the lawyers. Life was much better for the stars themselves when they were spread out over twenty or thirty well-thought of offices. But that was sometime after speech replaced sign language, though well before the last millennium.

Large agencies are, in general, not a good place for a beginning actor. Mid-size to small agencies are more helpful and smarter places for young actors to be. Most actors who are with mid-size to small agencies sit around and scheme about what life will be like when they are with a large office. (So do their agents.)

Almost all of the highest-earning actors in show business are with the four largest offices. If you have a bunch of stars, you have more power than somebody who has no stars. Lew Wasserman figured that one out. But the power which exists *because* of the star, accrues to the *agent*, not the star. Jack Nicholson's small agency has just as much power as Josh Brolin's power agency and probably more because Jack Nicholson is a bigger star. I personally think most actors have no interest in power, they just want to work. And that suits the agents just fine.

There was a point when Meryl Streep and Glenn Close were both represented by the same office. And because Glenn Close is not an idiot, it didn't take her that long to realize that everything she was being offered had been offered first to Meryl Streep. For anyone missing the point, Meryl Streep had a higher price than Glenn Close (still does, I would imagine) but the agency was a force to be reckoned with because both Meryl Streep and Glenn Close were there. Not because they had an agent who had holes in the elbows of his sweater and ate lunch every day at The Russian Tea Room. So Glenn Close left the agency. I think Streep did, too, ultimately.

So we were talking about packaging. Actually, the agency that used to represent both Streep and Close is very fond of saying that they package. My feeling is that they don't. At any rate, they certainly don't in any way that will affect someone fresh out of school or off the bus who is trying to break into this business. You should be so lucky to be in a position to be part of a package. Assuming that's the kind of career you want. And if you are just out of school and an agent starts talking to you about putting you in a package, you should tighten you chastity belt and prepare not to believe a word of what you are about to hear.

Let's talk for a moment about loyalty. Glenn Close had a

perfectly good reason to leave that large agency. Not every actor has such a good reason to leave their agent but actors leave agencies all the time. I never used to understand why. However, I have developed a theory. Somewhere the actor knows when decisions are being made on their behalf that are dictated by the bottom line and not what is best for the actor's career. (What is that anyway? Might take some time to figure out. But that kind of time is at a premium these days.) I believe that if an agent were to listen to what the actor wants to do next, and took into consideration all that would feed what the actor wanted for himself (along with a soupcon of what would be good for the agency), actors would be far less flighty. An agent must honor the client's instinct, but that instinct must be educated by experience.

I am not suggesting that what all actors really want to do is go to Cleveland and gorge themselves on Chekhov and their poor agency can just lump it. Nor am I suggesting that actors don't want to do big budget gladiator movies where they get to wear jock straps and togas and cool sandals and take home a pile of money. Who wouldn't want to do that? But there is a balance and there is work that can help an actor grow and become a better actor and there is work that will let you buy another Warhol for the family room and both kinds of work ought to be considered valid. At the large agencies, that is not the case. Barring keeping a prestige client happy. (If Ryan Gosling wants to do a little low-budget movie a friend of his wrote, where's the harm? At least he doesn't want to do some freaking play off-Broadway.)

But you know, sometimes it might be better to do a play

or take second billing or cut your price in order to do a part that would make you a better artist. (At this point, any agent reading this book would probably hurl it across the room. A better artist? Give me a break. What kind of crap is this?) Incidentally, I think most such moves (plays, weird parts in low budget movies, workshops even) only serve to enhance an actor's career. But that is long-term thinking. In today's world, long-term thinking is not the norm nor is it considered productive to the business at hand. Why make a move for an actor that might pay off in a few years when, in all likelihood, that actor will be with another agency in a few years? I suspect this may have something to do with there being fewer careers that last the course of a lifetime anymore. I'm talking about lasting with dignity intact.

You can say horror movies are cool all you want. No amount of rationalization will convince me that horror movies are anything other than dumping grounds for actors who are trying to stop a downward spiral. I know Brad Pitt made a good zombie movie but it was only good because he made them reshoot the end and it was only made in the first place because he wanted to do it. So he kind of does what he wants. He's cool. Every once in a while a piece of trash movie is cool. They are cool because every once in a while a talented star or director or writer pulls off a good one but then he or she is onto better things and Jessica Lange is still clumping around in zombieville. And being awfully good. I know. And with an Emmy. Several Emmys. I suppose that's some sort of consolation. It's a hit. She's a star. She's rich. I know. Maybe if I liked the show better .... Of course, Ms. Lange just won a Tony for "Long Day's Journey," a very different role indeed.

But it's the mavericks like Brad Pitt who set the tone for everyone else. Why not be a maverick? Why not have your agent try to keep up with you rather than the other way around? If an actor is smart enough to constantly reinvent himself or direct his own movies or write and score his own projects, the agent may not be such an important part of the equation. But not everyone is Clint Eastwood. Does Clint Eastwood's agent actually do anything? What does Clint even need with an agent at this point? Well, I'm sure that agent has plenty to do but it must be a lot more fun to be Clint Eastwood than it is to be his agent. On the other hand, I'll bet it's a lot more fun to be Bruce Willis's agent than it is to be Bruce Willis. You think?

What do big time agents do anyway? Well, for one thing, they are always on the lookout for people they do not represent who are for one reason or another unhappy with the people who do represent them. Or someone who can be made unhappy with the people who represent them. Sometimes they go after someone else's client just for fun. Sometimes it works. Most actors, no matter how famous they are, don't have that confrontation gene that would let them say to their agent: "You're not doing enough for me," or, "You're not doing what I want you to do." So it's easy for *another* agent to say to a star, "What would you like to do next?" And then, when they tell you, you say to the star, "I can make that happen." And voila, you've got yourself a star. Now maybe their actual agent could have made whatever they wanted to happen happen but their actual agent never asked. Simpler to just leave and go with the new guy. Even if the star knows you were just chasing them for fun and they, at first, had no intention of going with you, hey, it's fun to be chased. Though in the long run it is perhaps more laudable to be chaste but, as we have noted, generally speaking, the long run has left the building.

This dance goes on not just with stars. It goes on big time with actors who are in the process of breaking out. The actor who just broke into a six-figure payday is possibly on his way to seven figures and the feeding frenzy is on. Now why, you may well ask, would an actor move from an agent who has been working well for him – well enough for that actor to have come to the attention of another agent (and convince a studio to give him $350,000) if perhaps not yet the public – why would that hypothetical actor (let's say it's you) leave the first agent and go to the second?

Why even consider such a move? Because an agent wanting you will always mean acceptance and the thrill of newness and of courtship which goes on in the dance between tempter and tempted which has been around since the beginning of time, though the tempter wasn't called an agent then – I believe the proper name was asp. Who asked the asp, um, agent, to the table anyway? In all probability, the actor, you, did something to bring favorable attention to yourself. Let's say you did a role in a play that was reviewed in *The Times* and you were mentioned favorably. Other agencies took note.

I was head of the New York office of a bi-coastal talent agency when I got a call from my boss in California at ten o'clock one morning. It was 7:00 AM her time so I knew she was reading the paper. She asked me if I had seen the review of last night's Broadway opening. I said I had. She said that was a very positive mention of the girl playing the star's daughter. Had I noticed? I had. She asked if I had seen the play. I said I had not. She asked when I was going. I said I would probably not go as we didn't have any clients in the cast and she always objected when I spent company money to see plays without clients. She said this girl was obviously very desirable and I should go see her. I said that since the girl was on Broadway in a very good role, the chances are she already had an agent and, after such a review, she was probably very happy. My boss said that I was an idiot and after such a review, this girl was probably dreaming of all the big things that were about to come her way and would be much more likely to come her way if she were to leave her (probably) small agency. My 7:00 AM caller pointed out to me that all the approval coming this young actress' way was going to make the girl vulnerable.

Nothing makes an actor more vulnerable than praise, said my boss not for the first time. They're used to rejection. It's praise they don't know how to handle. Tell her she would be our top priority. Tell her...oh, don't make me tell you how to do your job. (Why stop now, I wondered.)

The answer to why our hypothetical actor – back to you now – would leave your first agent is because someone comes along and seduces you with the promise of a rosier future. Why does anyone leave any relationship? More and better benefits. Let's drop that hypothetical actor, you, and let's jump on the bandwagon of this girl who got the rave notice in the paper. She, I can promise you, will be wined and dined and, if the stakes are big enough, a few gifts may even be thrown into the bargain. (The lead of a small movie called "Wish You Were Here" looked like she had what it takes for fame and was sent a very expensive watch from an agency, which had

had it engraved – Wish You Were *Here* – and signed with the name of the agency. She did not sign with that agency though I heard she kept the watch.) This actress in the Broadway play will be told she will have access to more projects sooner and at a higher level than at her current agency. I know this because it looks like I'm going to be one of the vultures feeding her this bullshit. (Aren't I ashamed? A little.)

The seduction is usually rounded out with the promise that very soon the actor will be as big as the agent's biggest clients, some of whom are very big indeed. In short, the asp makes clear, he and his office have more power than the actor's current agent, who is a loser, and if she wants to be in the big time, she had better get on board right now. It will not occur to the actress that if she has come to the attention of the powerful soon-to-be-circling-her agencies, she has also most likely come to the attention of studios, networks and independent producers who will seek her out for work no matter who her agent is. Still, she wishes one of the four large agencies had come after her. They probably would have if she were prettier, she told me when I took her out for a drink after I saw the show. I should have known she wouldn't choose me. Who wants an agent you can trust? (All right. So I'm bitter.)

Truth is, the four large agencies will probably never go after her. She is a very talented, better-than-average character actress. She is not a star. She was on the verge of going with me, she told me, when the star of her Broadway show told her he'd really appreciate it if she'd meet with his agents. Well, I couldn't fight that. I didn't even have any clients in the show. Not a great advertisement for my omnipresence in the business.

What happens to her next? Six months later, she shoots a pilot. Not the lead but a pilot nevertheless. Ah, see! Changing agencies worked! Her first office had never even sent her on a pilot. In fact, the network had asked for her on this one. (They go to the theatre, too.) Her new agency had nothing to do with it. The pilot doesn't sell. (Oh.) She gets a great small part in a studio movie. Turns out there is a lot of buzz on this movie. Which has yet to even start shooting. She's still annoyed that her pilot didn't sell. She thinks, as an agent who randomly made a play for her implied, that the pilot would have sold if her agency had more clout. Well, how dumb is that but the thought got inside and it rankles. Then the movie starts to shoot and her four days go well. She's happy. The studio, according to her agents, is happy. Life is good. She is being considered for everything. She is on the list.

You Bet There's A List

Is there a list? You bet there is a list. And her getting this movie assures that she is on it. The truth is, she was probably on the list as a result of that rave in the *Times* before she even left her old agency. Now the word is that when the movie opens, she will be huge. (Everyone says so.) Then it won't matter how pretty she is. (Yes, it will. Just ask her.) Maybe then she will even have enough clout to be desirable to William Morris/Endeavor which, truth be told, she has wanted to be represented by ever since she was a little girl in Duluth (when it was called just plain old William Morris.) But the movie tanked and William Morris/Endeavor did not come calling. These days she does a lot of guest stars. She is not a star. (Told you.)

Sometimes actors are incredibly loyal. The legendary agent Ed Limato's extraordinary list of stars – Denzel Washington, Mel Gibson (who Limato stuck by during his travails), Richard Gere, Michelle Pfeiffer – stayed with him while he went from ICM to William Morris and back to ICM and once again to William Morris. It could hardly be said that these were unknown actors but it is remarkable and gratifying to note that, successful as they were, they felt the man who represented them might somehow be responsible for their *continued* success. Limato was a particularly colorful character – going shoeless at big parties, screaming like a maniac in negotiations, passionately loving his clients and saying so, living alone in a mansion with his mother. In a profession filled with people who may be fierce but are not terribly interesting or creative themselves, Ed Limato was a passionate practitioner of his trade and deserved his clients' loyalty.

There was a time when the two most important agents in Los Angeles were Stan Kamen at William Morris and Guy McElwaine at CMA (which, several incarnations later, has morphed into ICM). It was said that when one of them had a client who was considering jumping ship, that client would only leave one for the other since they were far and away the two most important agents in town. So whenever one of them was discovered to have a restless client, whichever of them was to be the potential beneficiary of this restlessness would take a meeting with that actor. Afterwards, either Stan or Guy would call the other to say he had just met with client X who was unhappy and his competitor had six months to fix it or he would sign client X himself.

Such gentlemanly fair warning is not conceivable today but it was not unusual then and cutthroat as the game was even back then, integrity had not completely departed the equation. I am not saying that all agents used to behave with such a sense of fair play but those two did and they were considered the best. And the dignity they brought to their profession was a large part of why they were held in such esteem. They had taste, they cared and they played by the rules. Bruce Savan was in that league, too.

You might have to go back to Leland Hayward to find an agent who got as much airplay as Ed Limato or who cared as passionately about his clients. (And by airplay, I mean nice things being said. I do not refer here to Michael Ovitz about whom I do not wish to contribute further ink.) Leland Hayward was a wonder. He represented Greta Garbo, Judy Garland, Ginger Rogers and Henry Fonda before selling his talent agency and producing "South Pacific" and "Mr. Roberts." They don't make agents like that anymore. I would venture to say they don't make *people* like that anymore.

Loyalty? Are You Serious?

The lack of actor loyalty to agents is almost a given in today's market. Years ago I visited my client Paul Giamatti while he was shooting "Man in the Moon" which starred Jim Carrey. I got into a conversation with the delightful Mr. Carrey on the set about precisely this topic. He told me to hold on tight to Paul. By way of illustration, he told me that shortly after "The Cable Guy" (a fabled flop of his own) had opened, an agent, not his, had called him at home to commiserate about the movie's terrible first weekend grosses. The agent added that the weekend that had been chosen for the film to open was a notoriously terrible weekend and his agent should never have allowed that to happen. Now, said Jim Carrey to me, "I am not a fool and I know perfectly well that my agent has no control over when a movie of mine opens but don't think I didn't twirl and call my agent and chew him out. I mean, that agent who called me must have stayed up all night just thinking of a way to make me unhappy with my agency. Good luck keeping Paul," he added.

A short time after that, a pernicious little predator at one of the Big Four got it into her head that she had to represent Paul. She took to calling him several times a day, sending him scripts, filling him with tales of what she could do for him that I couldn't. This porcine upstart was relentless. You may say that Paul could have told her he was perfectly happy with the agent he had who had overseen his career from college to the present day, that he had never been out of work, that the size of his roles and the money he earned for them increased yearly by leaps and bounds and thank you for thinking I will be wildly successful but my current agent thinks the same thing and please go away. These are words that do not come easily to an actor. Paul finally gave in and went with her. I have to say, it hurt like hell.

I am happy to report that he left her a few years later. Probably because he noticed that while he had been on track to become an over-the-title star, something that none of Ms. Big Four's other clients were then, he wasn't breaking through to that exalted place where he could make his own rules. Frankly,

I think most of her clients deserve to be more famous than they are but the business has decreed they are all excellent character actors and that is enough for them. This actually may be the business's assessment of Ms. Big Four herself but sadly it transfers to her clients as well. In fact after Paul left me for the Big Four bandwagon, she was fired by her Big Four agency.

If she has such great clients, why was she fired? She had prestige clients which is not the same thing as a great client. Deeming this agent expendable sent a message that her clients were expendable as well. Paul got the message. All those good actors and all in static careers. I recognize that there are a large number of actors out there who would be happy to have David Morse's career. I can't help but feel that Mr. Morse must want more. He is certainly worthy of more. That's the thing about the large agencies. They tend to accept the status quo and actors who come to them on the cusp tend to stay on the cusp, or fall off altogether. Remember Julia Ormond who Clifford Stevens at Paradigm helped shepherd to the lead in the remake of "Sabrina"? Well, she went to CAA. Julia who? Plus Paul Giamatti is a *great* actor which is no small thing to be. He ought to not settle for being a feather in his agent's cap.

You may be thinking you wouldn't mind being a feather in some agent's cap. Please don't. You are better than that. You need a defender and a champion, not someone seeking to enhance their own prestige.

The first time I ever met a big deal agent from one of the big deal agencies was back when I was first starting as a manager and had a client whose career was taking off. This client didn't have an agent. He hadn't needed one but now that his career was taking off the big deal agents were coming to call and I was semi-open to it. He was desirable and people were starting to desire him. This agent wasn't the only one but he was the first one and he made an impression. He had an engaging personality – most agents do.

We're like hookers, not flashy – just really easy to talk to. So this guy came by and we got along like a house afire. He asked me all sorts of questions about my office, about me, about how we worked. I could see he was looking for weak spots. He wasn't subtle about it. He was more powerful than I was. Period. The truth is, I like guys like that. Streetwise, fearless – so he wasn't subtle. Big deal. The guy was a bully in a two thousand dollar suit and I thought he was fun. (Adjusted for inflation, that would be a five thousand dollar suit today.) Anyway, I saw his game and I intended to show him that neither he nor his suit was going to push me around.

I rather proudly told a story about how I had just laid waste to a studio's attempt to ride roughshod over my client's welfare on his latest picture which he was then in the midst of completing. This had happened just a few weeks before. My desirable client was shooting in Idaho or Wyoming or some right to work state. Mr. Big Deal Agent said he knew that. (I said I knew he knew that.) So my client and his leading lady (who was a star) were scheduled to shoot a love scene the next morning but the night before, over a drink in the hotel bar, the star had let slip, in an off-hand remark, that she had facial herpes. She wasn't contagious now, she hastened to add, but she did have herpes. Well, my client freaked out. He called me the second he got back to his room (this was before cell phones, duh) and told me there was no way he was going to shoot that love scene in the morning. How could she know for sure she wasn't contagious?

He was married, his wife was pregnant and he was damned if he was going to risk passing herpes along to his wife and his unborn child. He refused to shoot the scheduled scene in the morning. Period. Well, I didn't know if it was possible to pass herpes on to a fetus and my client's wife wasn't even at the location but I certainly didn't blame him for not wanting to expose himself. I promised my client I would take care of it. So I got the producer's number – he was staying in the same hotel as my client. It must have been midnight. I woke him up. He started yelling. (He was a yeller.) I presented the problem and he commenced yelling some more. I suggested that putting an actor in a position where he was in danger of catching a sexually transmitted disease was asking too much of that actor.

"Well," said the producer, still at full volume, "I guess that's what you sign up for when you kiss people for a living." Wow. It seemed the wrong moment to point out that this guy's wife was an actress who also kissed people for a living so I did not. I did suggest they bring a doctor to the set in the morning and have him determine whether or not the female star was in a contagious phase. If not, the love scene could proceed.

The producer screamed he wasn't going to humiliate a highly respected actress by having her examined like some cow in front of the cast and crew! I said there was no need for her to be examined in front of everyone, it could happen in her trailer and furthermore, my client wasn't going to kiss her until a doctor said she was symptom-free and that was that. End of story. The producer relented – after a lot more screaming – and my client was mollified and the next morning he kissed the girl.

The big deal agent just shook his head. He seemed deflated. I had not impressed him with my story. He had other concerns. Such as? "They could have lost shooting time," he said. "Yeah," I agreed. "And I could have lost a client." The big deal agent was a company man, a studio stooge, who pointed out to me that it wasn't about the clients. Clients came and went. We remained. It was all about us and our relationships with the studios and costing studios shooting time was a no-no. Never forget that. Oh. Was that what it was like in the big leagues?

Just as a coda, that movie wasn't much of a hit. Kind of a flop really.

How Agencies Really Work

Let me give you a nuts and bolts summary of how agencies really work. First of all, they usually divvy up the casting community among the agents in the office. The important agents work with the important casting directors. One very important casting director hates to work with important agents because she can't push them around as easily as she can terrorize an assistant. Generally, though, the big deal agents work with the big deal casting people which assures everybody involved that they are as important as they think they are. And the heads of the big deal agencies work with the heads of the studios and the networks.

Agents are sellers and casting directors are buyers. In a

larger agency, an agent probably works with a smaller number of buyers since those offices tend to specialize (movies, TV, independent movies) plus they have the luxury of having more agents – and the liability of more information getting lost and not being communicated to people who need to have it. Of course, most of the large offices persist in telling you that they seldom work on the casting director level thus implying that there is no space at all between them and the heads of all the studios and networks. As if the heads of those companies gave a tinker's damn about who is in the new Will Smith movie. Will Smith is in the new Will Smith movie. That's why it's being made.

You will not be dealing with these honchos who don't – or who say they don't – deal with casting directors at the beginning of your career. The only time you will even meet one of them is if several agencies are fighting over you. Then the big guys, the agents you have heard of, will come and sit in the meeting the agency has to tell you how crazy about you they are. Then you will never see that agent again. Until your first important paycheck.

In the smaller offices, most of the agents know most or all of the casting people and they will happily claim so. (They may not know all the film casting directors.) This can be helpful as they have an overview of what is going on. The trouble is the smaller offices don't represent a lot of actors who could benefit from an agent with an overview. Those offices are simply scrambling for every job out there. That's healthy, too. Agents in the large offices don't do a lot of scrambling – except when they are stealing someone else's client. They "field offers" as Sydney Pollock said so memorably in "Tootsie." This is helpful when there are offers to field. Even then, a fair amount of taste and discretion is involved. Or ought to be.

Let's say a character actor (someone who is less than beautiful) gets a star-making part in a movie and gives a star-making performance. Let's say it's you. What should you do next? Anything that will solidify you in the public's mind as someone who is thought of as a star. In other words, a great role. At the very least, a *big* role. Carrying a small movie would not be a bad idea. Hey, it's the lead. Not that you should or will get to carry your next movie but the movie and the role should be seen as canny choices. You could be the villain in the new "Mission Impossible" franchise. That's always someone special.

You should not be a supporting actor in a Julia Roberts movie in a role that could be played by anybody and nobody could do anything special with anyway. (No disrespect to Julia Roberts, OK?) And if you are capable of carrying a movie, that will be plenty obvious to the taste-makers when they see you on screen. Brad Pitt and Matt Damon have no trouble playing supporting parts. Nobody is rethinking if they ought to be stars or not. After "Thelma and Louise" Brad Pitt actually waited longer than lots of people in that break-out position before he risked carrying a movie on his name alone. Now he seems to relish small parts. But get to be Brad Pitt and Matt Damon before you start doing favors for friends, or yourself.

Of course, casting directors do not, for the most part, hire above the title actors. A casting director did not give Jim Carrey the job. The studio gave Jim Carrey the job. Jim Carrey has to worry about the studio's concern that Mike Meyers might bring in more money. What do Mike Meyers and Jim

Carrey have in common? Practically nothing except they are both stars and they are both funny. Which one gets the job will be based more on bottom line economics than how right they are for the part. Who has a bigger demographic in the South where the story takes place? Although, since the story takes place in the South, maybe the Middle-West's feelings ought to be considered. Forget New York and LA. What about China? Suddenly being at the mercy of a casting director's opinion doesn't seem so bad. And we needn't shed tears over Carrey and Meyers's talent being reduced to numbers on a demographic poll sheet. Twenty million a picture ought to smooth over any absent consideration for artistry. (But, you know, I'll bet it doesn't.)

"No Turned Up Noses"

Even though agents and casting directors' functions are naturally intertwined and each needs the other, they are natural adversaries as well. It's too bad, and it's really too bad when the actor is the one who suffers. There was a casting director who once famously would not bring in a well-known actress for a role because she didn't like her mouth. Ouch. I had a casting director say to me when I suggested a client, "With those pop eyes of hers? Never." And a big-time director told a casting director friend of mine, her voice dripping disdain, "No turned-up noses." But it isn't always just some silly physical prejudice that gets in the actor's way. Sometimes it's political. Sometimes the casting director wants to do a solid for an agent friend (who can help her land her next job because he represents the producer) at the expense of my client who is more right for the job. But then, half the time the actor the casting director is pushing for and my client who I am pushing for will lose out to another actor who nobody was pushing for but it simply more right for the role. So good. The right actor has been found. Wasn't that always the point? Well, maybe. Let's face it, we are all in it to prevail.

Casting directors are type cast as much as actors are. Some of them are considered better for theatre (where the least amount of money is so naturally they would like to be considered for film and TV every bit as much as the actors they cast), some are considered good at finding kids, some are even considered better at comedy than drama. Don't let your agent's negative attitude toward casting directors color the way you interact with them at an audition.

I quite like most casting directors. I have some friends who are casting directors and they are wonderful people and wonderful friends. Why not try and befriend some of them yourself? Not in some calculating way but if you sense that you like one of them and one of them likes you, say something friendly. We are all people here. If you are a geek, you can say to the casting director who seems to specialize in geeks – and would probably like to cast a few beauties now and then – "I know I'll always be a geek but you won't always be *casting* geeks." She might smile at that. She might even say, "Oh, I think you could do a lead." "A lead geek?" "No, a lead *guy.*" Resist the urge to ask her out on a date then and there but this person could be a friend. You have bonded on one of the most basic problems in show business: type casting. And you have just been typed as a lead!

If the business can pigeonhole you, it will, no matter your

field of expertise. Each new job will be your pigeonhole. Keeping your options open, making sure the pigeonholing doesn't *stick*, used to be the agent's job. Not so much any more. Most agents these days are only too happy to keep the jobs coming even if it's the same job over and over again. Never mind that the career possibilities for their client (you) may be narrowing. Or even fast approaching the end of their shelf-life. The appealingly goofy young guy might start to come off a little creepy as he approaches forty. It's not so much that the agent has become less concerned with the arc of an actor's career (though that certainly is true since most actors don't stay with an agent long enough for the agent to even feel a part of that arc), it's more forgivingly seen as a result of agent's simply not having as much time as they used to because they have too many clients. That's one of the ways in which a manager can be helpful.

But let's first talk about agencies and my highly informed, extremely jaundiced view of them. They have remained mysterious in order to remain formidable and I'd like to help you draw back the curtain, at least a little.

First of all, what do you *think* agents are looking for? Let us consider the agent's plight for a moment. Let's say you were an agent, with your own agency. Who would be on your dream client list? Would *you* be? Would any of your classmates be? How many clients would you have? How many stars? All stars? Really? Boring! Before we next get together, I would like you to email me a dream client list and at our next workshop we will discuss what you have done. A dream client list speaks for itself.

WORKSHOP FIVE:
Walk A Mile In My Shoes

Before we get to your dream client lists, let's do some improvisation. Not an acting class, I know I promised, but I lied. But not really. This is basically a chance to burrow further into an agent's mind, although in this case it will be your mind standing in for the agent's. Let me explain.

How can you possibly expect to be wanted, let alone sought after by someone whose priorities you have never even considered? Someone who is a complete mystery to you. Someone you very possibly even resent? What do you think the agent is looking for? Bottom line: someone who will make money. How does he know when he is talking to such a person? Well, after a while, agents develop an instinct, or hope they do. The truth is, while *no* agent is infallible on the who-is-going-to-succeed front, there are signs. These signs are interpreted differently by different agents.

An agent who has no use for you in the morning may be shrugged off thanks to the one who flipped for you in the afternoon. While the morning agent's rejection might sting less thanks to the hours-later acceptance, the morning agent's reaction should not be dismissed. They each had their reasons for liking and for not liking you. You need to know, or at least think about, what those reasons might be. Why the one in the morning did not like you is every bit as important as why the one in the afternoon did.

What do agents want? I always go for someone I like personally, which makes me a sucker and destined for heartache but that's me. Obviously, I always tumble for someone I think is gifted. How can I tell? I guess! I suspect and then I go see work. I look at their reel if they have one or I see them in a play when they get one. Do I insist on waiting till they are in something? Yes. I only signed one actor in my life whose work I had never seen because he was irresistible in the office. He proceeded to star in one movie and was little-heard from after that. But if I have responded favorably in the office, it is more than likely I will respond favorably to their work. What makes me respond favorably in the office? I look for someone who is pleasant to be around, who is passionate about the profession and who deeply wants me. (Deeply? Really? Sure. I'm a person.)

I like it best when I want them first. There is no substitute for seeing someone in a play or on film and falling in love with their talent. If they have forced themselves upon me in the office, it always takes me a while to warm up to them. But if I have seen someone in a play, loved their work and called them into the office, they would have to go a very long way to screw up their interview with me. A few have managed that feat, however.

There are agents who would prefer to talk to an actor in an office than watch that actor act in a play. I suspect these are people who have no idea what good acting is and are much more comfortable proclaiming that someone gives great interviews and you're gonna love 'em, baby, I promise you, you're gonna love 'em. This is how they sell their clients. And it works. For them. I had a very successful LA manager try to interest me in a client of his thusly: "I only want her with you for theatre – you know, Broadway. None of that eight hundred dollar-a-week crap. She probably won't even want to do Broadway but she'll want to know that people are talking about her. You know? Look, she's drop-dead gorgeous and she's got a million dollar personality. People love her. Fantastic body. Legs for days. Plus she's not a bad little actress." As I said, people have different priorities.

Anyway, let's talk about what we'll be doing today. Improvisations are fun. At least, this one is. One of you will be the agent, one of you will be the actor. Here is your back story:

Agent: You work for the head of the legit department at a mid-size bi-coastal talent agency. Her name is Jane Jones. You are her assistant. An important casting director has asked your boss to meet with a young actor and your boss has asked you to do it for her. The last time she asked you to interview someone was six months ago. Your verdict then was that the actor had no talent, was a tough sell and would be a waste of the agency's time. He is now a series regular on an HBO show. Your credibility is, shall we say, suspect and at stake. Safe to say, this is your last chance to spot talent – at this agency anyway.

Actor: At the restaurant where you work, you waited on an important casting director who took a shine to you and called you in to meet and read. He liked you and has set up a meeting with a highly respected agent named Jane Jones.

Where are you? Let's say that Jane Jones has told you to use the agency's conference room for this meeting.

Clearly, the agent's objective is to find out if this actor is someone the agency wants. The actor's objective is to get signed. So let's start with Ms. Harris as the agent and Mr. Zawadski as the actor. Don't forget your picture, Mr. Zawadski. Yes, Ms. Harris?

Ms. H: Couldn't someone else go first?

Me: No, Ms. Harris. All right, let's go.

Mr. Z: (enters, holding his picture and resume): Hi. I'm Jerry Zawadski.

Ms. H: You'd better be. I'm Naomi Harris.

Mr. Z: Ha! What a great room. Is this your office?

Ms. H: This is the agency's conference room.

Mr. Z: Oh, duh. I guess that was pretty stupid of me.

Ms. H: Medium stupid.

Mr. Z: I thought I was going to be seeing Jane Jones.

Ms. H: Ms. Jones was called away.

Mr. Z: Great. Then you and me can get it on.

Ms. H: We can try.

Mr. Z: You're funny.

Ms. H: No, you're funny. (*A pause.*) I'm told you were very rude to our receptionist.

Mr. Z: (*A longer pause.*) That's not true.

Ms. H: (*Laughing*) No, it's not.

Mr. Z: Always be nice to receptionists. I know that much. You want my picture?

Ms. H: Of course.

Mr. Z: (*He puts it on her desk.*) Here you go.

Ms. H: (*Picks it up, looking at the resume*) Brown?

Mr. Z: (*Nodding*): You sound surprised.

Ms. H: I am.

Mr. Z: How come?

Ms. H: Do you really want to put me on the spot like that?

Mr. Z: Yeah, well, I realize my whole thing here, my whole aura, you know, I mean, it doesn't exactly scream Brown.

Ms. H: What does it scream?

Mr. Z: Oh, I guess working-class stiff, big heart, maybe fun in the sack.

Ms. H: You've thought about it.

Mr. Z: You bet.

Ms. H: Describe me.

Mr. Z: Tough cookie, bruises easily.

Ms. H: That's very...forward.

Mr. Z: Accurate though. Right?

Ms. H: (*Smiles, in spite of herself*): Perhaps.

Mr. Z: Hey, we like each other.

Ms. H: You're very seductive.

Mr. Z: Just having fun.

Ms. H: Have less fun.

Mr. Z: Got it. Really appreciate your seeing me. I'm in a show over at the Tiffany if you want to come check it out.

Ms. H: And what are you playing? A big-hearted guy?

Mr. Z: You got it.

Ms H: Why should I go to the Tiffany? I can see you're a big-hearted guy in my office.

Mr. Z: In your conference room. But, you know, come see me in my lair. See me do what I do. Maybe want to represent me. Could happen.

Ms. H: Why do you think this agency would be right for you?

Mr. Z: I don't know. This agency is a big deal. I want to *be* a big deal. Sounds like a good fit.

Ms. H: We have a lot of very big stars here. Aren't you afraid you might get lost in the shuffle?

Mr. Z: Never gonna happen.

Ms. H: You're very sure of yourself.

Mr. Z: Trying to impress you. Is it working?

Well, I think this interview is very promising and I'm going to leave it there. Was his charm working on you, Ms. Harris?

"I wasn't sure."

What about you, Mr. Zawadski? Was she having it?

"I think I needed more time with her."

I think you needed to back off a bit. But that's me. Who knows where you and Ms. Harris might have taken this exercise. The point of the exercise is to try to imagine how an agent thinks and if you can do that, you might think of them less as the enemy and more of them as a partner – or a potential partner. This would be helpful to your cause. And by the way, Ms. Harris. I have no idea why you were so reluctant to go first. You clearly have no problem with assertion. People are full of surprises. Why don't we next invite Mr. Fitz-William to interview Ms. Paley. Mr. Fitz-William, kindly take a seat at the conference table and Ms. Paley, take your picture and go out and come in. Go.

> **Ms. P:** (*Poking her head in the door*) Am I in the right room?
>
> **Mr. FW:** Depends on who you are.
>
> **Ms. P:** Oh. Of course. I'm Nan Paley. I'm looking for Jane Jones.
>
> **Mr. FW:** Well, you've got me, honey.

Ms. P: I don't... understand.

Mr. FW: Jane Jones had other fish to fry. You're talking to me.

Ms. P: Oh.

Mr. FW: My name is Lonnie Fitz-William, if you care.

Ms. P: Well, of course I care. There's no need to be rude.

Mr. FW: I'm not rude. That's just how I am.

Ms. P: Oh. Can I sit down?

Mr. FW: If you're staying, it might be a good idea.

Ms. P: (She sits.) Um.

Mr. FW: So tell me about yourself.

Ms. P: Well, here's my picture and resume.

Mr. FW: Where did you go to school?

Ms. P: Um, UCLA. It says on the resume.

Mr. FW: Screw the resume. Why don't you just tell me about yourself. What audition scenes did you do for UCLA?

Ms. P: Oh, well that's actually a funny story.

Mr. FW: Let's hope so.

Ms. P: I did something from "Hedda Gabler" and then Lady Bracknell.

Mr. FW: Those are both terrible choices for you.

Ms. P: That's what they said.

Mr. FW: What's the funny part?

Ms. P: I got in.

Mr. FW: So you won. That is pretty funny.

Ms. P: I thought so.

Mr. FW: You won me over there for a second there. Don't go back to being Miss Priss.

Ms. P: I'm so nervous.

Mr. FW: That's kind of obvious.

Ms. P: I'm sorry. It's just that guys like you never like me.

Mr. FW: Excuse me? What is a guy like me?

Ms. P: Oh, I don't know.

Mr. FW: Big old queens?

Ms. P: No. God no. I've got…

Mr. FW: Do not say you have tons of gay friends.

Ms. P: I wasn't going to say that.

Mr. FW: Bullshit you weren't.

Ms. P: Maybe I was. It's just, funny bitchy guys never like me.

Mr. FW: That's funny because sullen, brainy bitches like you never like me.

Ms. P: Oh. Maybe now we're getting somewhere.

I would say yes, you are now definitely getting somewhere. It was something of a train wreck up until then. Do you all see why? Ms. Paley, you had several opportunities to turn that around before real emotion entered the room and did it for you. And Mr. Fitz-William, why were you being so difficult?

Mr. FW: I wanted to see what she'd do.

And the truth is, you are not crazy about women like her, am I right?

Mr. FW: Yup.

And that's fine. That's even good. Not everyone you meet will be your cup of tea and you are going to have to turn them around. That does not make you a phony. It makes you a professional. It is not your concern if the director appears to be a sexist pig, if the script is second rate, or scene partner is talent-free. Your job is to act and to be affable enough to be given the chance. A student of Sandy Meisner once objected to a scene Sandy assigned him because the play it came from was so poorly written. "Oh," said Meisner, "you're a critic. I mistook you for an actor."

This exercise is a source of never-ending revelation to me. It is your job to let someone know you have talent and it is the other person's job to find out if they agree. I never cease to find it extraordinary how far afield the discussion can veer given those intentions. This is something you can do at home with a friend. Take turns being the agent. I would suggest that you ask other friends over to watch you as you work on it. Better yet, tape yourself as you and your friend find your way through this exercise. Watching yourself saying cringe-worthy things and behaving in a manner you would disown in a second had you known how it was going to look to anybody else is an invaluable, if sometimes painful, way to learn something new. But we all know what happens when there is no pain. I am not going to give you further examples of what my admirable students came up with to torture and engage each other. The point of this exercise is to do it. So find a friend and do it.

Put yourself in an agent's shoes. What are their priorities? What they are looking for? Have you researched them? Who is on their roster? Don't you know? Why do you want to be on that team? Agencies have personalities which are expressed in their client lists. What would your agency say about you?

How do agents think? What are their priorities? You may never really get to know your agent (or he may become your best friend, doesn't really matter) but if you want to get an agent's attention, you would do well to consider that they have a few needs of their own and think about how you might fit into what those needs are. There are actors who define an agency. Try and be one of those actors. If I were to see Adam Driver on an agency's list, I would know I am dealing with an office that cares about acting.

Let us turn our attention to your dream client lists. What have you come up with?

Ms. Harris is the only one of you to have separated men from women, just like a real talent agency. I would suggest that with only ten clients, your resemblance to a real talent agency ends almost as soon as it has begun, though you might be able to keep the wolf from the door with just George Clooney. Generally, however, ten clients sounds like a manager. You can afford more; you actually need more if you want people to call you for ideas. And you do want that.

Mr. Fitz-William, you came up with a name for your agency. You actually envision yourself doing the things that you do even before you do them. I find this the sign of a rich artistic temperament. Your list of fifty clients – a nice round number – leans a little heavily on youth, Mr. Fitz-William. In fact, the only people I see over fifty are Meryl Streep and Robert De Niro. Is Susan Sarandon chopped liver? Is Steve Martin not capable of making a buck? There are roles for people over fifty. As an agent, it would behoove you to be known for having good clients, good taste and a wide selection rather than specializing in just one demographic area. Not that a talent agency is a department store but if it were, Barney's is a better model than Sears. Only the best but the best of everything. You want to cover the waterfront even if you restrict yourself to the Gold Coast. Of course, you cannot be expected to think of everything. If Hollywood decides to start making movies about the Inuit Nation, you cannot be blamed for being caught with your pants down but, generally speaking, a diverse list is a healthy list.

LARGE AGENCIES

The common wisdom is that if you want a large career, you need to be with a large agency. And most actors who already have large careers are. Jack Nicholson and Harrison Ford are not. Harrison Ford and Jack Nicholson are the only two major names in the business who are with small agencies. (Or, rather, were: Harrison was his agent Patricia McQueeney's only client until she passed away in 2005.) When Jack Nicholson accepted one of his Oscars, he said he wanted to thank his "one and only agent, Sandy Bresler." Nicholson is the only actor in America even close to that stature who could lay claim to having had only one agent in his career. Even Harrison Ford kicked around a bit before recognizing the advantages of fidelity to a consistent mind at the helm and went the loyalty route. She served him well.

Loyalty doesn't seem to have hurt Nicholson or Ford's luster in any way which is my point here. Could they have better or more exemplary careers? I cannot see how. And do they seem like the kind of guys who would leave themselves unprotected? I will attempt not to mention either one of them too often. I have a soft spot in my heart for each of them.

How powerful is Jack Nicholson's agent? When Nicholson made a movie called "The Pledge" with tons of name actors who were willing to work for less than their usual quotes because Sean Penn was directing, Mr. Nicholson's salary was twelve million dollars. An homage to his iconic stature, I suppose, since everybody else had a ceiling of $100,000. Everybody else included the likes of Sam Shepard, Robin Wright, Benicio Del Toro, Helen Mirren, Mickey Rourke, Vanessa Redgrave, Aaron Eckhart, Harry Dean Stanton, Michael O'Keefe, and Lois Smith. Even Sean Penn had the same salary cap as the actors. One day one of those poor beggars with the $100,000 ceiling was complaining to the producer about how much money doing this movie was costing him in lost revenue. The producer pointed out that the actor should stop complaining since he and all his famous fellows were the second highest earning people on the picture. "No they are not," the actor snarled. "The second highest earning person on this picture is Jack Nicholson's agent."

"You Know I'm Going To Be A Big Star"

Back when "Star Wars: A New Hope" was still in the editing room (where George Lucas had been tinkering with it for months on end), Harrison Ford was represented by an agency I used to work for. His name came up in a meeting one day and the owner of the agency (a notorious hot head) said, "That damn movie of his is never going to come out. Let's drop him." And they did. Then when Harrison's manager wanted to talk about shopping for a new agent, Harrison said to her, "You know, I'm going to be a big star when this movie comes out."

And, like any good manager, Pat McQueeney said, "Of course you are, Harrison. You're going to be colossal." Ford suggested that she drop her other clients, get herself franchised, represent only him and he would never leave her. And that's what happened. I am not sure, nor is anyone, if that never leaving her bit was ever put in writing but he never did leave her. 10% of twenty million dollars a picture at the average rate of a picture a year is an OK living. God knows what he gets on the back end. Commissionable, I would think.

There are four large agencies: William Morris/Endeavor, International Creative Management, Creative Artists Associates, and United Talent Agency. They are all known by their acronyms. They are all headquartered in Los Angeles and each of them has a New York office. The New York offices are quite nice. The LA offices are impressive which is precisely what they are supposed to be. Come unto us and live large.

Agencies used to informally categorize their individual agents' skills as falling into one of the following four categories: Signers, Bookers, Negotiators and Hand-holders. Those terms are all pretty self-explanatory, right? Well, these days, it's really every man for himself. The agent is basically told: make money! The finer points of how that is to be done will be sorted out on a case by case basis, if they ever even are, by the attorneys. Sound like a zoo? It kinda is.

The large agencies more formally separate their agents into categories of concern – either film or television. There are no theatre departments worth speaking of at the large agencies (except at WM/E there is an excellent guy who signs hot kids and keeps stars happy by looking out for projects they might be suited to and can pass on). God forbid he should let one of them actually do a play. And CAA says, oh, we do theatre. And sometimes they do.

These agencies do not develop talent. They send stars or established actors on interviews and meetings for starring parts or they field offers (thank you Sydney Pollack) for their mega-stars. No one is going to be offering a beginning actor a role of any size in a movie anytime soon. Unless they starred in some indie that took off or they leapt off the screen in one scene in a studio movie. Yes, I have heard of Lupita Nyong'o. She leapt off the screen in a studio movie ("Non-Stop"), she went to Yale and she is gorgeous. And "12 Years a Slave" for all its brilliance, was a small independent movie and the director could hire whomever he wanted without some studio executive breathing down his neck saying the actress he had chosen didn't have enough credits, wasn't screwable and who knew if she could even deliver a performance?

But let's say, for argument's sake, that a large agency is interested in a very talented young actor (like Lupita) from an MFA school (like Yale). Let's throw in that the young actor is great looking (like Lupita). So why is the large agency interested in a rank beginner (like Lupita)? Because sometimes the beginner will get a break (like Lupita). A big one (like Lupita). Sometimes (rarely) it will happen that the agency has caught lightning in a bottle. Though it seems to be taking Lupita's hot shot new agency (CAA) a while to be lining up her next job. (It has to be perfect, you know.) She's the face of some fragrance so she's probably OK with her rent. Oh. Wait a minute. Lupita just got something. Whew! She'll be fine.

The fact is, the chances of lightning in a bottle are about as great as making a video that goes viral on YouTube or winning the lottery. Yes, it happens. Of course it happens. But don't bet on it. Hey. Lupita won the lottery. I am not saying she is not gifted. She is unbelievably gifted. And beautiful. But she won the lottery. You can't plan on that happening. But, increasingly, unknown actors are signing with large agencies. Is it a good idea? I don't think so. But it happens. Sometimes it will work out in the actor's favor. Mostly not but what you want to know is: when that *does* happen, *how* does it happen? (Because it could happen to you.)

Well, let's say the young actor has one of those aforementioned famous parents or is spectacular looking or has managed to attach some kind of buzz to their name. Other people in the industry may have heard that buzz and so there is interest. Lloyd Bridges once had a couple of kids who wanted to act. So did Henry Fonda. Always worth checking out to see if the genes have traveled to the next generation. Charlize Theron was a model. Having a famous parent can result in instant buzz and everybody notices the appearance of a beautiful new model. (Well, don't they?) The difficulty here will be keeping the buzz at bay until the chrysalis is capable of living up to its buzz.

Lloyd Bridges made sure those boys had some camera time before they went out into the world. A downside to a famous dad is that it can signal entitlement and an unwillingness to wait. There are several just-give–it to-me brats out there right now. Not so in the case of the Bridges boys (thanks to Bridges pere) but people are wary of it happening so, if you have a famous parent, be sure to behave well. Even if you don't have a famous parent, behaving well is a good plan. Though if you have a famous parent, I would bet you are not reading this book.

Instant buzz can happen sometimes with a young person coming out of the MFA programs. The studios will have become aware of this buzz because buzz is what they inhale with their first joint of the day and they will ask to meet this young person. They won't do anything as mundane as attend the buzz person's school showcase. They'd have to wait for that. They can't even spell 'wait'. They will call the young person into their offices. An assistant will put them on tape and, if anyone in the agency is interested, that person will be called in for a meeting. Almost always that young person (of great beauty or talent or sex appeal or good genes or *something*) is found to be simply too green. They lack seasoning. They lack whatever assurance comes from even a modicum of struggle in the business and actual time acting in front of an audience or a camera. There is no substitute for such experience. None.

"I Would So Nail That Audition"

Except when there is. Billy Crudup was less than a year out of school when he auditioned for the lead in "Arcadia" at Lincoln Center. I was Billy's agent at the time. He did not get a call back. The casting director told me that Billy simply wasn't ready for such a role. There were actors flying in from Los Angeles to audition for this part. There were actors flying in from London. It was a big role. A great role. They could have anyone they wanted. What was needed was experience. What was needed was seasoning. Billy was simply too green. So I told that to Billy. I always try and pass on feedback when it is offered. (Unless the casting director asks me not to.) Billy said, "Hm." And he thanked me and hung up. The next day he called me and said he thought he knew what had been missing from his "Arcadia" audition and could I get him seen again? Now there are actors who routinely say, "God, if I could just get back in the room, I would so nail that damn audition." That would be most actors. Billy had never said that to me before so I listened to him. I called the casting director, who is a reasonable man, and relayed Billy's thoughts. "I will see him again," said the casting director. And he did and Billy went on to read for the director and was called back for the director and got the job. How did he do that? I don't know. Can you act having years of experience? Billy Crudup could.

Gary Oldman spent nine years doing theatre after drama school before he ever went near a camera. But Gary Oldman is not our prototype here. We are talking about our to-die-for-looking starlet or studlet fresh out of an MFA program. Although, wait a minute. Gary Oldman was kind of a dish when he was young. There must have been film opportunities for him which he passed up. But he had trained as a theatre actor and so goddamn it, he worked in the theatre. It is a different world over there in the UK. Faye Dunaway came out of school with that breathtakingly beautiful face and starred in an off-Broadway play and then in a movie and then in another movie and then another. I read recently that she was suing her landlord to keep her rent-controlled New York City apartment. Gary Oldman is still a star and a role model for younger actors.

What The Hell Is Buzz?

Let's go back to buzz for a minute. What is it? It is an inchoate, intangible but audible chattering among the opinion makers in the business that something (a film being made by a supposed wunderkind in Santa Fe) or someone (Carroll Baker's granddaughter in college in upstate new York) is worthy of attention. It's kind of like what is supposed to happen when you hire a great public relations person – but without the public relations person. Public relations is all about manipulating public opinion. Buzz is supposed to be purer – like the theatre. Nothing (in show business) beats the high of being the first to know that: "The Graduate" is going to be huge; Brad Pitt is the sexiest guy to come along since Paul Newman; Tom Cruise blew it on Oprah; Ovitz was fired; "Twelve Years A Slave" is going to get the Oscar; "Jaws" is going to be a dog. Oh, did I mention that buzz, while pure, is not always accurate?

If you are a young actor, you will want to generate buzz and the only way you will get it is by attracting the attention of someone who everybody listens to. Like a big deal casting director who is always finding somebody new and terrific. (Which is how a casting director gets to be a big deal in the first place.) Like a director with the taste and the power to cast an emerging actor in a great role. There aren't too many of those. Or by being nobody from nowhere who manages to sign with one of the four large agencies. Let's assume for a moment that you would even want to do that. I've already said it's a bad idea, right?

When an unknown signs with a big agency, everybody else waits for that person to fail. You would think they would root for them to succeed. That ain't human nature. But if you want buzz, if you want the smart money paying attention to you (smart and wise are not the same thing but who cares about wise?) screw it, sign with the big agency.

How would you go about doing that? Well, why not find out who cast the highest grossing independent film of last year. Find out who that casting director's assistant is. Make it your life's work to get to know that assistant. (While you are still in school? Yes. Where will you find the time? Go back to Toledo.) You ask the head of your MFA program to write a note to the casting director about you. Why would the head of your program do that? I don't know. You tell me. Because you are going to be famous and the school will be able to claim you as a graduate? Somebody who teaches in your program will be willing to write a note. Ask the casting director to come to your showcase. Beg them to come. Write a whole bunch of people.

Get your name heard. Cultivate a hungry young casting office that is dying to work on better projects and get them to call a large agency about you. Do you think Barden/Schnee was always the hottest casting office in New York? Send them tape of you being brilliant. You may very well get a meeting with a big agency (since that's what you say you want). You will at least get a meeting with the casting director. If you get to meet with the large agency, and you have a million dollar personality, and are gorgeous or dripping with sex, they may sign you and you may get to audition for every young leading role in every movie made during the next year. All of those roles will probably go to stars. If you haven't worked at all, you may be dropped. The agency had been hoping for lightning in a bottle but, hey, not this time. Although for a while there, you had buzz.

A Real Juicy Role

All right, let's give our story a happier ending. Sometimes (rarely now), if the beginner is good *enough*, or funny *enough* or gorgeous *enough* – and let's say you are all those things – *and the right part comes along*, and the beginner – you – will get a really juicy role. Much celebration all around. Of course, your life changes completely. (Try not to develop a drug habit.) Then the movie comes out. First, it is sneaked at the usual places. Then it is shown in the usual private homes. Then agencies start to get copies. And it acquires buzz. Is the buzz good? Yeah, it's pretty good. What about the young actor? What about you? Do you leap off the screen? Are you compelling (a favorite word of the executives)? Everyone in town knew this was a star-making part. There were rumors Liam Hemsworth wanted to do it because, sure it was small but it was a great part and people might take him more seriously if he did it.

So what's the verdict on you? Are you going to be a star? Nobody wants to be the first to say yes. What if they're wrong? What if they love you and the public doesn't? What if they hate you and Steven Spielberg thinks you're great? Then sooner or later somebody who knows his own mind without having to consult anyone else (let's say Joseph Middleton – who? – look him up, he's got clout) sees the movie and judges that the new guy, that would be you, falls a little short. Well, that's what everybody had kind of been thinking. He wasn't bad. But he wasn't great. And the business, yes, the whole business, will write that person, you, off. And good luck next time taking the next good part away from some poor deserving star who's trying to deepen his image. So the young actor is dropped from his agency. Just like in the first scenario. But this time he at least got the job. You got up to bat. Aw, and I promised you a happy ending. (Actually, I said *happier*.)

Won't the large agency give that young actor some time to develop? I mean, are they just going to write him off after one wrong move? Everyone had such high hopes. Most likely. Probably, he's had his shot for now. If the actor blows a really good shot, definitely no. The grosses might have been higher on that picture if the actor in that break out role had actually broken out. So your not measuring up has cost people money. Really? Well, not really but it could be spun that way. (You can bet whoever greenlit the picture will spin it that way.) The agency had been really talking you up, this picture was going to make you a star but people do not become stars in flop pictures.

All of a sudden you're the *reason* it's a flop? That's not fair. Hey, it's Chinatown. After all, it's up there on the screen – you are not compelling. The alchemy of the agency is at stake here, not to mention the studio's coffers.

We don't want the studio blaming the agency. When something is not working that could hardly be the agency's fault. It *might* have been the director's fault for hiring the actor in the first place. Not because he didn't know how to direct but because directors don't usually get blamed. Maybe it's his fault, maybe it isn't. Not relevant. Studios keep hiring the same directors (almost always guys) who put together their last mega-million-dollar colossus. Hey, he brought it in on budget, didn't he?

Unless it was a *famous* director in which case, it goes back to definitely being the actor's fault. And the agency doesn't want that actor around, tainting the agency's name with that stinko performance trailing after him wherever he goes. See how you went from not compelling to stinko? Yeah, that happens.

Very Compelling Agents

It seems impossible to write about the large agencies without mentioning at least a couple of the mega-agents. The truth is that agents are faceless by design. The Agency has a face, the agents do not – a few superstars notwithstanding. Many folks think that Mike Ovitz dreamed up the model of the black-suited foot soldier, indistinguishable from his or her fellows, doing battle in the service of the agency. Actually, Lew Wasserman came up with that one when he was running MCA, far and away the most powerful agency in the last century. Black suits, white shirts, black ties, almost all men, faceless. Including Wasserman himself. Read "When Hollywood Had a King." Terrific book. Fascinating man. Scary, too. The government broke up MCA in the '50s (something about not being able to own a talent agency and a movie studio at the same time – not fair apparently). Then in the '80s, CAA emerged as leader of the new pack and they are still teetering there.

These days CAA is run by a small group of agents the most visible of whom is Bryan Lourd. I don't think he tries to be visible but he was once married to Carrie Fisher and marrying Princess Leia tends to draw some attention. He also has a staggering client list which would set him apart from the competition no matter how much anonymity he may claim to prefer. He is responsible for: George Clooney, Robert De Niro, Robert Downey, Jr., Sean Penn, Naomi Watts, Natalie Portman, Arnold Schwartzenegger, Steven Spielberg, Oprah Winfrey, Jamie Foxx, Josh Hutcherson, Meryl Streep, Kate Winslet, Peter Joback, and Nicole Kidman. That list may not be up to date but you get the idea. (No list, no fact I lay claim to in this book will ever be as up to date as if it had come out of my printer tomorrow. And lists of who represents who change faster than Paris Hilton's sheets.) Lourd's client list changes though not as often as most, I would bet. He keeps his clients. He's good. I doubt CAA is making much money from Arnold Schwarzenegger these days but the muscleman works. Muscles never go out of style.

Anyway, look at Bryan Lourdes's list! How does he even have time to sleep?

Who is Peter Joback? Funny you should ask. I used to represent Peter Joback. He was sent to me by a wonderful casting director who had seen him in a show in Sweden while on vacation with her husband. Peter came to see me when he was in New York. He is an extremely handsome man with a superior personality who sings like an angel. (He had a CD. He did not sing for me in my office.) I was charmed by him and sent him to several people who were not impressed. I couldn't get him arrested. People didn't find him compelling. Well, there were other things: he was going back to Sweden soon, therefore not really available, he didn't have a green card, he had an accent – yada yada yada. There were good reasons I was no help but bottom line – I was no help. Couldn't make him a star in under a month. However, I am delighted to see that he is now with a big time agency and I have no doubt you will be hearing his name before too long.

The only other visible-to-the-public agent is probably Ari Emanuel on whom the agent Ari Gold in "Entourage" was based. Word has it, the characterization is not in the least exaggerated. In which case, he deserves any celebrity which has come to him since he is so colorful and so, what, flamboyantly driven? Good luck getting him to mastermind your career. (Do you really want him to? Oh. OK.) His brother, Rahm, His Honor the Mayor of Chicago, did a pretty decent job as Obama's chief agent in the White House.

If you cannot pique the curiosity of Bryan Lourd or Ari Emanuel during your early years in show business, do not despair. Do something visible without their help and they will find you. If you are compelling, you may have a hard time keeping them away.

"Honey, You Are One Of Thousands!"

Why do big agencies drop people? You may not even notice you've been dropped. When your star starts to wane, they just kind of ignore you to death. All agencies drop people when they are not making money for long enough. It seems somehow more ruthless when big agencies do it but all agencies do it. And rather than the agency examining what might be wrong with the way the client's career is being handled – or the parts the actor is being suggested for – they just drop him or her. You don't want one actor's failed – or even stalled – career reflecting poorly on the agency. It's not as if there were no one to take that actor's place. Plenty of fish in the sea. As Sue Mengers (a very successful agent from the last century) once put it to an actor, "Honey, you are one of thousands." Frequently, clients who are about to be dropped can feel it coming – so they jump ship before they can be marooned. Not before they have found another agent though. Never do that.

If the young actor doesn't catch on in the first year (first two years if the agency is feeling magnanimous), she will be dropped. If you really want to know why a big agency is not a good idea for a beginning actor, most of that beginning actor's competition during their time with that agency will be stars (frequently from the same agency) and it is a rare director, an even rarer studio that will go with an unknown over a star. (One definition of a star is: someone you can blame if the picture is a flop. Didn't we just discuss this? Johnny Depp must be looking over his shoulder a lot these days.) The unknown actor will be seen for roles the business does not feel they are ready to play. And in most cases, the business will be right. While you are an unknown is your best time to learn.

Since the unknown actor is with a large agency it will be felt worth taking a look because the large agency signed the actor in the first place; so ergo the unknown must have *something*. But if some hapless director doesn't cast him in the blockbuster movie he has been handed to direct after his art house hit (and why should he?), that actor will not be perceived as prematurely being positioned for starring parts. He or she will be seen as just not having the right stuff and, in the end, the known quantity will prevail in a business which is not fond of risk. Why go through the charade in the first place? Because once in a blue moon it works. In a risk-averse business, some maverick director takes a chance on an untried actor and the actor delivers a brilliant performance and a star is born. (See "The Graduate".)

The great producers in the last century knew that making a star didn't happen overnight. When they found somebody like Lana Turner, they took the time to develop her. Their risk was in focusing on her in the first place. But having focused on her, they did not lose all interest at the first sign of unreadiness. They addressed that unreadiness. More acting classes. More speech classes. More grooming. They watched like hawks in her first few outings. And as she started to succeed, they watched even more closely. Their hopes (and their money) were on her. So they took care of her. She really did have what it takes, right? Right. She sure did. What was her agent doing during this grooming and then flowering process? Probably negotiating, then renegotiating Lana's contract with the studio. What was Lana doing? She was working. She wasn't thinking about changing agents, for God's sake, she was thinking about her career. I'm not saying Lana Turner was Meryl Streep. But she was compelling. It is safe to say that these days no one has much interest in the actor's development. They deliver or they don't.

When Rules Do Not Apply

If you've been mulling all this over, you might well ask, why not send the neophyte out for smaller roles? To which the large agency would ask, where's the money in that? I was at a small agency and sent a client on a small role and he wound up playing the male lead in the movie. But the director was Sidney Lumet, one of the few directors who knew what he wanted and had the clout to get it. So with directors who have clout, as with actors of genius, the rules do not apply. If you are meeting with Mr. Scorsese, whether or not you get the job will have nothing to do with your big agency. But, you protest, your big agent got you to Martin Scorsese in the first place. Yes, and I got my client to Sidney Lumet. Your large agency got you to Scorsese for the lead and when Scorsese says he feels you might be right for a smaller role, you're going to feel a little like the agency let you down. The fact is, whether or not you get the job has nothing to do with your agent. But how you are positioned when you are seen for the job matters quite a bit. And if you are continually positioned for roles you are not deemed ready for, eventually you are going to start getting the blame.

Bottom Line: Not Compelling

Let's say that a studio is interested in a great looking young actor who went to a top MFA school and is now with a powerful agent to play the lead in a big new comedy because the studio's casting department heard that this actor is a comer. Let's say that the agency has more than a sneaking suspicion that the great looking actor is not exactly funny. What are they going to do? Tell the studio to go away? Who even cares if he's funny? They might try suggesting bigger stars (who may or may not be funny but sure as hell make more money). But let's say the actor gets cast in the movie, does a lousy job and the movie bombs. Do you think allowances will be made for the untested actor who doesn't have a funny bone in his body? No.

The business will write the actor off. Not funny. Can't handle a lead. Too theatrical. Too gay. Too strange. Bottom line: not compelling. Is that the agency's problem? Are you kidding me? Possibly in a few years, after doing time in independent films, maybe even some theatre, and with a smaller agency of course, the actor can return and be noticed and given another chance. Assuming the actor has that kind of determination. Or luck. Or clout.

Now let's say that same actor was with a small agency. He's still great looking and he still went to a top MFA school but for some reason, he decided to sign with a small agency. Let's say he knows what he's got. And he somehow managed to come to the attention of the casting department of the studio shooting that comedy. Maybe the small agency did their job and submitted him. Maybe his manager got his name in the mix. Anyway, it happened. And let's say the small agency also suspects, just like the large agency, that this paragon of acting they managed to sign is not exactly funny. What is the small agency supposed to do when their client is offered the role? Turn it down? Are you nuts? They are no more going to do that than the large agency.

You will notice that nowhere in this discussion has there been any consideration of how right the actor may or may not be for the part. That is not even in the equation. Well, who gets to decide that? You do. Can you handle the part? If it is a good part and you are nobody from nowhere, it is impossible that you will feel you cannot handle the part. So you say *yes*, of course. And let's say you do a bang-up job. You get major buzz. Agents are all over you. Ryan Gosling's agency among them.

Now there's a career you wouldn't mind having. But that career is taken. (He's not very funny either but he *is* Ryan Gosling.) What's his agency going to do for you? Make you bigger than Ryan. Bet on their saying that. But the picture comes out and it still flops and large agencies are crying for you anyway because you just starred in a studio movie. BUT let's say hell freezes over and you decide to stay with your original small agency.

Does The Role Speak To You?

Then what is supposed to happen starts to happen. Two projects come along with interest in you. Not offers but interest. Now is the moment when you should start thinking if you are right for the part. Which one are you going to go for? You hear they are also talking to Ryan Gosling for one of them. But the other one feels righter for you. The agency acts as if the choice is obvious. (The most money, knucklehead – yes, your pure, small agency goes for the predictable choice. Actually, the money isn't *that* different.) And the Ryan Gosling one may really be the better choice. It's got a better director. This is where you have to know who you are as an actor and all those years of training and waiting on tables and taking bad direction from student directors and turning commercial copy into gold will start to pay off.

Choose the part that you will have the most fun doing and that plays to your greatest strengths. They may not even offer it to you. But if they want Ryan Gosling, shouldn't you have gone with his agency? You think his agency would push for him over you on this movie? Are you nuts? Of course they would. Be glad you stayed with the small guy. But that's not the issue here.

The issue is the part. This part needs someone funny. Are you funny? Oh, you're funnier than Ryan Gosling? THAT'S NOT THE QUESTION. THE QUESTION IS, ARE YOU FUNNY ENOUGH FOR THIS PART? THAT WILL ALWAYS BE THE QUESTION. SUBSTITUTE DANGEROUS FOR FUNNY OR CLEVER FOR DANGEROUS, OR SEXY FOR ANYTHING. ARE YOU RIGHT FOR THE PART? EVEN IF YOU ARE NOT RIGHT FOR IT, DOES IT SPEAK TO YOU? COULD YOU PLAY THE HELL OUT OF IT? These are questions you should ask throughout your entire career. I could make a long list of some very famous people who should take heed. (Is the character a know-it-all? I am right for that part.)

Look, nobody, not a large agency, not a small agency, not your manager, not your lawyer, not your grandmother is going to tell you to turn down the lead in a comedy because you aren't funny. Only you can do that. And do *you* think you aren't funny? You liar. You know you're a laugh riot. I read some interview with Sylvester Stallone who was complaining that the public didn't want to see him in comedies. Clearly, he thinks he's funny. I...don't. Pretty compelling though.

The core problem here, what I am trying to address, is that even if the studio is casting a movie (we're talking above title talent here) and they are looking for the lead in a new movie, probably the last thing they are going to consider is how right for the part is the star they have decided to go after: Chris Pratt or Vince Vaughn or Andrew Garfield? What do you mean Andrew Garfield isn't funny? "Spiderman 2" grossed over $200 million domestic! (It is so a comedy. Ask the Golden Globes!) And who at the agency is going to tell Andrew Garfield that he is not funny or Vince Vaughn that he may be a little old and shouldn't do the picture because if it tanks he will be blamed and it *will* tank because he will be too old. Gotta go with Chris Pratt. Who is funny and is compelling and has been kicking around for more than a few years with absolutely nobody believing he had the stuff to carry a movie, let alone a movie with a $200 million plus budget. HA! There is nobody hotter in town right now.

Now let's say a star is offered the lead in a comedy. Is he going to tell his agent he's not sure it's a good move for his career because this girl he went out with before he was famous told him he wasn't funny. I can promise you, the agent will say, "What are you, kidding me? Dude, you are HYSTERICAL." So I guess what I am saying here is: *when you are famous, make sure you have someone who still talks to you as if you weren't.* Keep in mind all the things you learned about yourself before you became famous. Because they will still be true. I once represented a *great* actor, who was also smart and whose first big break was a featured role in what happened to be a comedy. I went to the set one day to watch him shoot and saw a young movie actress wipe my brilliant client off the screen because she was funny and he was not. He has subsequently had a very successful career but since he has been able to choose his roles, I have never seen him do a comedy. (Did I mention he was smart?)

Coverage

A final word about the large agencies. They all have something called Coverage, an ever evolving, very thick (when printed out) tome with descriptions of all projects at all studios and all networks and all the important independent producers with an assessment of each project's readiness to go into production. The coverage also itemizes the above and below line talent (in front of the camera/behind the camera) who have been attached to (and sometimes who have passed on) each project thus far in its life. This data is compiled by some peon who has recently left or desperately wants to break out of some mailroom and woe to whoever he or she may be who has overlooked some point in the development process. (Julia Roberts turned this down? Good to know but not vital. Everything is offered to Julia Roberts first. Shia LaBeouf turned this down? Kid's a freak show. Finn Wittrock turned this down? Essential information. That kid shouldn't be turning anything down. That's bad advice. He can't be happy. Get him on the phone.) Coverage will be talked about and that's what it is. Some important managers also have their own coverage or access to the Coverage from a large agency. Everybody talks about Coverage and how it is absolutely essential when building any career. It's not absolutely essential. It is helpful.

A last word on this topic that won't die: Coverage also includes the summaries of the plot lines of every project mentioned. Curtis Hanson once asked a young actor of reputation who was auditioning for the lead in "Wonder Boys" what he thought of the script. The young actor replied that he had not read the script but he said very proudly that he had read the Coverage and he thought it was terrific. He did not get the job. Tobey Maguire had read the whole script (the only name actor who met the director who had done so) and got the job.

Poaching

Of course, one of the biggest things I have against large offices is that they steal smaller office's clients. They steal from each other as well but that doesn't bother me so much. When Spalding Grey was getting to be a thing, CAA came knocking on his door. Probably other agencies did, too but I know about CAA because Spalding told me. (I was his agent.) When CAA reached out to him, he was understandably curious. He went to the meeting at their offices which was held in their large conference room. There was a large round table at which were seated a large number of men in black suits and black ties and white shirts. No one was speaking. Just as Spalding was thinking that the choice of a round table was interesting because it was impossible to tell who was more important than whom, one of the men in a black suit began the meeting by saying that according to the agency's calculations, Spalding would be making five million dollars a year just two years after signing with CAA, were he to do so, which the gentleman speaking, dearly hoped he would do. However, CAA's concern, the gentleman continued, and it was not small, was that Spalding had no interest in earning five million dollars a year. Would Spalding care to comment? Spalding laughed – then and as he was telling me the story. I asked what happened next. Spalding laughed again. "Does it matter?" said Spalding. "Wasn't the whole path of the meeting obvious in that man's opening words? Don't worry, Philip. I'm not going anywhere." Gotta love Spalding Grey.

Spalding did not leave me then though he did a while later when ICM, who handled his monologue engagements, insisted they also needed to handle his acting career because it was just too monumentally difficult for them to work with an outside agency (me) to coordinate his schedule. As I was neither capable nor equipped to handle Spalding's one man bookings, he left me. Obviously, he had to. He said it pained him and I'll bet it did. He was a prince. And ICM left him no real alternative. And no acting career, either.

Summing Up

A powerful agent representing even the most gorgeous and gifted young actor is like a 60-carat diamond hanging from the neck of a spectacularly beautiful woman. What does a spectacularly beautiful woman need with a 60-carat diamond? (I know Elizabeth Taylor would have begged to differ.) Most big time agents only know how to reflect wattage that already exists.

Work on your wattage before you turn yourself over to the polishers. Sure, it is within the super-agents' power to launch a career and some of them have done so – when they got lucky and felt the urge to make a star out of someone who was ready to be a star; but the casualties along the way ought to give any young actor pause. Those failed efforts aren't laid out in some killing field for young hopefuls to see. Ask around. There are cautionary tales. Take heed. You know many of them yourself because you have heard of them – briefly. As a general rule, none of the four large offices are the natural habitat for a beginning actor.

MID-SIZE AGENCIES

I was once speaking on a panel of agents to the graduating class at NYU. One of the other agents ran the New York branch of one of the ten mid-size offices. I ran another. We were direct competitors. We were both inevitably asked by the students how many clients were in our stables. This guy would always say 75 without blinking. Now I knew his office was packed with at least four hundred clients! I knew this for certain because a former assistant of mine had gone to work there and he'd told me. The first time this agent laid claim to 75 clients in front of a room full of impressionable acting students, I laughed out loud. He asked me what was so funny. I've waited until this paragraph to answer him. "You charlatan, you do not have 75 clients, you have at least 400 and you don't work well for any of them."

Small offices have between 100 and 200 clients. Mid-size offices look after double that number. Large offices? Fuggedaboudit. These figures are approximately double what they were twenty years ago. How come the inflation? Twenty years ago supporting actors used to make quite good money for a week or three of work. Today the star, the person who gets the movie made, makes extremely good money and everybody else makes scale. Less money for actors, less money for agents. Simple.

Bi-coastal mid-size offices are worthy of your time. Not too much internal politics, not having to go outside the agency to get information about LA, lots of time to try and find work for actors. I ran the New York Legit Departments of three excellent bi-coastal, boutique-type talent agencies. Today they are all out of business. But why? No time anymore for that kind of customized care. "Does your client want the job or not? Take it or leave it. No, I haven't got time to meet that new girl. Oh, wait, the studio says I have to meet her? How did the studio get involved? You went behind my back? You are dead to me. How's four o'clock tomorrow?"

Each of those agencies had a good long run. None came a cropper because they were bad agencies. The business changed and mid-size agencies had to struggle to keep up. Some of them closed their doors rather than change their standards. Some of them were bought by slightly larger agencies. Some of them merged with each other. That's still happening. Some of them just became meaner.

The minute most actors start to make serious money, they leave the agency that brought them to the serious money for a larger, name-dropping agency. Yes, those agents left behind by ungrateful clients are bitter. Who could blame them? Wouldn't you be bitter? Soon there may only be small agencies and big agencies. One of my offices was known for its truly superior actors, none of whom were stars. The owner was fond of saying, "I don't represent people who can get your movie made but you can't make your movie without the people I represent." But the actors at that agency who used to make $25,000 and $50,000 a week when the agency was at its peak are making scale today. No wonder the owner threw in the towel. She became a manager.

Of course, it kills the mid-size agencies that they are not the large offices to whom they tend to lose their emerging stars – though not as frequently as the smaller offices lose theirs to the mid-size offices. But generally, mid-size offices have stronger client lists than the small offices. Therefore, having more to defend, they are more aggressive than the small offices. This makes them appear tough – which most actors like because most actors are afraid to appear tough themselves.

Most people don't want to tick people off but actors would rather die. And it's O.K. that those offices are tough so long as they are tough on your behalf and not tough on you.

Several small offices are known to be outright mean to their clients. Reprehensible, but it happens. Do not stand for it. It is hard to be a small agent. Most of them do what they do because they like actors and want to help them. Not the bitter bullies. Look for someone who is aggressive but not a jerk. Most agents in mid-size offices fill that description very nicely.

The main mid-size offices are The Gersh Agency, Innovative Artists, Paradigm, Agency for the Performing Arts, Abrams Artists and Don Buchwald & Associates. They can all get the job done. If you have a champion who works there, let her do her work. There is an excellent agent at Paradigm named Sarah Fargo who told me, when I asked what she looks for in a new client, "I'm looking for a connection. Even if an actor is talented and I know they are going to work, if there's no connection or pull, I know I'm not the right agent for them." Well, Sarah is a very smart woman but it is also the relatively manageable size of her office that allows her the luxury of making choices of the heart.

No Young Actor, Who Is Not A Star, Should Lose A Deal Over Money — Period

In television, a young actor can clean up – if the network wants him badly enough. The agent has to guess how badly the network wants his client. And if the agent has decided his client is worth a certain figure that the network will not step up to, some of those mid-size offices will blow the deal rather than lose face.

No young actor, who is not a star, should lose a deal over money. Period. Young actors should work. I lost a deal over money and it still kills me. I lost it because the studio pulled the offer before I had technically passed – in other words, they screwed me over but I was powerless to complain. Even their own casting office agreed. I (and my client) had been treated badly – but the casting office wasn't going to back me up if I called the network to complain. I (and my client) were victims of an internal fight between the producer and the network (who had never wanted my client in the first place). I was trying to appear tough but I had not meant to blow the deal. The mid-sized office willing to blow a deal for a young actor is maintaining their own reputation for toughness, not struggling to establish a going rate for an emerging actor (as they would claim).

Pilot Season

There are mid-sized offices famous for keeping actors away from theatre jobs during pilot season. Think about the mid-size office that would deny a budding theatre director access to a young actor for a play during pilot season because they're fairly sure the actor will get a pilot. They will have some 'splainin' to do when that theatre director gets his first movie job and refuses to see that young actor because he holds a grudge for having been shut out when he wanted him for that play two years ago. Meanwhile, the young actor never even got the mythical pilot that the agency was holding out for. And he certainly never heard that this director was interested in him for a play.

Mid-size offices tend to make much of the fact that they are bi-coastal which means, in theory, that you will be covered for projects on both coasts. In practice, this proves not to be quite so fluid a process as it is meant to appear. I know I said a moment ago that I like having access to LA's information, and I do, and it may very well play out that way for you. But I could do without some of their attitude. If New York signs you, there is the question of getting the agents in California to know you and your work, not to mention be enthusiastic about you and your work. Not to mention having to get around the way they think in Los Angeles: "Why did you sign her? She'll never work out here, not with that nose."

The Reel

If you have been around long enough to have put together a reel (six minutes worth of you being brilliant in scenes from film and TV shows you have done), then the New York office that is interested in you can send that reel to their California office and, again in theory, everyone out there will fall in love with you and start combing the woods for jobs for you. If they do not fall in love with you, New York will never be allowed to sign you so don't worry about what California thinks. If they haven't nixed you, they're fine with you. (Which is not the same thing as being enthusiastic.) Not everybody in LA may have responded to you as positively as everyone did in New York (and, by the way, it is *unlikely* that *everyone* did in New York). So when the New York office of a bi-coastal agency blithely informs you that you will be covered in LA, take that with a very large grain of salt. A bi-coastal office makes life simpler for agents, but it may not always be the absolute most beneficial choice for an emerging actor. Should you turn it down? Not on your life.

Pilot And Take Off Are Not The Same

When I went from that small New York-only management office to what I imagined would be the luxuries of a bi-coastal mid-size agency, I was beside myself with the possibilities. I signed a young actress everyone in the New York office was crazy for. She was very new. She didn't have a reel. But she had sit-com written all over her and all she wanted out of life was to be on one. We all loved her and since it was December, we advised her to go to LA for pilot season, which started in

January. She was thrilled. Never mind that a new face should go to LA *before* pilot season when casting directors have time to meet them in a general interview. I hadn't known that. It wouldn't have hurt for the agents in my office to get to meet her first as well. I didn't want to wait because I was crazy for this girl. But my enthusiasm for her was counterproductive and not professional. I was an idiot. Reader, I am telling you all my mistakes so you don't have to make them yourself. Are we still friends?

A few weeks later, my counterpart in LA called to say that none (none!) of the agents out there got what was so special about this girl and they were going to tell her to go back to New York. In the middle of pilot season? I was completely unprepared for what to do if LA didn't like someone that New York did. I mean, how could they question our (my) taste? You know what? It happens all the time. Especially when it comes to what actor has sit-com written all over them. New York and Los Angeles's tastes (if you call the instinct that drives most California agents taste) are seldom in agreement with each other. Why is this so? Well, can you think of ten stars you can't stand? Sure you can. I've got news for you: they are stars. *Somebody* likes 'em. But nobody in LA (or at least in my LA office) liked this poor girl. We (I) should never have advised her to go out there without having met at least two of the agents in our office there first. I should have had the sense to tell her to stay put. I was afraid of losing her. I did anyway. Can you see me wringing my hands here? I still feel badly about that girl. She left my agency soon after that little sojourn in LA and rightly so. She had the guts – and the brains – to go to a smaller office. She didn't need bi-coastal representation in the first place. I would suggest that almost no one starting out probably does. (And today, by the way, that actress has a very nice career.)

Make Them Love You

A mid-size office is staffed by four, five or six agents. When you sign with a mid-size office, it is unlikely all of the agents will have seen you work. Unless you have a reputation or a reel in which case you probably think you know everything I know. (You don't.) The agent who *does* know you, having seen you in a play, or met you at an opening night party or whom a friend called on your behalf, will likely be the only person you meet on your first trip to the office. If that goes well, that agent will arrange a meeting for you with all the other agents. If *that* goes well (and we will talk about how to *make* it go well), they will probably sign you. The agent you originally met will be your responsible agent. (In a large office, you would deal with only your responsible agent. In a mid-sized office you deal with everyone.) Your first order of business should be to cultivate relationships with all the agents who have not seen you work and get to know them.

Make them love you. And when they do, don't forget to love them back. But not too much. Drop by the office. Not too often. Call once in a while. Email occasionally. Do not make a pest of yourself. Do not ask why you don't have more auditions. *Do not mention auditions. They know you want auditions.* Trust me, they know. If you are showing up too frequently, you will know. You will feel it. If you are making a pest of yourself and you don't feel it, you have no business being an actor.

Brad Pitt's first agents used to run and hide when he came to the office, which he did almost every day. Why didn't they tell him to get lost? Well, he looked like Brad Pitt. And, apparently, a little birdie told him he was going to BE Brad Pitt. So if you drop by your agent's office every day, make sure you look like Brad Pitt and are going to the same place.

Look Good

Even if you don't look like Brad Pitt, do look good when you stop by the office. ALWAYS look good when you see your agent. This does not mean put on a suit and tie or high heels and pearls. Look good. Look hot. Be relaxed. Be easy. Be funny. Got all that? Good. Do it.

There is rarely any need for an actor – with a career of any size – to ever leave a mid-size office. I know how hard the agents have to work at mid-size offices to make sure that everyone on both coasts knows everything that is going on. And I know how often communication between the coasts gets screwed up and balls get dropped. I cannot even begin to imagine how often the ball is dropped at the large offices. At one office the East and West coasts had a two-hour meeting each week and discussed *all* the clients. That office was far and away the most effective place I ever worked. We all hated that weekly meeting but, boy, was it helpful. If the large offices did that, it would take them all week just to get through the client list. So they have other meetings. Sometimes momentous-sounding meetings. ICM has meetings with each other all day long. When you call, no matter whom, he or she is in a meeting. Some say ICM stands for In Constant Meeting. Bless them for trying.

There is no reason to leave a small agency – if your career is growing. Why stars leave big agencies for other big agencies is beyond me. But they do. All the time. Leaving your agency is something that has become a routine thing to do. It may be a status thing. We are an impatient nation. But would you leave your wife and the mother of your children just because you didn't want to appear complacent?

The War Of Art

It is generally wise for anyone in this business to be wary upon waking up in the morning. Not for nothing was CAA built with "The Art of War" as its bible.

It's not just actors who leave agencies. Agents leave agencies. Agents leave mid-size offices for other, temporarily more attractive mid-size offices and for large offices. Agents do this because they are have been offered more money and assume they will automatically acquire more prestige at a bigger office which is what they have been looking for all the time they have been taking care of you. And this is their pay-off. Be happy for them.

The other office wants them because of the clients they will be able to bring with them and this will, you hope, include you. If it is your responsible agent who is doing the leaving, he or she will have asked you to follow them. In so many words. Most agents are contractually forbidden to solicit clients when they leave. This means nothing. If they have not approached you with the news of their departure and asked you to follow them out the door ("Should I leave with you?" "[Nodding their head forcefully] I couldn't possibly advise you to do that."), then leave the agency. But wait. If the owner of your first agency takes you out to dinner and says he knows what is going on with your responsible agent and he hopes you will decide to stay right where you are, well, then you have a decision to make. The owner may even offer to become your responsible agent – if you are important enough. You may feel good about the owner. Or you may not. If you feel good about where you are, it will be a difficult decision. Your responsible agent has become a meaningful person to you. There is no such thing as the right decision. There is only a decision that feels right to you. But if that dinner invitation doesn't come, get the hell out of there. Your champion has gone.

Let's say you are with an agency and one of the agents, *not* your responsible agent, decides to leave. So what, right? No biggie. Well, probably not. But it is up to you to find out how and if this change will affect you. Actually, your responsible agent should have called you to tell you it was happening and it was no big deal. But let's say he doesn't and you call him. You ask what this change in the agency will mean to your career and he will say: believe me, sweetheart, this change will not affect you. This is probably the best thing that could have happened. Nobody liked him – or her – anyway. Wait until you see who's coming in. This change will be, your agent will say in an unwavering voice, very, very good for your career. And perhaps it will be. But pay close attention. Never stop paying attention.

Summing Up

If you find an agent or an owner at a mid-size office who wants to represent you, go for it. They are an endangered species. And where better to be than at a place where – at least in theory – you will never have to leave. Large agencies will rip each other's throats open to get at your famous body and friends will ask you why you are not leaving your small agency but a mid-size perch can keep you warm at night and make sure you have somewhere exciting to go in the morning.

Henry VI Part Two:

"Small things make base men proud."

SMALL AGENCIES

There are over a hundred small agencies in New York and over 400 in Los Angeles. Some of them are excellent. Some of them are great for some people and not for others though that is true of all agencies whatever the size. An important actor with a big career might be very ill served by a large office which did not understand or care about that actor's priorities. Not all actors even have priorities. Agencies do: money. This is not a bad thing. It is simply a fact. There is not a lot of money flowing in the small offices but, in the good ones, there is pride.

Clout — My Agent Doesn't Have Any

Before getting into the mechanics of small agencies and how they do and do not work, let me say a few words about clout, as in: "My agent doesn't have any." This expression drives me bananas. Actors, especially beginning actors are forever whining that their agent doesn't have any clout by which they mean they get few to no auditions for movies and television. Clout is passionate belief in your client. Plus an enviable Rolodex. Plus hard work. That is all you need. OK. Gross exaggeration. But there is truth there and more than a kernel. More than the big offices would care to admit. If you have a client list full of stars, of course you have clout. How hard is it to find a job for George Clooney?

Many small agencies may not have massive clout but maybe that is because they don't fight hard enough for their actors. Or maybe they don't have actors worth fighting for. And whose fault is that? Maybe they are signing the wrong people. If everyone they had were as good as you, they would have clout, right?

All actors who deserve to be seen for film and TV projects are not signed exclusively to the large and prestigious mid-size offices. Many wonderfully deserving actors are not even signed to anyone. If your agent does not get you seen for projects you feel you to deserve to be seen for, change agents. Do not whine that your agent has no clout. Don't leave where you are until you know where you're going. And do not leave where you are in a huff. Never leave anywhere in a huff. Nothing is personal. Naturally everything is personal but behave like a grownup. It's the right way to behave.

Other Agents Will Always Want You Because You Are Fabulous

Small offices usually consist of an owner, another agent, sometimes two, and an assistant. Sometimes it's two owners and an assistant. And probably an intern. Everybody has interns these days. You used to have to beg and plead to get an intern if you were a small office. Now they are lined up around the block. Small agencies do not generally have offices on the other coast but they have affiliations with a few such (comparable) offices which means that you get to pick and choose whom you want to work with, should you find yourself 3,000 miles from home. The office which is affiliated with yours will probably not work for you when you are not in their city, unless you are an actor with a reputation or you have a great reel which that office can use to get you jobs. This is frequently a very happy arrangement. Your commission will not increase. The agencies will work something out between them. Sometimes that's a hornet's nest but it is not your concern. Do not get roped into taking sides.

Small offices are often staffed with young would-be sharks who have their sights set on making a million dollars a year at CAA. This is not a bad thing for the clients of the small office. The sooner the young shark makes you famous, the sooner CAA will come knocking on that agent's door (who will then offer to take you with him to CAA because you are the reason, or one of the reasons, they want your agent in the first place). But CAA may knock at your door first. If they can steal you without having to pay your young shark's salary into the bargain, so much the better for them. If your young shark has half a brain, he will have prepared you for this scenario. He will have told you that other agents will want you one day. Other agents will always want you because you are fabulous. But, hey, he saw you first, right? He loved you first and he wants you forever. Maybe you should stick with him. Maybe.

Most small offices don't even deal with the concept of a responsible agent. There is the owner and there are the employees. Sometimes small offices are staffed by veterans of earlier eras who can't get hired by the cool, young, hip agencies. Some small agencies have many more clients than they are capable of servicing. But they still love talent. I promise you. It's not their fault that they don't have big fat careers that make you want to beg them to represent you. Well, maybe it is their fault but they can still help you. They still *want* to help you. They still have rent to pay. They still believe in lightning in a bottle.

Everybody in show business believes in lightning in a bottle. Let's say the veteran (anybody over 45) sees something in you and wants to work for you. Is that a bad thing? Let him work for you. Is anyone else beating down your door? If they are, check them out and then go with who is best for you. How do you know who that is? Oh, for Christ's sake. Grow up. It is possible you may have to cohabitate with a few agencies before you marry one.

Not infrequently, at these small offices, there is a person with taste who cares deeply about the profession. Who *gets* actors. Who, more importantly, gets *you*. Do not rest until you have found such a person. Often, it will be the owner of the agency. Often, that person's taste and zeal and caring is what made the reputation on which that office is still eking out a living. Sometimes they still have that spark. If you sense that and they respond to you, you may feel this will be a good match. Trust your instinct. There may be difficulty when your star starts to rise and the large agencies start swarming, and your small agent who still has a spark will likely get his or her heart broken, when you leave but you will still have had Paris.

Does Small Mean Small-Minded?

There is the view that the small agency thinks small and when an actor's career threatens to become sizeable, the small agent will get all flustered with actual success and not know how to handle it. Important careers demand mega-watt agencies. This is total nonsense but it is generally held to be true.

There used to be several small offices capable of thinking big. Thinking huge, in fact. Robbie Lantz represented Elizabeth Taylor, Richard Burton, Leonard Bernstein, Michael Blakemore, Montgomery Clift, Yul Brynner, Milos Forman, and Alan Jay Lerner. He was the only agent in the office. He and his one excellent assistant handled hundreds of major deals. Robbie was one of the most gracious, civilized and discerning men in our field. He has also, sadly, gone to his reward. If your small office doesn't have some gigantic star in their stable now, have they ever? Do they want to? What are their hopes and dreams?

A small office may prove a stepping stone, or it may prove your home for life. The larger offices, when they come calling on you, are practiced in the ways of dismissing the small offices while being forced to acknowledge that small offices even exist. Hell, the larger offices are practiced in ways of dismissing each other. But they save a particular vituperative scorn for their low rent step-siblings in arms.

"Does your agency get the Coverage?" they ask with a smirk knowing full well that your agency does not get the

Coverage and that the very idea of trying to have a career with no access to Coverage is, well, beyond laughable. It is sad. "What's the biggest deal your agent has ever done?" they ask. Then they start in with the jargon. They talk about "pay or play protection" and "artwork title floor," which applies to only about ten people on the planet. ("Paid ads" means that your name is guaranteed to appear in any advertisement for the film – or any advertisement larger than ¼ page – or whatever your agent negotiates. "Artwork Title Floor" means that if the title of the film is spelled out in artwork, say a snake, as opposed to standard lettering, the size of the artwork cannot exceed the size of your name by more than 25%, 50% – pick a number.) And how come you didn't have paid ads for the part that put you on the map? Paid ads? For a three scene part? Give me a break. But the actor doesn't know that you don't get paid ads for a three scene part. Did Brad Pitt get paid ads for "Thelma and Louise"? Did Mickey Rourke get paid ads for "Body Heat" (a one scene part)? Did Channing Tatum get them for "Step Up"? (And he was the star of that.)

Now you start freaking out because you have a movie coming out that has buzz and your performance has buzz and everyone says it's going to make your entire career and you don't even have paid ads! Your miserable agent didn't get you paid ads for this movie that is going to introduce you to the world. This is a big moment for you. Must you be presented to the public in such a tawdry way? Without paid ads! You might as well be naked.

"I would consider you an important client," says the high rolling agent as he presses his pitch to you. Well that is flattering to hear especially coming from someone who represents several people you idolize and is therefore self-evidently important himself. But then again, anyone who represents people he calls important must also have a few he feels are unimportant. You wouldn't want to be one of those.

Terms like "important client" are usually chosen for their power to flatter or impress. And why on Earth assume your agent who has brought you this far cannot take you further? If you can become a movie star after working your behind off for a couple of years, there is no reason to suppose that your agent who started in the mailroom a few years ago himself cannot become a mover and a shaker along with you and continue to represent you in your new and greater celebrity.

Where do you think big-time agents come from? Do you think they were born with Angelina Jolie on their client list? Why should these strangers with the gold watches be allowed to come along and have you on their team when they did nothing to get you to where you are today? How dare they suggest you walk away from the guy who helped get you there. That is precisely what they will suggest. And they will be relentless. You may want to be seduced, and after a lavish seduction scene, you might just stay put.

There is a jewel-like agency in New York called Cornerstone which is capable of representing any size career and does. They are not unique in this ability among small agencies but they are rare. If you cannot get in to see them, find the others. Who are they? Do your homework.

Negotiating 101

The first sizable deal I ever did was for a young actor who everyone in my small office thought would be a star. And sure enough, sooner rather than later, he was offered a starring role, *the* starring role, in a studio film. It would be his third starring role but he had never been paid more than minimum. His first picture had been scale. Nothing to be done about that. Everybody's first picture is for scale. Second picture had been for Robert Altman. Nothing to be done about that either. (The guy didn't pay. Period. A genius, yes, but what a racket – if you ask me.) But here, finally, was a studio movie and my client was not a beginner. Business affairs called and offered my client $25,000. I asked for $200,000. The person in business affairs seemed taken aback and said she would get back to me.

Five minutes later, the producer himself called back screaming. I mean screaming – I didn't know what the hell I was doing; I was an amateur. I was going to destroy my client's career. He suggested – still at full volume – that I call some other agents who knew what they were doing and find out what this part was worth, given the budget, given the director, given all sorts of things that I was too stupid to even know about. And, in the meantime, while I was at it, I should learn how to negotiate. So I did call a few other agents and the general consensus was that I should get something approaching $100,000. I got $125,000. Thank you very much. No, you are too kind. Thank you.

You grow with your client – if you are capable of doing so and if your client is willing to stick around. My client stuck around for a few more pictures. Jack Nicholson stuck around with Sandy Bresler forever. If agents have a patron saint, it is probably the Knicks number one fan. (I promise I will stop mentioning him.)

Truth is, I think many small offices fight harder. They don't always have the guts to go for it but they have less to lose when they do. Sherry Lansing told Alec Baldwin that she would just be so much more comfortable if he were with a big office rather than his medium size one of which she had never heard. Baldwin's agent kept asking for contract points they should know Sherry Lansing does not grant. A larger office wouldn't dream of offending Sherry Lansing. (Alec's mid-size one didn't care.) Well, of course she'd be more comfortable with a big office. She was practically a shareholder in the Big Four. She had history with the big offices. She knew how far she could kick them. Steven Spielberg told a client of mine he'd appreciate it if she would take a meeting with his agency. What??? Will these whales just please back the heck off?

The big offices are too much in bed with the studios for my taste. I had a beautiful young client who was starting to take off who left me for William Morris. I had just gotten her $75,000 for a movie. On her first job through William Morris she got $35,000. She was happy just being with William Morris who never really thought she'd be big. Though she is now. And she didn't stay with William Morris for long.

Some actors think there is something shameful about being with a small office. It marks them as a beginner. Most small offices have a few clients who bring in some serious money. Tyne Daly was with a small office and never left. How come I don't revere her the way I do Mr. Nicholson? Well, the stakes aren't as high with her as they are with Jack. She's just as good an actor, though. I'll tell you that for nothing. And she's a bigger name than most small offices have on their list. All right, I revere her. A lot. However, most of the recognizable names on small office's client lists are not that big. They are, dare I say it, wonderful actors who may have had a heyday a decade or two ago and are still hanging on. The young actor may be afraid this will reflect on him – he's not some has-been, after all – and his career will have a ceiling while he is at that agency. If this turns out to be so, leave. But first get to whatever you imagine that ceiling is. It's higher than where you stand now, I promise you that. In the meantime, if an agent at a small office responds to you and to your work, and wants to work for you, be gracious; be smart; let her.

Not Famous ... Yet

Maybe you'll wind up doing plays for a couple of years. Be prepared to wait on tables. Nothing wrong with waiting on tables. The tips are great and so is the information you get from your co-workers about who's casting what, who's leaving what show, who's in from LA and doing general interviews. Most young actors wait on tables at some point.

The idea of a career taking time to develop or, God forbid, that an actor might need a little time to become capable of dominating a stage or screen has become an almost prehistoric concept. Young actors come on the scene today, especially the MFA and conservatory grads, snap their fingers and wonder where the hell their career is. They thought perhaps it would be waiting for them? Where does this entitlement come from?

Partly from their own arrogance and utter lack of experience. Actually, a little arrogance is healthy. Being noticed takes time and a little bluster while you're waiting can help keep you warm. You'd think being as beautiful as Jessica Lange would be all the credentials anybody could ever need. Think again. Getting good enough to instill confidence in those who seek to hire you because you have developed and learned to radiate some confidence of your own – it takes time.

Dustin Hoffman was in New York for ten years doing theatre before he was cast in "The Graduate," for which he was recommended by the director of a play he was doing at the time – Alan Arkin – not an agent at all. John Malkovich had been kicking around with his own theatre company in Chicago before he came to New York at twenty-eight and blew everyone's socks off off-Broadway in "True West." And he still had to wait five years to appear in his first movies, "Places in the Heart" and "The Killing Fields" (both in the same year). Messrs. Hoffman and Malkovich are both great actors (and played father and son on Broadway before the younger one became as huge as the older one) but it was a given back then that even a great talent needed some seasoning. The Brits always expect to pay dues. They consider it fitting. So long as you do not doubt your ultimate recognition, paying your dues is fine. Knowing you belong can be a comfort.

Tenacity

All right, here it comes. The key element Dustin Hoffman and John Malkovich share, aside from the colossal talent they both have, is tenacity. Since you will very likely start out being represented by a small office (Dustin started with a wonderful guy named Jerry Kahn who was his own one-man office), your most precious gift, aside from your talent and a superior 8x10, will be your drive to succeed. I am trying to make you feel good about your small office. I am trying to give you the tools for them to help you.

Your agent will not automatically be as tenacious as he should be for you. He may and should fight for you but he will get his clue about how long and how hard that fight has to be from the way you present yourself and behave. The large agency will think they are too important to have to work up a sweat in order to get you seen for a project. The small agent may feel they don't have a prayer of getting you seen so they don't even try. Neither of these eventualities bodes well for you. The thing is, if you assiduously tickle their fancy (in the nicest possible way), you stand a much better chance of being heard by your small agent than by a large one. And they have just as good a chance of getting you seen as the large agency – if you keep after them. Yes, really. Though if you have chosen a large agency, you will still have to speak up. Yes, really. Your voice has to rise up above the million-dollar clients on the phone that day. Maybe even more loudly. And more, well, diplomatically.

The small agency has more to lose – you. So they will bust their hump to get you seen for a project you have a shot at. Do not go to the mat on every single project that you come across which has a part for you – choose your battles. When I was nobody from nowhere in that small management office, I had clients seen all the time for roles in major movies because I believed in them. And it became evident my belief was well founded because many of them started getting those roles I was getting them seen for. So studios and networks and casting directors started listening to me. I hope this doesn't wind up sounding like a story about me because the winners here were my clients. I'm only talking about myself in order to talk about the subject of this book – namely, you!

No One Works Harder Than You — For You

The clients who succeeded in building careers were working right there along side me, frequently ahead of me. Everyone to whom you give money – your agent, your manager, your lawyer, your PR person, your stylist (!) – will claim they are busting their butts for you because that's what you pay them to do. And since you are paying them, it is also going to be up to you to determine whether or not they are all earning all that money. The more time they spend telling you how hard they work, the less time they have to do the work they say they are doing. Don't let them snow you into letting them go at their own pace. Actors with good careers usually wake up each morning wondering where the next job is coming from and make strategic plans for the day ahead. Have I said: be wary? Choose wisely.

Your gently and diplomatically cracking the whip will probably be most necessary when you are with a small agent. In a large agency, with presumably more money at stake, it is safe to assume your agent will be more motivated to get you work. Safe but not fail-safe. The need to do battle on your own behalf does not end when you are finally at a large agency. (You still want that, don't you? Why won't you listen to me?) Who knows how that large agency will perform on your behalf? What if they go off half-cocked trying to turn you into the fourth Hemsworth brother? Is that OK with you? Then fine. If you really want to be Michael Stuhlbarg, it is not OK. (Though a klieg light shining Michael Stuhlbarg's name onto the nighttime sky couldn't hurt that career any.) What if they don't go off cocked at all? Do you think they will remember that you wanted to be told the second the Salinger estate started granting film rights to the "Nine Stories"?

Now that you are bankable, do you think they will remember that you wanted to remake "Shoot the Piano Player"? Are they on the phone about that to whomever has the rights to "Shoot the Piano Player" the day after the *Variety* review declared you were a shoo-in for an Academy award nomination? The rights to "Shoot the Piano Player" are held by a law office in Philadelphia which knows nothing about movies. Is it possible your agent will lose patience in dealing with them and just not bother with the damn rights to some goddamn French movie only ten people have ever even heard of? Is your agent known for his patience? (Are you?)

How on earth can agents at the big agencies ever get any peace when that great part that Bruce Willis just got was lusted after by Kevin Costner and Dennis Quaid and Kurt Russell into the bargain? What are Costner's and Quaid's and Russell's agents going to tell their clients? Did the studio tell Sam Rockwell's people that he just wasn't a big enough star for the investors and did Sam Rockwell's people tell that to Sam Rockwell? Did that shut him up? They probably told him he was too young. That's easy. Was Kurt Russell's manager told that his client was too old? Did the manager tell that to Kurt Russell? Probably not. And even if it were true, the studio probably never told that to the manager. Bruce got the job. That's the whole story. Everything else is just face-saving bullshit. Gotta keep the client happy, right? Can't let it seem like it was *his* fault he lost the job. Can't let it seem like it was the agent's fault either. Well, that's why they call it work and that's what the ten percent is for.

Now, all of a sudden, we've got to worry about Michael Keaton again. Think he'll stay back on top? Stay tuned.

Practical Ambition

So what can you actually *do* to get an agent? You mean apart from trying to go from play to play to play so that people – Agents? Agents' assistant? Casting directors? Casting assistants? – can see you and fall in love with you and want to meet you? Your small theatre should inform you every time that someone from the business is in the audience. If they do not do this, ask them to. Ask someone in the box office to let you know when an industry person has come because whoever it is will surely have asked for a comp.

Ask friends with agents if you could meet their agent. Actors are snarky about this. Do it anyway. Can't hurt.

Contact casting offices and offer to be a reader. If you get in anywhere, ask them which agents they like. Ask if they would call one or two on your behalf. Don't push it and establish a relationship first.

There are those places that ask you to pay them money and then introduce you to an agent. I think those places are reprehensible. But they will introduce you to an agent or two (or an assistant or two). I think those places are more effective with meeting casting directors. After all, casting directors are actively looking for good new people. The agents are generally looking for some spare change.

Did any person who is now an agent go to your college? Write them. Did (does) your acting teacher have an agent? Any help there? Who are your five favorite actors? Who were their first agents? Write them. Tell them you love their eye. (Is that offensive? I don't think so.) Everyone you meet who is capable of doing you any good at all will know that you want their help. Ask for it.

And always and forever: Work. Act. What are you selling? You. Gotta be visible, dude.

Let's say you have an agent and a pretty good one at that. Don't let your job just be keeping after your agent. It's not all up to him. Lift a finger already. Find out what is going on in the business and get your name out there. Make a list of parts you could do in current projects. In future projects. Notice that part on "The Good Wife" that you could have done but weren't seen for. Mention these parts when you talk to casting people, or people who know casting people, or people who work in production. Let people know how to use you and make it clear you want to be used. You are ambitious. You cannot be gotten rid of with a compliment or two to your agent. You want a *job*. Better, you want a career.

The smart money will try to stop you at every turn. Everybody wants to find the next big thing and nobody wants to have to deal with whomever that turns out to be. What does that mean? It means that people are ambivalent about people who start showing signs of becoming important. A Universal executive told me she had seen an early screening of "The Graduate" and she couldn't get over how strongly she was able to sympathize with and care about the funny looking little guy who played the lead. He was so odd looking that he probably wouldn't get another movie after this – which was too bad because he was a good actor but just not what the public wanted to see. If Dustin Hoffman had to find ways around entrenched, myopic thinking like that, what hope is there for anybody else? An earlier time you say? I don't think so.

How many years did Mark Ruffalo have to languish in LA before a break in a New York play put him on the map? And Mark Ruffalo is handsome. Before Mr. Ruffalo's break happened, I remember a wonderful casting director complaining to me that her studio wouldn't consider him for a movie she was casting because he wasn't handsome *enough* to play opposite Leelee Sobiesky. (See – casting directors fight for actors, though, like agents, they don't always win.) So does everybody have to pay dues for nine years and give the world lessons in why they are physically attractive before the business will cut you a break? Obviously, not. But stellar talents like Malkovich and Hoffman and Ruffalo had to wait that long, so you might, too. If your response to that is: it won't take *you* that long, then good, you are in the right business.

Can We Stop With The Bad News, Please?

Why am I telling you all this negative stuff? Well, call it tough love. I don't want you to get discouraged when it turns out to be hard. Because it *will be* hard. You have to know that so that you can persevere in the face of more rejection than any human should have to bear. If you belong in the business, it will all be worth it, I promise you. But whether or not you belong in the business is your call: no one else's.

Even a very gifted person eventually gets terminally discouraged. When that happens it breaks my heart. I am thinking in particular of two former clients, both women, who did get discouraged and left the business. And the business is the poorer for it. It is natural to feel, and I would seem to be encouraging you to feel, that if you can't take the pressure, well then, you should leave while the leaving is good. But these women were both so extraordinarily talented I can't help feeling that their separate retreats were tragedies. I also feel that, in both their cases, they simply had no idea how tough it was going to be when they got here and never quite got over blaming themselves that they were having such a hard time. It is my hope that if you are armed, you will fight harder, smarter and longer.

The first hope for surmounting these hurdles, both real and imagined, is to recognize that the business does not owe you a career. Go out there and find some work. Learn who you are when you are working. Learn how other people see you. It will take as long as it will take. And it will happen when you unequivocally feel that you deserve for it to happen.

Bill (William H.) Macy used to come to my office on practically a daily basis and complain that he wasn't getting seen for the parts he wanted to play. He wasn't being seen for "The Guy" and he wanted to be "The Guy." He WAS "The Guy." Why didn't people see that? I felt for him but I wasn't quite sure that he was "The Guy" either. Boy, was I wrong. He became "The Guy" but not on my watch. I didn't deserve him. Maybe I can cut a few years off my time in purgatory if I just admit it.

Let's say you get a part in an off-Broadway play. It's a good play and so is your part. It fits you like a glove. You love playing this character. And, as I promised you, the business takes note. I am not saying there is a full page spread in *The Times* about your play and your breakout performance but there is a small review in *The Times* and *The Village Voice* and the one in the *Voice* singles you out. In the first week of the run, a casting director's assistant, an assistant at a talent agency and an actual agent actually come to the play. The agent's reputation is kind of skeezy but they all three want to meet you. And you make appointments to meet all three (yes, including the skeezy one).

For next time, we are going to do mock interviews with an agent. That would be me. You will each have ten minutes to come in for an interview with me. Let's say a mutual friend of your family asked someone in my massive circle of friends to meet with you as a favor. How would you behave? What would you want to know? What impression would you want to make on me and how would you go about that? Bring a picture and resume and dress as if you were meeting an agent. Because you will be.

DECLAN DONNELLAN tells an acting story about Constantin Stanislavski:

"The best story I know isn't about an actor at all but about a dog. An actor had a dog. This dog used to come to rehearsals and, being rather lazy, would sleep in the corner all day long. Strangely, every evening, just before the actors were to finish, the dog would be ready at the door, leash in mouth, waiting to be taken home. What astounded Stanislavski was that the dog would wearily haul himself to his feet several minutes before his master called him. Regular as clockwork, come the end of rehearsal, the dog would trot to the door and wait there patiently.

Now how could a dog know the rehearsal was over before anyone went to the door? Finally, Stanislavski figured it out. The dog could hear when the actors started talking like normal human beings again. The difference between the fake and the living was just as sharp as Pavlov's bell. Stanislavski told his company that they would have succeeded in their craft when the dog went to the door while they were still rehearsing."

WORKSHOP SIX:
Agent Interviews

The Sixth Workshop is my favorite – it's where we talk about meetings.

A n interview with an agent is a meeting. After you have signed with an agent, every time you sit down with that person will be an interview. (Do I mean you are still on trial? No, but your agent will always be assessing you. She will be looking into you.   Are you taking care of yourself? Are you gaining weight? Are you in a good frame of mind? Are you happy with the agency? Are you thinking of leaving? Is the agent thinking of dropping you? Do I mean it never stops? Yes, that is what I mean.) Every audition and callback you have is, by definition, a job interview. What happens at the audition and the call back when you are not actually acting is a meeting.

Kicking around career strategies with friends, bitching about your career with co-workers at the restaurant, these are pow-wows. The difference is the agenda. And the degree of trust in the room. With friends, trust ought to be a given. In a meeting, trust has to be earned. And in show business, the only time it doesn't matter how you look is when you are with your friends.

Take A Meeting

Learning how to take a meeting is at the heart and soul of your first year in New York. Any time you spend in the presence of someone who can get you work as an actor should be considered a job interview. I don't think it requires its own MFA program but there are skills that come into play in an interview and you should know them. Agent meetings are different from casting director meetings. Let's deal with agents first.

An agent wants to know how to market you. Whose career would you like to have? An agent also needs to know who you are when you are acting. Has the agent seen you act? For the purposes of our little exercise today, the answer is obviously no. If she has not, ask her to come see you in the play you just happen to be in. That's why you have got to always be in a play. The first four plays you get cast in that agents say they will go to, they won't go to. They don't automatically go to your fifth play. Those are just the odds. Agents are not fond of going to plays that they do not have to go to. (They have to go to plays their clients are in.) Why do they have to go to yours? Well, for one thing, if you've been in five plays in the last year, you might be an interesting actor. Not many actors are in that many plays. Make sure you are in the first act. The agent will probably leave at intermission. Make sure you are not playing an 80 year old Russian peasant. Is that how Scorsese is going to cast you?

Speaking of Scorsese, audition for student films. NYU and Columbia have excellent film programs and they need actors all the time. Maybe you will luck into a good script. Maybe you will have a nice scene or scenes from a student film you did that you can show to an agent. If it is not a good scene and you are not good in it, do not show it to anyone. You will have gained some camera time in any event and you can be grateful for that.

I worked on a student film when I was a young actor in New York. The director was: Martin Scorsese. (So how come I'm not famous? Well, as I have endeavored to point out, talent ultimately gets factored in.)

So you finally got an agent to come see you in a play. The agent calls you the next day and asks you to come into the office to meet. (Actually, you probably call him but this is a fantasy so let's credit him with a little enthusiasm.) What should you wear? Are you dressed comfortably or are you dressed the way you imagine the agent wants you to be dressed? And where did you come up with what you think that is? Are you a mind reader? This agent hasn't a clue who you are. You will have to tell him. Wear your favorite shirt. Wear the shirt that makes you feel relaxed and attractive and very much yourself.

Give yourself a crash course on that agency and, if possible, on that agent. Whom do they represent? Whom have they represented? Who do they have whom you admire? What do you want this agent to know about you? Is that necklace really appropriate or not? Gather a few 8x10s, take a copy of your scene from the student film you did, leave your apartment and go to the meeting. Be five minutes early. On time is late. Late is not acceptable. Postponing the meeting is totally unacceptable. Not getting enough sleep is self-sabotage. Having a pimple erupt that morning is fate. Go.

Now we shall actually do it. Do we remember our premise? You are all more or less at the start of your careers. None of you has an agent. A family friend or a college sweetheart of one of your parents or a teacher knows someone who knows someone who knows me. Would I do them the favor of meeting with you, the child of that dear friend who has just moved to New York? And because I am the nicest man in the world, I have said yes. Each of you will have ten minutes. Only ten minutes? Believe me, the world can be revealed in ten minutes. Those minutes can breeze by or they can be excruciating. The choice, I think you will see, will be up to you. Incidentally, you will learn as much from this exercise by watching each other as you will from the actual process of your own interview. You are dressed in something which shows you off to good advantage and which makes you feel at ease.

Please do not let me do all the talking. God knows, I am capable of making conversation but please do not make me. The meeting is about you. Bring a picture and resume with you when you enter.

The meeting begins the second you walk in the door. Who's going to go first? Ah, Kendra. I love your enthusiasm. Go out and then come in.

Kendra (*knock, knock*): May I come in?

Me: Of course you may come in. Tell me your name, please.

Kendra: Kendra Logan. It's really great of you to see me.

Me: A pleasure. Did you bring me a picture?

Kendra: Sorry. Yes, here.

Me: Thank you. It's not a bad picture. It's not a good picture, either.

Kendra: Most people have liked it.

Me: Oh. Tell me whom else you've met.

Kendra: Well, my acting teacher likes it.

Me: That's so important.

Kendra: I guess it isn't really.

Me: Where are you going after we're done?

Kendra: Just home.

Me: You seem to be dressed for lunch at the Plaza.

Kendra: I'm dressed for you.

Me: Pearls for me?

Kendra: Well, yeah.

Me: I'm flattered. Granny's pearls for me.

Kendra: How did you know they were my grandmother's?

Me: Lucky guess. Where are you from, Kendra?

Kendra: New Orleans.

Me: Really? What was that like?

Kendra: It was great, really great.

Me: In what ways?

Kendra: Oh, well, the music, you know. It was just great. Except in the summer. It gets so hot.

Me: It sounds glamorous. The Big Easy.

Kendra: We don't really call it the Big Easy.

Me: I see. I don't detect an accent.

Kendra: Oh, we don't really have a southern accent.

Me: We?

Kendra: People from New Orleans.

Me: I stand corrected.

Kendra: That's OK.

Me: So how can I help you here today, Kendra?

Kendra: Well, gee, I need an agent.

Me: Let's pause here. Class, somehow we got off track, didn't we? I asked Kendra where she was from. And from there we spun into small talk. If she's not careful, we're going to spend her entire ten minutes without getting to her acting, the reason she's here today. Soon, I'm going to say, "How nice to meet you. And good luck," and Kendra is going to go home with her grandmother's pearls.

Kendra: But I was just being polite.

Me: Noted, and thank you. Where could you have steered the conversation back to the purpose of our meeting?

Kendra: But it's your meeting. You're in charge, aren't you?

Me: Am I?

Kendra: It's your office.

Me: And it's your life. Does anyone here have a suggestion? Yes, Mr. Fitz-William.

Mr. Fitz-William: When you asked Kendra where she's from, she could have said, "I'm from New Orleans, but I've played a soldier from Cincinnati in Iraq, Mirabelle in Moliere, and Helen from *The Cripple of Inishmaan.* I do a mean Irish accent.

Me: Brilliant, Mr. Fitz-William!

And we'd be off and running toward the goal of Kendra's career. Don't let small talk derail your ten minutes. A couple minutes humanizes you. Five minutes, and half your meeting's over.

When you walk into my office, I have no idea who you are. Unless I have seen you perform and have called you in which is not the case here. Make me a little present of yourself. Maybe I'm in a rotten mood, maybe I'm on top of the world. None of which should matter to you. What matters is to get me on your side. Make me fall in love with you. Make me want to see who you are when you act. Maybe I will ask you to do a monologue right then and there. Unlikely. A monologue in an office is a horrible thing to contemplate but have I asked for it? Yes, I have. And it was horrible. Once it wasn't. Once someone completely captivated me.

There are several agencies which will rent a studio and see monologues and scenes from people they have recently met and in whom they are interested. Not all agents do this but some do. Even some good ones. Find out who does.

How are we going to get to see you act? How else are we going to know what you are like when you are acting? That is what, at bottom, we are selling. If you have a reel, that would be perfect but most of you do not. If you are in a play, that would be superb because I could go see you. On the other hand, it would be a drag because I would have to schlep to wherever your play was and sit there for at least one act. You'd better make me love you a whole lot if I am going to sign up for that. You'd better make me forget what a drag it would be. You'd better make me think it would be fun. And you'd better be in a play. Always be acting.

I Assume You Can Act

I don't need to see if you can act. I assume you can act. I need to see what happens when you act. If you cannot act or if you act badly, that is another and a much shorter story. I am looking for someone who finds glory in his work.

Do we get the idea of this exercise? Do we get the point? An interview is an unnatural encounter between two people, one of whom wants something from the other. It can go well or it can go badly and the onus of whether or not it goes well usually falls to the person who wants something. In the case of an actor and an agent or a casting director, that would be the actor. That would be you. The agent or the casting director wants to like you, of course. But you want them to love you. You are the needy one. There's nothing wrong with that. Just recognize it. Do not deny it. And go with it.

What makes for a good meeting? Even an audition (and we will get to auditions) usually has a mini-meeting before the audition itself begins. It might be very short. It might consist of the following dialogue: "Hi, how are you, what are you going to read for us today?" "Well, I thought I'd do the St. Crispin's day speech." "Oh God, have you got anything else?" "Gee, no." That is a meeting. It does not bode well for the audition that is to follow but it is a meeting nevertheless. A meeting happens when you have an agenda and the person you are meeting with has an agenda. In order to get what you want, you offer a little piece of yourself. Most of us do that automatically with friends. You will have to learn how to do it with strangers. This will not make you a tramp. Unless the piece of yourself that you offer is literally a piece of yourself. (Don't do that.) One thing you might add to the little exchange above is: "Yeah, I used to think the St Crispin's speech was a chore but then I remembered the first time I heard it and I realized how great it is." Well, you have certainly redirected their expectations. Now all you have to do is live up to your advertisement.

Interview each other. Tape those interviews. You will be appalled at first. Watch for what you do well. See what throws you. Fix what you do miserably. It is frequently terrifying to see the traps into which we fall. How do we learn not to fall into those traps? The same way we learn anything. By falling into them. Being forthcoming in an interview, seeming at ease while someone who can help you is trying to figure out whether or not they want to – these are skills. They have absolutely nothing to do with acting but it is necessary for you to master these skills if you are going to be allowed to act.

The days of the pathologically shy but brilliant actor are done. I love actors like that and I've represented a few in my career but these days, I'm afraid I wouldn't have the time.

When an interview goes well, it is a wonderful feeling. It is like a performance. You do everything you can to prepare for it and then you throw all the work out the window and just sail. How do you prepare for an agent interview? Well, you find out all you can about the agency and about the agent. How do you do that? You do research. You ask around. You go to the Drama Book Shop. You scour the internet. Show some initiative, for God's sake.

Do not show off to the agent what you have learned from your research. Do not ask the agent how she enjoyed Skidmore. Just know that you are prepared. There is much confidence that comes with proper preparation. Also remember that the agent knows nothing whatsoever about you. Unless, of course, they have seen you act. If they are seeing you as a favor to a friend they have probably just been told that you are fabulous. It is up to you to actually *be* fabulous. It wouldn't hurt to know who the agency represents and what other people in the business think of them, which you may share, should it be favorable and which you will keep to yourself if it is not. Be curious about the other person. Isn't that some sort of cardinal rule in acting? Put your attention on the other person?

Tommy: Can I go next?

Me: Of course you may go next, Mr. Younger. Go out and come in.

Knock, knock, knock and he comes in.

Tommy: Hi, sir.

Me: Sir is not necessary. But I wouldn't mind seeing your picture and resume. Thank you. This is not a good picture.

Tommy: Yeah. I apologize. It's not really me. When I heard I was going to be able to meet you, I was kind of kicking myself I didn't have a picture I was proud of but I'm seeing a photographer next week. Maybe I could show you some of the best shots from that session?

Me: If our meeting goes well today, I'd be happy to look at them, Mr. Younger.

Tommy: So no pressure.

Me: Oh, was there no pressure before, Mr. Younger?

Tommy: Ha! That's funny. Wish you'd call me Tommy. I had a Latin teacher always called me Mr. Younger. I think the guy hated me. He was Welsh, so that's interesting right there. But he really didn't like me.

Me: Why not?

Tommy: I dunno. Nothing to do with my being a mixed
   race mutt. He just didn't like the way I looked.

Me: Where did you study Latin?

Tommy: Exeter.

Me. Really?

Tommy: Yeah, but I'm not a rich kid. I had a full ride.
   Not athletic. Not that Exeter gives athletic
   scholarships. I'm a pretty good athlete but I'm
   not disciplined enough. You know? I can't pick
   a sport. I'm *kinda* good at all of 'em but not
   great at any of them. Hope that doesn't sound
   too arrogant. My scholarship was just based on
   my grades. And need. Obviously. I'm a poor kid
   from Florida.

Me: Did you like Florida?

Tommy: I liked the surf. I'll tell you that. But I always
   had this dream about New England. "Dead
   Poets Society" hit me right between the eyes.

Me: You couldn't have even been born when that came out.

Tommy: Netflix.

Me: And were you Ethan Hawke or Robert Sean
   Leonard?

Tommy: Easy. Robert Sean Leonard.

Me: Whose career would you rather have?

Tommy: Robbie Leonard's. I know it's seems like Ethan
   Hawke is more successful but RSL has this

really dignified career, you know? They both still do theatre, though, which I really admire. I just feel closer to Robbie. Probably because of his character in "Dead Poets".

Me: You call him Robbie.

Tommy: In my mind I do.

Me: Who cast "Dead Poets Society"?

Tommy: Howard Feuer. He did some really great stuff. "Billy Bathgate," "Hair".

Me: "Ishtar".

Tommy: Hey, they can't all be winners. He died young though, poor guy.

Me: And why do you think I might be the right agent for you?

Tommy: Anybody who signed Philip Seymour Hoffman when he didn't have any credits is someone I want to represent me from now until forever.

Me: A little heavy on the flattery but otherwise, I got a good sense of you.   Well done.

A good interview is like a good conversation. It flows. Thoughts, points of view are exchanged. Evaluation takes place. Agendas are accomplished – or not. Ideally, humanity, or a sliver of it, puts in an appearance.

The Casting Director Meeting

Meeting with and auditioning for a casting director is an altogether different kettle of fish. Therefore, preparing for that meeting is different as well. Most preparation for a meeting goes on inside your head. Simply *meeting* a casting director on a general interview is not that different from meeting an agent. You are there to communicate who you are so that the casting director can determine what kind of stuff she thinks you will be right for.

What kind of stuff are you right for? On an audition, obviously, you are right for the role you are there to audition for. Do not bore the casting director with your range by telling her other totally different things you think you are right for. If the casting director suggests that she sees you as edgy and urban do not rush to tell her you are from Oklahoma. If she wants to think of you as edgy and urban, why muddy the waters? She does not care that you may be a great actor capable of playing anything humans are capable of feeling. She is not looking for *anything*. She is looking for something specific. If you are lucky, it might be someone edgy and urban. I am not saying casting directors are superficial idiots who only care about how you look. Of course they care about how you think, too. Just not while you are in their office. While you are in their office, they want to know how they should think of casting you.

Casting directors are in the business of codifying what's behind your eyes. Do not announce what a chameleon you are. Great actors are a category, too, like blondes. Do not even think of mentioning what a good actor you are. They assume you are a good actor. Why else would they be talking to you? An agent has sent you to them, right? The better the agent's reputation, the better actor the casting director assumes you to be. (Reality has nothing to do with anything.) If the casting director called you in herself, as a result of seeing you do something, she has already decided how she will be able to cast you. This meeting is to establish a relationship. Really? You thought you were auditioning for a role? You are but she doesn't think you're right for it. She suspects you'll be right for the one she is hoping to be casting in a few weeks. (Her landlord and I both hope so.) She wants to see if her hunch about which role you're right for is right. Why doesn't she just call you in for that if she gets that job? Because by then she won't have time to pre-screen actors she doesn't know so today is essential. What if, in the future, you are sort of well-known around town and you have to make a choice between roles – something she's casting and something someone else is casting. She would like you to choose what she's casting. She's thinking ahead like that? Maybe there is some buzz on you. Ask her about directors she likes. Talk to her. You might learn something. This is the heart and soul of the meeting. This is the quest you are on. To discover and reveal who are you when you walk in the room. And while you're at it, to get someone else in your corner.

Jerry: Mr. Carlson?

Me: Yes, Mr. Zawadski?

Jerry: Doesn't acting matter at all? I'm an actor, for God's sake.

I have never met an actor worth his salt who did not feel that if he was sufficiently brilliant in the reading, he would get the job. THIS IS SIMPLY IS NOT TRUE. You will get the job because you fulfill their expectations for the role. How do you do that? That is out of your control. A good audition helps. What helps even more is your conviction that you are right for the part. After that, it's in the hands of the Buddha.

The Audition Begins The Second You Walk In The Door

Do not say "hi" as the adorable person you are and then switch into character. They will think you are acting. And you will be. And no matter how well you act, they will not buy it. They want the person on the page to be the person who walked in the door. I know it is called acting but casting directors think it is called casting. Producers and directors think this as well. If you are brilliant, that's a bonus for them. Mostly, they want you to embody the vision they have of the role in their heads. You cannot possibly know what that is. Half the time they may not yet know themselves. They will know it when they see it (as Justice Stewart said of pornography). So show it to them. Maybe not in the full extremity of the character's behavior in the scene you are about to read but in your heart. Accommodate your heart to the character. How do you do that? Some might call it acting.

Many actors feel if they are sufficiently *malleable* they will get the job. That is not only not true, it is destructive. Do not ask the honchos what they are looking for. Do not suggest that whatever they are looking for, you can do. What are you, a prostitute? Alan Arkin's reply to this question – is there anything you want to tell me? – when he is auditioning is: "Do you want me to do your work for you?"

Surprise Me

Frequently, especially with some juicy star-making role, the person who is cast is a surprise to the people who cast him. "Well, we thought we were looking for one kind of person," they say, still kind of in shock over their decision, "and then this person came in and just blew us all away." That is because the actor was living up to his or her own expectations of the role and not what he or she imagined were the producer's expectations. (It may also have something to do with its having been a good reading.)

One of New York's most successful and best casting directors once told me,

"If I am talking to an actor and I turn the camera on and the actors' voice changes in any way when they start to read, I can promise you they are not going to get the job." A former assistant of hers, now very successful herself, completely disagrees. So who should you listen to? Well, your heart, I would say.

If your personality changes slightly each time you meet a casting director, the casting director is not going to think that you are a big fat phony; they are going to think that you have done your homework and you want the job. Obviously, if you're auditioning for an axe murderer, leave the axe outside the door.

Billy Crudup and Paul Giamatti caught on to what people on the other side of the desk needed to see and hear faster than anyone I ever represented. They just got it. It helps that they are both superior actors but that isn't what made people think, hey, this is the guy we *need*. Not: this is the guy to keep an eye on. Not: this is the guy who we will want to hire someday. No. Now. This is the guy we want right *now*. Today. They were simply ready to be hired.

How did Billy and Paul communicate that? I have some suspicions. First and foremost, they believed it themselves. They didn't do some hocus-pocus con job on themselves or the people in the room. They did not say out loud, I can handle this part. Or I was made for this part. How cheesy is that? They communicated they could handle it by embodying it, by being fun in the room, by being forthcoming and then by acting extremely well. Maybe the people in the room got a glimpse of their ambition. Maybe they liked it. Maybe they thought they had caught lightning in a bottle.

Keep in mind, casting directors do not give you the job. Producers and directors (who hire casting directors) give you the job. Casting directors are trying to please the people who have hired them by bringing in actors who they feel stand the best chance of *being* the characters called for in the script. Some casting directors read their employer's minds very well and are successful. Whether or not the casting director is insightful and brilliant or a complete boob has absolutely nothing to do with you or your audition. When you walk into the room, your job is to do the best audition you can do, not to size up how worthy the people in the room are to judge you.

There is a danger of walking into the audition room with a chip on your shoulder. Especially if it's just you and the casting director with no director or producer in sight. Most film and television auditions for casting directors are taped – unless you are really just starting out or the casting director wants to stick it to your agent or she genuinely just isn't sure if the talent (that would be you) is right for the job.

Most actors who have been around for more than a minute feel they shouldn't have to be screened by the casting director before getting to the producer and director. Well, get that chip off your shoulder right now. Actors will accept being put on tape because they trust that the tape will be shown to the producer and the director. Not true, by the way. Or not necessarily true. But they will not accept that the casting director has final say over whether or not they will be considered for the role. Is there anything you can do about that? No.

It begins to look as if the actor has to swallow a lot of pride on his way up the ladder. Is that not true in any profession? Casting directors are not an obstacle to you getting the part. They are there to help you get the part. (And get their next job.) You have to believe that because that's the way it works. Unless you just KNOW that you were robbed and insist that your agent make some noise and get you in for the director. I don't advise such diva-like behavior because if that happens and you do get in for the director, you will probably still not get the part *and* you will have made an enemy. Think twice.

Philip Seymour Hoffman's agent:

"You think this part in 'Twister' is good enough for Phil?"

Philip Seymour Hoffman's manager:

"What else is he doing?"

MANAGERS

E ven if you're a remarkable actor, you may still be hard to cast. Philip Seymour Hoffman was brilliant, but he looked like Everyman and no man in particular so initially people didn't know what to do with him. It was simpler for them to ignore him. What do you do when people ignore your client? What does anyone who is ignored, and does not want to be ignored, do? If you are an agent and a good one, you redouble your efforts. (There are agents who would have dropped Phil. The initial reception was not rapturous.) If you are an actor, you think of ways to let people know how to cast you; you give off some clue about who you are when you walk into a room.

In distant days gone by, many character actors were stars – Charles Laughton, Edward G. Robinson, Claude Rains – they were also immediately identifiable. When they walked into

271

a room, as a specific kind of guy. They brought a complete dramatic aura with them. Laughton was formidable. Eddie G. was scary. Claude Rains exuded power.

A character actor who was a chameleon was a different story. (A leading man who is a chameleon would be a still different story. And rarer than a cold day in June.) Phil could literally be almost any kind of guy you wanted him to be. This is where a manager makes his entrance into an actor's career. Someone who could beat the drum, encourage him to work in stuff that wouldn't necessarily make him a star but would get him out there, get his face and his brilliance known to as many people as possible. Frankly, that kind of strategic thinking is not what you will get from most agents. Agents are looking for a payday. Managers are looking for a career. (And naturally that is not 100% true but it is *generally* true. It's *supposed* to be true.)

Who Could Use A Manager?

These days, almost everyone can benefit from the services of a good manager because agents have too many clients and a manager can, at the very least – and in theory – take the time to break his or her client out of the pack because the manager has fewer clients.

Let's say you're not the greatest actor the world has ever seen but you are pretty damn good. And you are not bad looking. Do you still need a manager? It used to be that a typical agent was responsible for 30 clients. A typical manager was responsible for ten. Today those numbers can easily be doubled and with managers maybe a bit more than doubled.

Managers used to do things agents didn't – like read scripts (some agents read scripts – Stan Kamen had two assistants who did nothing but read scripts for his stars), have relationships with independent producers and directors, go to auditions and meetings with their clients, maybe even produce a movie once in a while. God knows they are fond of saying they are *allowed* to produce movies. (Agents aren't. Union rules.) Not many of them actually do. (Phil's did.) Nowadays, with agents doing so much less (not necessarily less work but less work for each client – more clients, remember), managers spend a lot of time just picking up the slack.

Whence comest this need, you may well ask, to have more clients? Actors make less money than they used to. It's as simple as that. We've said this before but it bears repeating. In large part, this is because stars are making grotesque amounts of money and there is less money left in the budget for the other actors. The result, if you ask me, is that the other actors are less interesting than in days of yore. Remember Sydney Greenstreet? How great was he? He made a tidy living, too. Today's supporting actors are mostly working for scale and if they are ambitious and as good as Sydney Greenstreet, they have turned to television, like Steve Buscemi or William H. Macy or Sara Paulson, where they can become stars. Less money for actors is less money for agents, ergo, more clients.

Mind you, there are actors who are not stars who have superior careers. Steve Buscemi wasn't a star till Martin Scorsese decided he was for "Boardwalk Empire." (Note – Steve Buscemi decided it first. Did he always know? Yeah, he knew.) Although, successful actors who are not stars probably spend more time hustling than they do passively waiting. (Steve Buscemi directs his own movies.)

I worked at an agency that represented a brilliant actress named Amy Ryan who kept telling us we were sending her out on the wrong kind of roles. We were treating her as a character actress when she was, she insisted, a leading woman. Well, we thought: poor deluded Amy. She's pretty enough to be Steve Carell's love interest on "The Office," but not pretty enough to be a leading woman. She's an unhappy client but what can we do? What we should have done was to start sending her out on leading roles because were we ever wrong. Now that she is 40, Amy is a leading woman. She may not be a star (though she deserves to be) but she plays leading roles. And stunningly. She has a new agent, too, by the way. And good for her. We didn't deserve her. Though I shouldn't be surprised to learn that a rival agency is trying to poach her even as we speak.

What Exactly Does A Manager Do?

As an agent's charge is to find work and negotiate contracts for actors; a manager's job is everything else. And how well the manager does everything else and what areas of everything else he is really good at varies from manager to manager. No one is good at *everything*. Of course, the manager who wants you will claim that *she* is. So you're going to have to do some research here. How do you know what to look for?

Well, what are the noticeable differences between an agent and a manager? Agents have to have an office. It's a union rule. Managers can work out their living rooms and many of them do. Yes, even good ones. Some of them work in glossy, glassy office buildings. Managers are neither franchised, licensed or in any way answerable to anyone – except their clients. And even then subject to the terms of their contract with the actor. Manager's contracts are different than agent's contracts. All agent's contracts are written by and generated from the actors unions. Managers contracts are written by themselves or their attorneys and they are very, very different from each other. Some of them are fair. Much like the managers themselves.

Let's say the manager represents someone who is starting to take off (lightning in a bottle). If scripts are starting to pour in, the manager reads them. If there are too many, the manager hires readers (or ought to). If there are several actual offers on the table, the manager helps the actor decide which one to do – and under what conditions. A rewrite? Approval of other actors? Of the director? Well, well. Clearly, we are talking about a star or a very soon-to-be star.

What Can A Manager Do For Someone Starting Out?

So glad you asked. I am not talking about the corporate-type managers who drive sleek cars and have sleek bodies and make sleek moves for their clients. Managers frequently tell actors who have no agents that they will be able to introduce the actor to an agent. You need to sign with a manager just for an introduction? What is this bull roar? In my never humble opinion, the unrepresented actor should just go out and act and not rush into the arms of an agent *or* a manager just because you feel naked without *somebody*.

Get yourself in something. So it's not a big deal production. It's something. Say you get cast in a play in a basement in

Brooklyn, or in some deserted hangar near the 405 (what are you doing in LA? get back East, goddammit) it's still acting. The agents will take note of your existence sooner or later. I realize many beginning actors might find such a prospect daunting and the sooner or later part unacceptable. I stand behind feeling that signing away 10% to 15% of your income (the manager's commission) simply to get to pay an additional 10% to an agent is ludicrous. However, if you insist on the manager-first scenario, there are valuable things a manager can do while you are both looking for that agent. They can introduce you to people. They can get you to a good class. They can get you a better acupuncturist. (Hey, I hear Daryl Roth goes to the same one.) They can certainly get you a better 8x10. Make sure they do all those things. Or some of them. They can help you *focus*. And that's worth money? Yeah. In this day and age? Yes. Of course, you haven't made any yet. If a manager wants you, hear them out. Clearly, they think you have something. What's wrong with that?

If we could cull the aspiring artist population the way they do deer on Fire Island, there might be fewer unhappy souls in the world but that's not how we go about managing despair in this society. Not yet, anyway. (Hey, in China over 30,000 students audition for one acting school.) Young people are still arriving in New York and Los Angeles by the hundreds every week. It's not just the spawn of the schools looking to take your jobs. It is all those kids, in even greater numbers, getting off the Greyhound who are hell bent on being the next Ashton Kutcher or Katie Holmes and why not? Ashton Kutcher and Katie Holmes once got off the bus themselves. And I *like* Ashton Kutcher and Katie Holmes. I lump them together because I think they arrived on the scene in the same year. Also, and without benefit of an MFA, they became stars. I also think they are *good* stars. They are fun to watch. Are you the next Ashton Kutcher or Katie Holmes? Then put down this book and get to work. I wonder if either of them ever worked with a manager. You can bet they do now. Why don't you find out if they did? Why don't you find out who it was?

Going Places

When I started out, I signed a young actor fresh out of drama school who started getting work fairly quickly and proceeded to star in *seven* movies in a row. And all but the first one were excellent movies. And no one tried to steal him from me – until the seventh picture. Enough was enough – he was making too much money. The big boys wanted in. More recently, I had a young client, also fresh out of drama school, who tested for the lead in a movie. (He was drop dead gorgeous.) While he was in LA testing, three of the large agencies took him out for breakfast, lunch and dinner respectively and pitched him to sign with them. He left me flat. Left his New York-based manager, too. He did not get the movie he tested for. The agency he went with dropped him a year later. There were a number of years when he didn't work at all and couldn't get arrested. Today he is on a successful television show and he just won a Golden Globe. My point? I certainly don't think that actor should have left me but I applaud his blind ambition. And I certainly do not approve of those three agencies trying to steal him because he *looked like* he might be going places. No, my point is today no agency is going to wait until an actor stars in seven movies to make a move on him. The industry radar that is trolling for new talent is hungrier than ever. There is no waiting anymore. Especially if you are drop dead gorgeous. Someone will show up on your doorstep and promise you the moon.

Actors are thrown into star parts these days before they're ready for them. When an actor has been in the business for ten minutes, he has had no chance to develop, to really learn his craft – to get good. All those stars in the last century playing twenty year olds when they were clearly in their mid-thirties. What was that all about? Well, it took them ten years to be strong enough actors to carry a movie. That's what that was all about. And they were some good actors, boy. Today no one wants to wait that long. You've got a part for a twenty year old? Get me a twenty year old. Get De Niro to play the father. Everything will be fine. And it probably will be, especially if the twenty year old is Jennifer Lawrence. But even Jennifer Lawrence – who I think is swell – is not Barbara Stanwyck. Not that she couldn't catch up. I bet she will. She's great. And she's made mostly very smart choices. Not sure about "X-Men." Am I saying a good manager would have told Jennifer Lawrence to turn down "X-Men"? Come on, I'm not an idiot. But I will say that she has never taken on anything she can't handle. She's getting good advice from someone, even if it's just her own heart. But maybe it's her manager.

Actor Loyalty Matters

Actor loyalty is an issue here. No one even expects it anymore. Agent loyalty is an issue, too. But it – or the lack of it – matters. If your agent drops you after a year and you become successful the following year, you are not likely to go back to the agency that dropped you. Until you are big enough to make them crawl – and they will. Do you think your first agent will suffer any regret for having dropped you? Think again. They will simply come crawling back to you and it will be for your money, not because they have any need for your forgiveness. (*Forgiveness?*) Agents drop actors and actors drop agents all the time. It's part of life. You should get over it. I should get over it.

One of my colleagues explained to me that I must never drop a client in person. I had to terminate a client over the phone. I asked why. "Because they cry," she explained to me. Agents are a different story. (Agents don't cry.) The real answer is that agents don't get their hearts broken. We develop armor. We concentrate on the process. This is healthy. We stop caring. This is unhealthy. How do actors bear it?

The agent/actor relationship is not a love affair. It's a business. The old school ones who actually did love their clients have had to learn to care less. Many of them have stopped caring altogether. (I'll bet Ed Limato never stopped.) This is harmful to the actor because it is difficult to make long-term decisions for an actor's career when you are reasonably certain that the actor will not be with you for the long-term. If an actor is starting to be noticed and is offered a job that he really shouldn't take (bad script, bad director, abusive co-star, the part is not a good fit), it is a rare agent who will say: Don't take it. That's where the manager should come in. For some reason known only to a very small number of people whom I have never met, actor loyalty is greater to most managers than it is to most agents. Presumably the manager, as the saying would have it, has your back. Willingness to turn down a fat commission might be a very good measure of authentic concern.

The only person who really has your back is you. Harrison Ford's manager has one client. I think technically she's his agent but that's just because she's been franchised and therefore is allowed to seek work and negotiate. (Have you been paying attention?) It is fair to feel she has Harrison Ford's back. If she had another client, do you think Harrison would feel he was getting less of her time? My bet is yes – because it would be so. But even if she had ten clients, that would still be a manageable (pun very much intended) number.

The manager with a small, elite client list is pretty much a thing of the past. Ilene Feldman in LA might still fall into that category. She's always had a reputation for caring only about the client. As if that were some sort of gimmick. Most of today's managers have almost as many clients as agents do and they are *still* perceived as having greater investment in the actor's well being than agents. If you can figure out why, please contact me. So who has your back? Well, hopefully your mother.

Coastal Disturbances

Is there a difference between LA and New York managers? If we can acknowledge that all generalizations are odious, yes, there is a difference. New York managers tend to be one man operations. Savvy, cozy, caring, tough – not so much into shiny and slick. In LA, the management scene is a much more corporate kind of situation. The offices are larger, more managers, more clients. Everyone dressed in that corporate (designer) black. Ubiquitous cell phone use. They travel in packs. Little armies. *Your* little armies, you are supposed to feel. And, after all, they are. Most of them are as faceless as the agents at the big four agencies. And most of them come to show business from even less of a background in anything that might resemble art than most agents.

LA managers are frequently attorneys – and they will tell you so frequently, or boyfriends or girlfriends of someone already important in the industry or former agents who think that life will be easier now that they are managing, though even they are not quite sure what this means. They think it's less work. I can tell you that because several of them have told me that. A large part of what it means is getting – by whatever means possible – clients and then holding on to them while they generate income. Do these managers have any particular standards for what *kind* of clients? Yes, clients who make money.

There is a management company in LA called 3 Arts which was begun by a guy named Erwin Stoff. They used to have Keanu Reeves and Winona Ryder. Those were their big ticket names. Now they have the likes of Amy Poehler, Louis C.K., and Rebel Wilson. Stoff and a female lieutenant came to my office one day to request a meeting with Billy Crudup. Billy had no interest in a manager and had asked me to turn down any who came calling. And many had. Well, duh. This was back before it became clear that Billy meant it when he said he had no interest in being a star. Everybody – me included- thought he was going to be huge. (And where prestige is concerned he is). Anyway, I politely told Stoff and the faceless woman that Billy did not want a manager. They politely said thank you and we gossiped for a while and they left. That night, I found myself at some damn opening night party. They were there. So was Billy. They made a beeline for him and chatted him up for fifteen minutes. (I timed it.) They were just doing their job. Unsuccessfully, as it turned out. Billy politely told them to get lost. Have I said how much I love Billy Crudup?

New York managers tend to be much more idiosyncratic. Two of the best managers I have ever worked with on either coast are Davien Littlefield (Philip Seymour Hoffman's manager) and Bill Treusch (who over the years has represented Christopher Walken, Eric Roberts, John Heard, Sissy Spacek, Richard Jenkins, Peter Weller and Melissa Leo – who jumped ship when she got an Oscar nomination after decades of Bill busting his hump for her). Davien and Bill are both thought of as characters which means that they have opinions, taste, intelligence and a need to prevail. And they work alone.

A manager once told me that he had excellent relationships with every casting director in New York and Los Angeles. I was not impressed. Knowing casting directors is the agent's job. The manager should know other people – independent producers, writers, development people, studio people. Television people, too. That's where the money is these days. Though still not the prestige. Though that may be changing. Claire Danes, Liev Schreiber, Paul Giamatti, Viola Davis – all doing television series (and all former clients, thank you very much.) Even Philip Seymour Hoffman did a pilot before he said his terrible good-bye. But the manager should know people who complement the people that the agent knows, not duplicate the same names.

If you already have an agent and you think you want to bring in a manager, be careful how you go about it. In all probability, your agent will not like the idea even a little. Your agency will probably say something on the order of: "You don't need a manager! Managers are a waste of money! You know, *we're* like managers!" Thus damning and praising managers at the same time. You may think, why should they care? They still get their 10%, right? Yes, right, but the client becomes one step removed from their control when a manager enters the equation. And no agent likes any loss of control. Control is paramount – it is also Universal, Warner Brothers and especially Disney. (My little joke.)

The manager has to do something to let you know she is on the scene. But how do you know she is really in there making a difference? How can you test her/him? Should you even test a relationship that is supposed to be about trust? Of course you should but you should do it without getting caught. And you will need the right moment. Let's say you hear about a part in a movie that an LA casting director is coming to New York to cast – a part you are really right for. Somehow she gets it into her head she will find that dream actor in New York. (Or they want a free trip. Maybe they want to see a particular Broadway play and they can get the studio to pick up the tab. Maybe they owe their parents a visit.) So you tell your agent you have heard that someone is coming to New York for this part and you want to be seen. The agent says he will look into it. You call your manager with the same news. The manager says she knows all about it and they have offered the role to a star who wants too much money and they are coming to New York pretending they are still looking and willing to settle for someone cheaper (New York actor/cheaper actor) just to scare the star into saying yes to the money the studio is offering. But might the part really be available? No. Might you be able to go on tape with the casting director for this non-existent part? Maybe, says the manager. The manager calls back with the appointment. Better yet, the agent calls back with the appointment – which was clearly generated by the manager. Ideally, you don't want your agent and your manager grabbing credit from each other every time something good happens. So that's a nice story because it's about a manager who actually knows things and who listens to her client and then actually does something. And the agent didn't even seem ticked off. Well done everyone.

After You Tie The Knot

After you tie the knot with your manager, you should feel better taken care of than you did before and your income and the number of days you work each year should grow. It comes about – when it does – in a slightly different way for every actor. The chemistry between the agent and the manager should enhance the size and luster of your career. An agent and a manager who compete rather than collaborate will sooner or later combust and the client's career will be the loser. I once had a successful client who asked his manager – with whom he was becoming disenchanted (and who was, in fact, worthless) – what he did for him. The manager replied that he was on the actor's team. Yes, said the actor, but what do you do? The manager said that he was part of the decision making process for the actor and he was on his team. "Not anymore you aren't," said the actor. "You are off the team."

You have the right to expect your manager to *think* about your career – short-term, mid-term, and long-term. Agents don't take the long-term into account but managers should. They should use that supposed smaller client list and that perceived advantage of greater client loyalty to make some decisions that might take a year or two to pay off. Advise the client to turn down a Lifetime movie in favor of a play at The Public, option a book for the emerging client, advise him to pass on auditioning for a 7/13 pilot role in a crummy script in exchange for a good role in a terrific low budget film, urge him to create a play with some friends from school. Take a development person to see that play. Take Steve Levitan to see that play. Does your manager know Steve Levitan? Why not?

Wait just a damn minute, you may say. You don't want to go turning down Lifetime movies. You've spent a lot of time in the gym, after all. You've got some abs to show off. Anyway, you've got student loans to think of. You certainly don't have money to option a book. So the manager can negotiate a free option. A friend of mine optioned a Doris Lessing story for not one penny down. And, what's this? Turn down a pilot audition? Maybe they'll up the guarantee from 7/13 to All Shows Produced – which they would never do if you didn't turn it down. And who is Steve Levitan? I renounce you.

I'm not suggesting you have to do all this stuff, especially give up money. I am proposing that there are alternative ways of thinking which can lead to the goal that everybody wants

– big roles in big projects. Wouldn't you rather take off your shirt in a studio movie opposite Amy Adams instead of on Lifetime opposite Meredith Baxter Birney?

People Who Can Help

What are these relationships I am telling you are so important to cultivate? Who are these people? I would call them People Who Can Help. A friend of mine is a talent executive at one of the studios. She is *head* of talent. She doesn't actually cast things. She hires people to cast things. So it behooves her to know *everybody*. When a brilliant young actor who was quirky and odd (not my client – I wish) who had been around for a few years, maybe ten, won a Tony for Best Supporting Actor, my friend asked me why she had never heard of him before. I said something knee-jerk and glib like his agent must have fallen down on the job. You may say, it was *her* job to have heard of this guy – and you would be right – but there are tons of young actors my friend should know that she doesn't know. Does that make her a bad person? No. Does that make her a bad head of talent? No. She can't know everyone.

As much as every casting director strives to give the impression that they know every single actor, they simply don't. Yes, that *is* their job but let's get real. It is the job of everyone who represents someone brilliant to know my friend. How many heads of talent are there? Well, there are six major studios. It's a hell of alot easier for me to know six people who can help my clients than it is for those six people to know thousands of young actors. And it's not so hard for me to call six people and tell them I have signed the next big thing.

If those six people trust me – and it is *my job* to make sure they trust me – they will meet my new client. Sometimes not without a fight.

These people are big deals and they know they are big deals and they are hard to get to. Even when they're your friends. And I do blame the agent of that quirky, odd actor who my friend hadn't known about before he won a Tony. Maybe he didn't know my friend personally. Maybe he didn't have the time to call her every day for a month to get her to take time to meet the odd duck. Truth is, I didn't take the time to get her to meet everybody I signed even though I always felt that each new client was going to be major. My response may have been knee-jerk but if not the agent, who? Well, then, the manager?

My friend is a Person Who Can Help because even though she does not cast individual projects, she can say to the people she hires to cast those projects that they had better make certain they see that quirky, odd actor for that quirky, odd role because she has heard from his manager – whom she trusts – that this guy is a major talent. And btw, she wants to see his audition tape.

Who is head of development for your favorite director? Thomas McCarthy makes wonderful movies. If I signed somebody I thought was special, I would want Thomas McCarthy to meet her. If she said to me that Thomas McCarthy was on her wish list, I would love her forever. (Do you have a wish list?) Who gave your favorite actor his first job? Ellen Lewis hired Michael Shannon first. And she brought him in for years for everything she worked on until someone finally bit. Well, she's on your list anyway because she casts for Scorsese.

You knew that, right? If you are special, you should consider it *your* job to know the names of everyone who can be useful to you.

You are not a star but you have just signed with a manager and you are, in fact, brilliant. No, really. You are the next Vera Farmiga. Or you are unbelievably hot. You are the next Channing Tatum. And your new manager calls up Donna Isaacson at 20th Century Fox and tells her he has just signed the next big thing and she absolutely has to meet him (you). The manager will put you on a plane tomorrow if Donna would just give you fifteen minutes of her time.

Find someone who believes in you and wants to work for you *that much*. So Donna says OK (this is a fantasy, right?) and the manager puts you on a plane, after lining up five more interviews for you in LA. Find someone who thinks it's *fun* to call up people and say:

"I have just signed a fantastic actor and if you don't meet him, you are out of your mind."

And that *is* fun. And you know what? Donna Isaacson will thank you and she will take your calls forever because when her bosses call her and say, "Why haven't we seen that new kid, the one who's supposed to be the next Channing Tatum?" Donna can say to her bosses that she has seen that kid, she has him on tape and he is on the list for their next picture which she is waiting to hear has a green-light.

News flash: after 23 years, Donna Isaacson is out. Not to worry, she will be replaced.

Good Managers Work Hard ... And Like It

Let's get back to that young actor my friend had never heard of. He came to the attention of the business at large when he won the Tony. What happened next? Not much. You were expecting phones ringing off their hooks? Hollywood folks don't really take Tony awards seriously as a significant harbinger of whom they should be hiring. The young actor kept working. His small agent got him a couple of small parts. Then a few years after the Tony, he got lucky when a couple of maverick filmmakers put him in a starring role in a movie. Then he got a really good television series. Shortly after that, not surprisingly, this Tony winner's manager told him to leave his small agency for one of the big four. And he did. Happy ending? Well, I haven't seen his name around much lately. Oh, he's got something coming out at Christmas. I don't think he's above the title.

There used to be a wonderful manager named Bob LeMond. He had great clients – Dianne Keaton and John Travolta among others. Travolta who became a gigantic star with LeMond's steadfast help – and his own outsized talent – was famous for turning projects down. He turned down "American Gigolo" (and handed Richard Gere a career). Not that LeMond took Travolta's 'no' lying down. He begged him to reconsider. Kicked, screamed and pleaded. Travolta was adamant. He didn't like the script. Obviously, it's up to you whether to accept a job or not but why have a manager if you aren't going to listen to him? If he gives you no end of bad advice, leave him. If he brings you scripts that you reject which became gigantic hits, maybe don't leave him. Travolta ended up leaving LeMond.

What did Bob LeMond do for Dianne Keaton? Well, for one thing, he took her calls at three in the morning. He said he realized one day that the more money she made, the later at night she would call him. If you need someone to obsess with at three AM, maybe you should have a manager. (Make sure you're famous.)

Mark Wahlberg's manager produces stuff all over the place and not just for Mark Wahlberg. He takes care of his other clients (and himself) as well, though I doubt Mark Wahlberg feels neglected. I hate to praise the guy because he once took a client from me but he is one smart cookie. And he and Mark Wahlberg make beautiful music together.

Managers can also be good at reinvigorating or even reinventing a career that is out of steam or stuck in a rut. If you came to prominence playing a gay axe murderer and that's all you have played since, maybe you should think about a manager.

There are really no end of ways for a manager to be helpful to an actor's career and only one way to not be: By doing nothing. You want someone who works hard and likes it.

Forces Of Nature

I used to say it was a good thing Marlon Brando had a good agent because otherwise we might never have heard of him. Some actors would give me a blank look. I had to point out that I was being ironic, that Marlon Brando was a force of nature and it hardly mattered who represented him. What matters about Marlon Brando's career is those performances. Look at them. Jesus. So perform already. Agents will come calling. In the end, they will find you. It may take a year or two or three. Just keep working.

The entire agent system is shrouded in an unhealthy amount of mystery and posturing which keeps actors from seeing how it all really works. Who talks to casting directors and who talks to studio executives and who talks to Jim Gianopulos doesn't really matter. It matters to all those people whose relationships are mired in severely structured layers of importance but it shouldn't matter to *you*. What matters to you is your next job and your agent's job is to find it for you. She's your *agent*, for God's sake.

The best manager's contract I ever saw took no commission from the actor until the actor's income exceeded $100,000. Then it was 5% up to $250,000. Then it was 10% above that. The man who created that contract felt that until you were earning at least $100,000 a year, you had no need for him. I have never heard of anything more reasonable or fair before or since. Not sure that guy is still around. I think he never made enough money.

Risa Bramon Garcia, casting director:

"Share your artistry above all else."

AUDITIONS – THE REAL SKINNY & PROTOTYPES

No one likes auditions. They are an excruciating and nerve-wracking process for all concerned. Let's try our best to say only positive things. Auditioning is one step away from actually acting. Auditions, I trust it is clear by now, in fact *are* acting. Both the second part where you act and the first part where you oh so effortlessly get to be yourself. Does it occur to you – it occurs to me – that the clearer you become as a personality, the clearer your acting will be? I stand by my disclaimer that this is not a book about how to act. But, you know, you could do worse than to listen to me when I bring the subject up.

An Audition Is A Chance To Act

An audition is – a chance to act. It is not a chance to suggest a way you might play the role – all the while implying that you have other ways you would be willing to show them. It is a chance to play the role. Fully and to the best of your ability. If the people you have said "hi" to when you walked into the room feel you are physically just not what they are looking for, the audition is probably over before you even get that chance to act. However, hope is not lost because you will have that chance to act. Take it. (It hasn't yet come to where they physically dismiss you after one look.)

Even though you may feel the vibe in the room is not in your favor, take your shot with gusto. Now you have even less to lose. You might change their minds. Not likely but *possible.* Don't wimp out now. If your reading has softened them up, they may give you an adjustment, which means they may ask you to do it differently. This will mean they are members of a small minority of people who hire actors who know what an actor does. If they like what you do after they have asked you to do it, they may hire you. Or they may hire someone else. They may hire someone else anyway. What you are there to do is to make an impression and to act. If you have done well at both tasks, maybe they will remember that they liked you. That's a lot. (OK. It is not a job.)

The Audition Begins The Second You Walk In The Door

If you are a young actor, your life is an audition. You never know when a friend will turn into a director, a roommate will turn into a star, an acting teacher will be called for a suggestion, everyone who crosses your path might potentially be of help to you. Everyone you meet certainly forms an opinion of you and whether or not they will be able to help you, why not insure that the opinion they form is a favorable one? And, at the risk of being didactic, clear. This may sound like: be a good person and lead a good life. Well, what's wrong with that?

When I was a young actor (have I mentioned I was an actor? Everyone was an actor), living in Los Angeles, my agent called with an audition for a movie called "Airport" produced by Ross Hunter. Hunter was an improbably powerful figure in Hollywood who produced glossy, big budget and usually very successful films. I went to the audition and did, I thought, a very creditable job. A few days later, I was home in the evening, stewing – impatient that my agent hadn't called with any feedback from Ross Hunter since I felt I had done a bang-up job at the audition. I was pacing. My (first) wife was watching television and knitting me a sweater. She made great sweaters. She suggested I sit down and watch TV with her. But I was restless. I was going out of my mind wondering if I was going to get "Airport." I needed to get out of the house. I felt a sudden craving for ice cream. There was none in the freezer. Since the craving wasn't going away, I decided to go to the store. I asked my wife if she needed anything from Ralph's Market. She said I could not go to the store looking like that. What, I demanded, was wrong with the way I looked?

I was unshaven (frowned on back then), I hadn't washed my hair, what I was wearing was stupid (there were reasons why she was my first wife), I could not go to the store. We proceeded to have a gigantic fight. I marched out of the house, went to Ralph's and ran smack into Ross Hunter at the checkout counter. I said "hi." He didn't appear to know me so I told him my name and said we'd met a few days ago when I auditioned for him. "Oh," said Ross Hunter, turning to his partner who was with him," Jacques, it's Philip Carlson who we saw for the film."

"He looks different tonight," said Jacques. "Yes," Ross Hunter agreed, "he does." I did not get "Airport." I never told my wife I ran into Ross Hunter that night at Ralph's.

Nerves

Everybody says don't be nervous. In this one case, everybody is right. Don't be. Put your attention on the other person or the other persons in the room. Make a choice. Don't be tentative, unless your choice is to be tentative. If your choice is what they are looking for, and you read well, you will get the job. If it is not but they are not ready to dismiss you altogether, they may ask you to make a different choice and if they like what you do then, you might get the job. Sometimes you may want to ask them if they'd let you try something different. Only do this if you are very sure they are with *you* but perhaps not with your choice. And then make sure you do something different. Nothing is worse than an actor who asks to do something different and then does the exact same thing. (Well, getting hit by a bus is worse.) At the very least, you will have given them a *clear* idea of who you are and how they may best use you in the future.

They want to like you – the cliché is true. They want you to be who they are looking for. They have seen your picture, the casting director will have told them a little bit about you, or if it's just the casting director, your agent will have told her a little bit about you. The person or people you will be meeting and reading for are predisposed to think you *might* be their answer. Otherwise, they would not be wasting their time. Know that. Believe that. They are on your side.

In The Room

Actors scare the hell out of producers. They're afraid all actors are crazy. It's up to you to assure them that you, at least, are not. Don't look like a troublemaker or a short-fused likely-to-get-in-a-fight-with-the-director type, or be-late-to-the-set type, or screw-up-in-any-way type, OK? So this is what you've been waiting for. You are in the room and everyone appears to be glad you are there and you don't look like a troublemaker. (Worth repeating.) You *talk*. You offer yourself to them. Then they ask you to read. This is it. This is your chance.

When Jason Robards Jr. auditioned for "The Iceman Cometh" he created something of a scene. He had been around the block a few times by then and after he read what he had been asked to read, a voice called out from the theatre, "Thank you. Next." And that particular day, Jason Robards Jr. had heard "Thank you. Next," one too many times. He is reported to have fired back to the people in the theatre words to the effect of, "That was the best damn audition you are ever going to see. Now do I have this part or not?" Well, he got the part. However, unless you are Jason Robards Jr., do not do this.

Feedback

After you have done the very best audition that you can do, your next job is to put it out of your mind completely. It will kill you not to ask for feedback but don't ask for feedback. Though actors long for it, most feedback is worthless. Do you think the casting director runs down the list of everyone they saw and says to the director, "Now why didn't you hire that person? They were great!" This will not happen. If the actor flew in from St. Louis for the audition it still may not happen. You think the casting director is going to challenge the director who hired her over five other casting directors just so she can give agents feedback?

What usually happens when the agent pushes for feedback, if he ever really does, is the casting director makes something up like, "Well, I think he felt your client didn't really have the humor they were looking for," or, "She just seemed too contemporary," or some other bullshit which is usually nothing more than a guess. The kind of feedback I like is feedback you can do something about: "He had an attitude," "She was late," "He was completely unprepared." Don't tell me that's all negative stuff. Of course it is – you didn't get the job, remember? – but it's stuff you can rectify.

Feedback is not going to be: Well, he was too wonderful so we're passing." The kind of judgment calls most actors think they are looking for – "Not funny enough," "Not pretty enough," "Not vulnerable enough," are subjective and even though the actor is dying to go back in and get that judgment reversed, there is very little *anyone* can do to change an initial impression. Get over it. That most excellent casting director Vinnie Liff used to tell agents, "The feedback is: your client is not getting the job." Positive feedback is getting the job.

Casting Directors

When you meet a casting director, be open to them. Do not judge them. That is not why you are there. You are there for them to judge you. That's how it works. Accept it. Be open to them. Do not come up with a quick and easy (and insincere) compliment (Oh, I love your hair). Just...let them take you in. Casting directors are hard to categorize as a group. It has been said that they look like people who were unpopular in high school. I think this is generally so but the implied conclusion – that they are out to get back at the popular kids – is not. Some casting directors are actually very attractive. Most of them genuinely like actors and want the best, the most qualified, the most suitable actor to get the job. They, like agents, are out to validate their taste. And in order for them to exercise that taste, they are going to have to see as much of you as possible.

A spur of the moment request for you to read cold is a superb chance for you to show them something unexpected about yourself. Do not treat it as a chance to fail. Let what is unique about you out of the box!

The thing about casting as a profession is, and this is crucial to remember, all casting directors are working off the same pool of talent. Anne Hathaway is as available to Universal Studios as she is to the director of a Columbia student's thesis film. I said she is available, I did not say she will want to do the student film. She may not want to do the Universal film, either. Casting directors to some extent are basically window shoppers for directors.

There are an increasingly large number of directors who have no idea about who the good actors are and what they can do, let alone how to help them do it; more and more directors are content to listen to the ideas of their sophisticated casting directors. David Fincher, who I think is brilliant, gives no end of credit for the cast of "The Social Network" to Laray Mayfield.

And, judging by the cast of "The Social Network," I would say that credit is deserved. The cast of "August: Osage County" was unexpected, wildly creative and brilliant. (I thought the movie was a stinker but the cast was fab.) Most people have never heard of a Robert De Niro picture called "Being Flynn." But the cast? Superb. Best use of the New York talent pool since… oh, say, "The World According to Garp."

There was a casting director who refused to see a movie star's wife (who was also a-sort-of-movie star) for a role because the casting director is reported to have said, "I don't like her mouth." The male movie star – who wasn't even in the movie his wife wanted to be seen for – tried to get the casting director fired. He failed. And his wife was never seen for the role. And life went on. Casting directors have a lot of influence. Most of them use it benevolently. Most of them care. Most of them have good taste. They don't always know what makes an ensemble but they at least know what makes a good actor.

Are There Any Secrets?

The secret is to be prepared. Know your lines (if it's film or TV), have the accent down cold (if there's an accent), know who you are and what you want and what the person you are talking to means to you and what just happened and all your actions and everything else that is part of your process and then throw it all away and act. It helps to be coached for important auditions. For all auditions, if you can afford it. Have a few coaches you feel good about. (Some of them may be out of town – working.) On the whole, great acting teachers are not necessarily good coaches. They are too focused on great acting and they will tie you up in knots. Good coaches know what the smart money wants.

Audition. After you've gotten a few jobs, you will begin to understand how you got them.

Hint: they will probably be the ones you didn't think you had a prayer of getting so you didn't try so hard.

Also see "Internet Resources for Actors" on page 356.

PETER BROOK, on acting for the camera
(from THE EMPTY SPACE):

"Acting begins with a tiny inner movement so slight that it is almost invisible. I make a proposition to an actor's imagination such as 'She is leaving you.' At this moment deep in him a subtle movement occurs. Not only in actors – the movement occurs in anyone, but in most non-actors, the movement is too slight to manifest itself in any way: the actor is a more sensitive instrument and in him the tremor is detected – in the cinema, the great magnifier, the lens, describes this to the film, so for the cinema, the first flicker is all."

WORKSHOP SEVEN: COLD READINGS

OMG Please Don't Ask Me To Do A Cold Reading

So here we are, back in our slightly grungy studio in the West 30's in New York City. I have picked you each a scene from a play with a role you may be right for. Or more accurately, a role you might be very right for. You will be doing a cold reading of the scene, with a partner that I will assign randomly.

First of all, you need to read a whole mess of plays. It is remarkable to me how little young actors know about actual plays. Become familiar with what has been written, what has been revived and what roles have launched some of your favorite actors. Look at theatrical history from a completely opportunistic point of view. Would that make it more appealing? Well, we're all human.

Becoming familiar with a large number of plays while hunting for one that feels right for you is an awfully good way to feel like you are part of the profession. Wouldn't you like to feel that way? Especially if you are thinking of training at one of the better schools, wouldn't you like to walk into your audition for that school feeling that they would be lucky to have you? Would it surprise you to learn that over 3,000 people auditioned for Juilliard last year (for twenty-some slots)? It surprised the hell out of me. What is there you can do that might set you apart from the pack? What is it you could say, feel or simply know that would make you feel – and make the school feel – that they just had to have you?

Wouldn't a thorough grounding in theatre history (from "Danton's Death" by Georg Buchner, to Eugene O'Neill's "Desire Under the Elms," or William Inge's "Come Back, Little Sheba") set you apart? Wouldn't it be nice, if when the school asked you what kind of plays you related to, you actually had an answer for them? Wouldn't it be clever of you to comment on their production of George M. Cohan's "The Tavern" last year because you really like it and you've never heard of it being done, or to blurt out at your ART audition that you have always wished you could have seen (their graduate) Peter

Sellar's production of the Sophocles play "Ajax" with a deaf Ajax? (Well, that might be considered showing off. But it's called acting, right? Is showing off a bad thing?)

Working on cold readings will be helpful to you in your bones. Let's say you are a working actor and you are at an audition. You read for the director and the director really likes you and wants to hear you do another scene. He asks you to look at this scene here. "Just go out in the hall for five minutes and take a look at it, then come back in and read for us," he says. What are you going to do? Plead for more time? Say that you need to break the scene down into beats and actions? Wrong! You are going to go out in the hall and look at the scene and come back in and read cold. And if you read well, you may get the part.

Cold readings. I have given you some reasons why this exercise might be helpful. Can you think of some others? Anyone?

"Don't you want us to be able to think on our feet?"

Yes, Ms. Harris, that's good. You might better say I want you to be able to *act* on your feet. Would you like to be the first to do a cold reading?

"No thank you."

Very well. So much the worse for you.

"Ouch."

I'm sorry but boldness is called for. And especially called for in a cold reading. What does your character want and what does he feel about the person he is talking to? And what just happened? Now I have said this is not an acting class. Does this sound like acting to you?

"A little," says Ms. Harris.

Ms. Harris, you may not want to go first but you apparently will be heard. Consider what I am asking you to do. Three minutes to put together a scene you have never seen before for a job you desperately want to get. That doesn't sound like acting to me; it sounds more like a magic act. And magic is precisely what is called for. But you want it to be a good magic act. You want it to be the best magic act it can be. You don't want it to be fake, or at least you don't want it to *look* fake – but how can it be real, deep and honest in only five minutes? Face it: you'll have to fake it. So decide what you want, how you feel about the person you want something from – with any luck it will be the same character from the scene you just auditioned with – and what just happened. What just happened is an extremely useful tool in this situation. It is something you should always ask yourself but for a cold reading it can be a boon. It can – ought to, really – lead you to some distinctive behavior that will lead you to do something that no other actor who is auditioning will do and may even get you the part. You want to stand out, don't you? You want to get the part, don't you? If you did something no one else did, wouldn't that wonderful? Surprising us is always desirable. What is so wonderful about Robert Downey Jr.? He never fails to surprise us.

Now who wants to go first. Ms. Harris? Still no?

"Still no."

Ah, you, sir. And what is your name?

"Rob Jackson."

And here is what you will be reading for us, Mr. Jackson. Turk in "Come Back, Little Sheba." I heartily approve of colorblind casting. Although, in this day and age, there is no reason why Turk couldn't actually be Black.

"I agree."

Turk is also supposed to be sex on a stick. Do you think you qualify for that, Mr. Jackson?

"I do all right."

How well you do is a matter of complete indifference to me, Mr. Jackson. I am asking if you think you are sex on a stick.

"Could be."

I will take that as a yes and I would agree. Mr. Jackson is not a traditionally handsome man but there is something... intriguing in his presence.

And who would you like to be your Marie? How about Ms. Harris here?

"Oh, no," says Ms. Harris.

"Hey, I don't bite," says Mr. Jackson.

"I'll read with him," says Ms. Paley.

And so they do the scene.

Well, that was very nice. What was your action, Mr. Jackson? To try and have sex with Marie? Well, yes, but why? Because that's what you do? You have sex with girls? Who is Marie to you? A hot girl. Isn't that kind of general? Are you in any danger of someone walking in on you? Wouldn't it be more interesting if you were?

What just happened? What just happened before the scene began? This is a terribly important question and you need to answer it with something that will galvanize you into the heart of the scene. Maybe Doc just told you Marie lusted after you and you should strike while the iron is hot? Never mind that such a thing is completely not in the play. It might, nevertheless, turn you on. Fill you with energy. What if Lola told you if she ever thought you had put your hands on Marie she would kick you out of the house forever? And what if Lola is due home in half an hour? Try it again. Now.

Nice. Much better. More focused. Do we agree? The point in any audition, a cold reading or one for which you have had adequate time to prepare, is to *do the scene* and do it better than anyone else. You don't want to do a good job, you want to do a great job. And that doesn't mean not being bad; it means being extraordinary. It does not mean over-acting. It means behaving.

Thank you both. Thank you Ms. Paley. You seemed to be enjoying yourself.

"I think he's sex on a stick," says the attention-getting Ms. Paley.

Is it any wonder people want to be actors when they can get away with behavior such as this? Interesting to look at the reaction on the faces of the other women in the class to this crack of Ms. Paley's. She has staked a claim here. Let's not give her any more immediate attention. Ms. Harris. Will you be next?

"Couldn't someone else go next?"

Of course someone else can go next. Who might that someone be? Kendra?

"I'd be happy to, Mr. Carlson."

Ah, my name, how nice. Here is your scene, Ms. Logan. Let the class know what you'll be reading for.

"Diana in 'Russian Transport' by Erika Sheffer."

A great choice, if I may say so myself. You know I agree with your Janeane Garofalo type which is probably why I chose it, although you're prettier than she is which conditions me to think that you are prettier than you actually are which is what makes this a smart and interesting choice. May I say that if it seems I am obsessed with how people look, that is an accurate description of me. I think it is an accurate description of everyone in show business. Narcissists, all of us.

"Russian Transport" is also not a play that is done every day. Erika Sheffer is not a playwright one hears from every day. Let's have you read with Tommy.

And they do.

Very nice but very ... tentative. Why so unsure? Tommy didn't do what you thought he would do? Listen, darling, you're lucky when the reader is breathing. This is your audition. Not the reader's audition. I know that acting is about what goes on between two people but an audition is about getting the job.

Most people you read with will be terrible. Not terrible actors. Just unprepared. Half the time, you will read with the casting director because she was too cheap to hire a reader. Or because she likes reading with actors. Some casting directors do. Do not worry that she is missing some of your best moments while she is looking at the script. This is your chance to shine. What do you want in this scene? You want to get him out of the house? So raise the stakes. Let's say if he does not leave the house immediately after this scene is done, you will not get a call back for this job. Motivation enough?

Quarterbacking The Seventh Workshop

If we are asking the world to be excited that we are in it, it behooves us to know what we're doing here. In other words – who we are. Know thyself. It is remarkable to me that some people just expect other people to be so happy they exist. It would be helpful for you to tell us why we should be so happy. The possibility exists that you will enrich my life but I need to be shown, at the very least, in what way. If Blake Lively walked into my office and told me her ambition was to start a theatre program for impoverished children in Gullah Land, I would probably look for an excuse to get her out of my office. If she told me she wanted to star in a nighttime soap and she had no problem with nudity, I would be texting my assistant to set up an agency wide meeting in ten minutes because I had just found us a great new client.

Very few of us are as staggeringly beautiful as Blake Lively. But every single one of us has something clear and distinct and God-like in us and it is our job, your job, to discover what that is and how to give it up when you walk into a room. Or do a monologue or do a cold reading. Or audition. By this I do not mean that it is an actor's job to be *on* all the time. This is a tiresome notion imperfectly understood by many actors and would-be actors.

I have met several *great* actors – Robert De Niro, Dianne Wiest, Bette Midler (yes, goddamn it) and there is a stillness about each of them away from work. It's rather wonderful, really. They are not *on*. They are the opposite of *on*. You may say this is because they are so famous, they can afford to not have to sell themselves at every opportunity. I would propose to you that they are so famous because they know precisely what they are selling and therefore have no need to display it. (They also have more talent than most humans but how much talent we have is out of our control.) And all this can be gleaned from a cold reading? Oh, this and much more.

Alec Guiness on beginning rehearsals for a new
play after being on a movie set for four months:

*"It's so nice to be back in the profession after spending so
much time in the industry."*

PRODUCERS, DIRECTORS
AND ACTUAL WORK

L et us get to know these all-important people who pull
the strings. As you progress in your careers, you will be
spending more and more time with these folks and you
will become more and more comfortable with them but they
will always be, first and foremost, The People With The Jobs.

There will come a time in your career when a producer or
a director, or both at once, may take you out to dinner to talk
about a role that they would like you to do in an upcoming
project. If you are reading this book, it is unlikely that will
happen to you this week or next. At the beginning of your
career, you will meet and read for the casting director long
before you are wined and dined by the producer or the director.
If the casting director feels you are what the creative team is
looking for, you will be called back to read for the director. If

the director feels good about you and how you read, he or she will then call you back for the Artistic Director (if it is a not-for-profit theatre); or the director and then the producer if it is Broadway or a movie; and the producer and the network if it is a pilot. Sometimes the writer gets into the mix. Particularly in television. The producer will almost always have the final say.

Steven Spielberg can hire you on the spot. There are only a few around who can do that. And now that Mike Nichols is dead, there are even fewer. I had a client who Sidney Lumet hired on the spot. "You've got the job," said Mr. Lumet. When the actor left the audition room, the casting director said, "Sidney, you can't just hire that guy. We've got a room full of actors waiting to read for you." "Well," said Sidney Lumet, "in that case, you'd better send them home." Most other directors will need the permission of their producer and, if it's a big enough project (i.e., if there is enough money at stake), the producer may need the studio or the network to sign off on you before you are finally hired. If you are being taken out to dinner to test your interest in the project, you will likely have been pre-approved by God.

The Reality Check

Let's skip the part about you being taken out to dinner since that's a fantasy, albeit a pleasant one. How should you behave when you meet these people at an audition? Should you act differently with each of them? That will be difficult if they are all in the same room. The answer, as always, is that you should behave professionally and well – you should know your lines (though that's not necessary for a play – but you should know them for the callback) and you should hold your script, even though you know your lines. This makes you appear flexible, as though what you will be doing is not all you are capable of doing – though it had better be.

It had better be an opening night performance. They say they don't want that. They lie. They do want that. Every single casting director I have ever spoken to about this says that is what they want.

You should be dressed more or less in character and you should be comporting yourself pretty much as the character would if you were he – and you are. We've been here, right? An audition is an audition, no matter for whom you are auditioning. After that, after you have made sure you are completely prepared and appropriately wardrobed, you should charm the pants off of everyone in the room.

Real-Life Examples

David Fincher said of one cast member's audition for "The Social Network," "He was so much fun we just had to have him on the set." The actor's name is Joe Mazzello and his being such a pleasure to be around should send a message to aspiring actors everywhere. Listen to that bouquet Fincher threw at him. What a gift that statement is. Because, of course, it's true. It's always true. I mean, the guy was a good actor but everybody who auditioned for that film was probably a good actor (I'm betting Justin Timberlake didn't audition). The point is, Fincher hired that guy for a very small run of picture role because he was fun (*and* good). What a good reason to hire someone.

Why should they choose *you*? What is so damn special about you? Will you be fun on the set? In what way? These are not frivolous questions. And they start to apply long before you audition for David Fincher. Didn't we hear the same thing from the people at the MFA programs? Yeah. We did.

I once had a client who auditioned for a movie that was scheduled to shoot for five months in Alaska. My client was brilliant (he may be my all-time favorite client) but he is distinctly a weird duck. He is also very, very shy, though not after he has decided to let you in. But before folks got the message that he was a great actor, it was his *job* to let them in before his comfort zone told him it was OK. It took him a while to figure that out. He lost the Alaska job which he wanted deeply just by acting weird. How do I know? The director told me so.

My client was convinced his audition had been first-rate and was stunned not to be cast. He insisted I find out why. Normally, I wouldn't have bothered but normally this guy wouldn't have asked. Plus he was my favorite client. So I called the casting director and asked her. She didn't know why he hadn't been cast. She said his audition was great.

I called the studio. They didn't know why. I finally got the director on the phone. He said my client had given the best audition he had seen for that role but he wasn't going to get the job because, "He's strange, you know? I wouldn't know what to say to that guy on location for five months in Alaska. We'll probably be spending a lot of time in bars." I tried to assure him, there would be no social interaction necessary or called for, just give my guy the job. He'll probably spend most of his down time alone in his trailer reading poetry anyway so that settles the problem of what to say to him. "No," the director said. Firmly. "No." He wasn't having it. He was looking for drinking buddies, as well as actors. Is that unusual? No.

So does talent matter at all? Of course it does, bubala. Stay calm. They are looking for the best possible actor but they are also always aware of how it might feel to work with you. Can't you be a good actor and a reasonably pleasant person as well? Would it kill you to appear easy going? My weird client was not easy going – but he wasn't difficult, either. How were they supposed to know that? A certain amount of temperament is expected from any actor, especially a lead actor, though not so much from a supporting actor and none at all from a day player. So if you have been working on your ability to assert yourself, I would suggest you practice on bus drivers or waiters or crossing guards or whoever you suspect is trying to hold you back in your search for the respect you deserve. I am not suggesting that you be completely docile or that ball-lessness is a requirement for getting an acting job, in fact, quite the opposite but a certain amount of, well, affability can go a long way.

Who Do You Think You Are?

Another client of mine made a gigantic splash on a television series. Producers were lined up around the block to put him in a movie on his first hiatus. An A-list director with a wonderful script wanted him for a wonderful role, not the lead, in his studio picture. A first-time director with a decent script wanted him for the starring role in his independent feature.

Hey, I love independent features but the studio picture had a better script – and a better director. I advised my client to go with the first one; he chose the second. I think that's probably when he took his first meeting with UTA.

My client shot the movie and several months later when he was back at work on his wildly successful series, I arranged for a special screening of the director's cut just for him in the town where his series was shooting. I told him I would come down so we could watch it together. He said no, he would take his own notes. I wasn't quite sure what he meant by that. I was more concerned about why he didn't want me to come down. Whatever he meant by his own notes didn't even compute for me. Turned out, it meant he wanted to take his own notes. He called me after the screening. I had been anxiously awaiting the call. He was upset. No, he was *extremely* upset because he couldn't get the director on the phone. He had left several messages. I said Brian (the director) would surely get back to him very soon but let's talk about the movie. How was it? Was he pleased with his work? "The movie was OK," he muttered. "Brian should be calling me back." Something was up.

My client was acting like a complete jerk. (Something he was not incapable of doing.) Had he invited another agent down there? Were they together right now? I would have bet money that was it. And I was kicking myself for not having gone down there to watch it with him. "What's going on?" I asked him. "I need to speak to Brian," he spat out. "I have five pages of notes for him. And we need reshoots." Excuse me? You have five pages of notes for a director of your first movie and you are upset he is not standing by his phone to

315

receive your thoughts? And you think you're going to be able to demand RESHOOTS? I attempted to insert reality into the situation – which I would not recommend doing with a teen idol who has just watched himself starring in a movie. Nothing I could say was going to get through in the face of such colossal ego. I'm sure I lost him when I did not immediately agree that Brian was a horrible person for not getting back to him immediately. I kept reminding myself this was work and there was money at stake. So I was supportive. But I lost him, of course.

Word got out about that young man's ego. He hadn't exactly been a day at the beach on the movie which came in over budget. Acting like a diva is one thing. A diva who causes unnecessary delays in shooting has no place on a movie set. Especially for a not-yet-movie star with no box office track record. Never mind the wanting additional scenes and suggesting how the picture be cut. If Tom Cruise has thoughts on how to handle any aspect of any movie he is starring in, people will listen. If some twerp on a hot TV show wants to talk about reshoots for his first movie, um, no. The kid continued to make a splash on his television show but it was a while before anyone asked him to be in another movie. He's on a series now. An OK one.

Artistic Directors – The Regionals

When you audition for a play at a regional theatre or at any of the prestige not for profits in New York, you will almost certainly have a final callback for the Artistic Director of that theatre. This tradition, to the best of my knowledge, began with Joseph Papp who created The Public Theatre in 1954 and ran it until he died. He was a control freak. Artistic Directors frequently are. Nothing wrong with that but it's good to know going in. Joe Papp was a giant and no one was going to act at his theatre on whom he had not passed judgment. Favorable judgment.

There is no better way to put your own personal stamp on a theatre's personality than through casting. Elia Kazan always said casting was 90% of a director's job. Artistic Directors are self-interestedly (and wisely) ever on the lookout for young people who might become well-known and make reference to the Artistic Director's theatre having given them their first big break. At the very least, the conquering young hero might return and participate in fundraising and other schmoozing festivities with board members. That's kind of an accepted quid pro quo. Actors, even famous actors, like to hang out with rich people.

Everyone likes rich people – except other rich people. If the Artistic Director spots someone at auditions for his theatre who he thinks is likely to break out and become famous, the Artistic Director may insist that actor be hired over someone who might be more right for the part – or is a better actor, but offers no long range benefit to keeping the doors of that theatre open. What's that you say? You think a better cast play might be a stronger choice in the long run? Go to your room.

Artistic Directors are also happy when you know they are the boss. Yes, the casting director may have brought you in; the director may have chosen you, the writer (if living and present) may be on your side, but the Artistic Director hired all of them. She will give final approval to you and your ultimate obeisance belongs to him or her. And even though the Artistic Director is probably making ten times what you are making per week which is a very good reason to resent them just a bit, keep in mind that what their salary really reflects is the Board's confidence in their ability to keep their not-for-profit theatre profitable and you must not hold that against them.

So that's the politics of not-for-profit theatre. For-profit theatre is no different. Be nice to everybody, especially the lead producer. And double especially the Stage Manager. On a movie set, that double especially applies to the DP (the cinematographer, you moron).

And those are pretty much your rules of comportment for theatre and movies. Then there is the zoo called television.

Television – Where The Money Is (These Days)

If it seems that people with power in the theatre are indirect, easily offended and hard to read, they are positively confrontational compared to those who sit in the corner offices at the networks (and mini-networks). Television is where you can come back from lunch and find your name off the door if you are an executive or your dressing room emptied out if you are an actor. And no one has so much as hinted to you that the end was near.

Television is a terrific way to make a living – especially on a sit-com – but those who guard its gates are inscrutable and mysterious. Their decision-making process is a secret. From you. From everybody. The only people who actually make decisions in television are those who have been able to create a structure around themselves which will make it absolutely impossible to trace any decision they make back to them.

Somewhere deep inside the bowels of the executive offices, a decision is made to make a particular pilot. No one will ever know who finally gave the green light (see above) – unless the show is a hit in which case cries for credit will be heard across the lot – or certainly from The Daily Grill to The Ivy. But the decision has been made. Now they have to cast the sucker. There is no decision that they will be called upon to make in their buttoned down careers that will make them more vulnerable than casting a pilot. Thus, final casting is always a group decision – made by the suits. In order to be a series regular, you will have to go to network.

Going To Network

The very phrase is the source of much longing and even more anxiety in every actor's life. The longing part is because going to network means you have a chance to become a series regular on a television show and make, oh, at least twenty thousand dollars a week (if your agent stands up for you and the crick don't rise) with loads more on the horizon if the show is a hit. ("Friends," "Seinfeld," "Big Bang.") And you will get to act every day. What's better than that? The anxiety part is because going to network is an excruciating process. But since being a series regular on a television show has become one of the most desirable, certainly the most lucrative ways to make a living as an actor, going to network is a devoutly to be wished for moment. It ain't easy. But it is worth it.

Even a beginner will start out at $15,000 an episode. (You thought I said $20,000? That's what I mean about your agent standing up for you. Though I have to say that series regular salaries are going down instead of up.) But listen to the hours. If you are on a sit-com, you will have a table read on Monday morning and then have the rest of the day off while the writers work on the script. Then you will rehearse all day Tuesday, Wednesday and Thursday and will be able to go home at five o'clock. Friday, you will work like a madman and your day will be very long but by day's end, you will get to tape the show in front of a live audience and you will really feel like an actor. You will have the weekend to yourself. Being on a sit-com is an absolutely fantastic way to make a very good living.

If you are on an hour show, you will make more money but you will likely work 14 or 15 hour days and, if you are on location, you will work 6 day weeks. Of course, you will pocket a pile of cash, which will be enjoyable when the series is done and you get your life back, assuming you don't have a heart attack and die first. Like Edward Woodward. (Who?) On your first television series, you will probably spend a good deal of time on the phone to your agent trying to understand why you are not getting a penny for all this overtime you are putting in (your salary has bought out your overtime); if you are somewhat more seasoned, you may wonder why your character is relegated to the same predictable two scenes each week and you never really get to bring anything to the party. (The answer is, it's not your party.) (Unless it's your show.)

Let's go back to the excruciating part where you go to network and get the job. Let's assume you are in New York and you audition for a series that will shoot in Los Angeles (where most of them shoot – although currently over 50 series shoot on the East Coast). You read for the New York casting director. She puts you on tape. The tape is sent to LA and they (whoever they may be) like it and want to do a test deal for you. This is basically a contract for you to do the role on that show with all the details of that contract negotiated, by your agent, with input from your manager if you have one. Every clause of your contract is sealed shut before you even get on a plane for Los Angeles to test for the role. The contract will be for the next six and a half years of your life.

Sometimes, when the budget allows, the producer will come to New York to read actors before bringing them out to California. If the producer wants you to change anything in your reading, he can ask you to change it. If he only gets to see what you have done on tape in his office or a screening room back in LA, it had better be exactly what he is looking for because neither you nor he will be able to change it. There it is on tape. That's what you did and that's what you would do with this part. Could you do it any differently? No one will ever know. So you'd better nail it. How easy is that? Not too. But it happens.

Even if you have read for the producer in New York, you will still have to test in LA. That's where the suits are. The reason why you read for the producer of a pilot and not the director is that the director is usually hired to solely direct the pilot. Another director may well take over if the pilot takes off. You will have to pass muster with the show's top honchos: usually the producer or the creator or the show runner. It just won't be the director. Unless a super star director is directing the pilot. Then he or she will have some say. Chances are, one of the reasons he's a superstar director is his expertise in casting. Just the news that Jim Burrows cast you in a pilot makes you more valuable than you were yesterday.

Step By Step

Going to LA to test for a series has become a two-step process. The new step is your first day where you will meet with the studio honchos: the casting director, the writer, producer and director, possibly the studio executive on the show. This will be a relatively low-key meeting. You will audition and everyone will pray that you are what they imagined you were when they saw you on tape – not shorter, taller, weirder or somehow less appealing. They will also be looking to reassure themselves that you will not cause problems on set. That you are fun in the room. Then you will go back to your hotel. If anyone has taken major exception to you, your agent will be called and you will be sent home. Otherwise, the next day, you will "go to network."

You will walk into a conference room in the network's headquarters with anywhere from 12 to 25 seated people, most of whom you have never seen before and will never see again. There will be the folks from yesterday plus a large bunch of scary looking people who are much more afraid of whoever they are sitting next to than you are of any one of them.

None of them will have a sense of humor. Do not try and test the temperature of the room. The temperature of the room will be toxic. Say "hi," be pleasant and knock it out of the park when you read. Then, unless someone asks you something, thank them and leave. You will hear if you have gotten the job anywhere from 48 hours to a week later. Possibly the same day. The length of time you will have to wait will depend on how short a time your agent has been able to negotiate for them to make a decision and how much they loved you in the room.

If they were crazy for you, they will say so immediately and you will have a job. What are you going to do, hold them up for more money? Ha! Why do you think the deal has already been negotiated? On the not infrequent occasions when they are not so sure, you may have to wait out the negotiated time. If the network had their way, they would dither for weeks. They always expect some perfect person, some god-head, to appear at the last minute. And sometimes one does. Several years ago, a role on a pilot was virtually cast with a client of mine until a teenager got on a plane in Australia and came to Los Angeles to go to network for a now forgotten series called "Roar." That was Heath Ledger. He did a series? Everybody does a series. Brad Pitt did a series. Get over it. Do a series.

Actually Being On Television

So you got the job. What happens now? If the show is "ER," you will have a very good chance of becoming George Clooney. If it's "Frasier," you are on your way to becoming Kelsey Grammer (though wouldn't you rather be David Hyde Pierce?). If this is like most of the shows that parade in front of the networks each spring, the network will not buy it, the series will never be shot and you will look forward to your next audition. Maybe the network will want to postpone their decision and hold your show as a possible mid-season replacement. Then they will hold you (meaning you cannot do another pilot) until, say November, or December, maybe January, depending, yes, on what you agent was able to negotiate.

Let's say the pilot sold and the series was picked up. Is it all wine and roses from here on out? No. Actors have been fired from shows for bad behavior. Frequently. Characters have been reduced to walk-ons because the actor pissed off the wrong person. Actors have been replaced because the network *suspects* it's an actor's fault the entire show isn't working. Actors have walked away from series which made them household names convinced that they were now stars who would be forever in demand and watched their career slowly erode after that. Each of us could name a few of those. Sometimes an actor is just wrong for the part and should be fired – and is. That's a good reason to be fired. But no extra points for a good reason. In fact, no points at all. Fired means you are now out of work.

But let's say you don't get fired, you don't get replaced and you don't walk away. You are on a successful series. That is so great, I can't even tell you how great that is. Congratulations. Then your series doesn't get picked up for a second season. No, screw that. We're on a happy kick now. Your show does get picked up for a second season. What are you going to do on hiatus? Does your agent have a film lined up? Or are you one of these pure types – do you want to do a play? Have you got one waiting? You're on a hit. Any theatre in the country would want you. Have you made sure that will happen? Your agent's first choice would probably not be for you to do a play.

What do *you* want to do? Lie on the beach? Your agent would prefer that to your doing a play. At least, if you were lying on a beach and something came along for you that would mean some nice money, you would be *available*. But look, you can lie on the beach when you're dead. You've got a career to look after now. Do something. Act somewhere. Hasn't some eager beaver independent producer been trying to get you interested in a movie script? Do it.

When You Get There ... Stay There

Maybe you're not looking forward to the second season as much as you were to the first. Back then, everything was new, everything was exciting. No one told you the suits might step on some of your acting choices. They do that sometimes. They don't want anything too out there. What does 'out there' mean? Oh, it could mean anything that gets them negative mail. Anything that upsets their mothers. Anything their *wives* don't like. (Husbands, too.) And they will tell you that *someone* doesn't like what you are doing and you have to change it. You don't always have to cave into such requests, you know. (But mostly you do.)

A client of mine was on a series where he played a character who was rather fey. The actor, my client, was in fact gay though not in the least flamboyant in real life. But he had the notion to turn his character up a notch on the show. In fact, it wasn't long before the character had become a raging queen. My client liked having America see a character like that. He felt it was his calling from the history books to etch this character on the American consciousness. Plus he was having a ball.

The network was not having a ball. The network asked him to tone it down. He said he would but he didn't. He was having way too much fun and he was the kind of guy who didn't give a damn what anybody thought so long as he was being true to his art. At present, his art was telling him to play an out-there gay character on a sit-com. He wouldn't have been surprised or even objected if the network decided to fire him. He just didn't want to be told how to do his job. He had been around far too long and given in far too often to compromise the truthful portrayal of a character whom he felt was a big sissy and proud of it. He would not back down just because he was making people uncomfortable in Iowa.

Every week the network came to him and every week he promised to butch it up. Every week, come tape day, he was practically skipping across the set. The network went to the star to see if he could do anything. Well, the star loved my client and loved what he was doing with the character. And the star was a real screw-you kind of a guy who wasn't about to tell my client or any other performer how to act. He was the macho version of my client in the screw-you department. He was, in a word, a mensch. So the network started leaving my client alone and, in the end, they let him do whatever he wanted to do. The moral of the story is, if the star loves you, you can do what you want. The hard part will be to find a star who doesn't care what the higher-ups think – and who loves you. Or maybe you could *be* that star. My client did that show for five years, went on to do several more series, act in a boatload of movies and win a Tony. It could happen to you.

Until then, let someone else make the waves. I am not saying be a wimp or give up your principles or whatever else you are asked to give up. Just don't become a monster the minute you get a little bit of power. Be aware, when someone suggests a direction, a way of behaving, a press junket, an AIDS benefit, they are not really asking anything so unreasonable. Not everyone is trying to take advantage of you. You get a lot of perks being a well-known person.

To be an actor is not a ticket to a secret kingdom where you don't have to play by the rules. The reason there is so much bad behavior in show business is that no one tells young actors the rules. Too many people stand to make money from an emerging star for anyone to risk pissing him off by telling him how to behave. Always have people around you who will keep you real. Is that part of breaking into show business? You bet it is. You want to *stay* in show business, don't you?

William Shakespeare:

*"There are more things in heaven and earth, Horatio,
than are dreamt of in your philosophy."*

Dorothy Fields:

"Life can be so sweet on the sunny side of the street."

GOOD TO KNOW

Breakdowns

Breakdowns are exactly what they say they are: a breakdown of every project and every role that anybody in the business is trying to cast. These are available, updated each day, to all subscribers of Breakdown Services, and available online but not usually to actors directly. There is a description of the project and of each individual character that is being sought. What did people do before Breakdowns? Well, they worked harder. The best agents knew about the best jobs because they had access to and the trust of the best casting directors and producers. Casting directors weren't quite so important as they are today. They became more important because somebody had to separate all the wheat from the chaff and that, for all intents and purposes, was the casting director's job back then. Oh, they had to bring in appropriate actors for whatever the character they were casting was but they didn't have nearly the say in who gets chosen that they do today.

That privilege began with a wonderful woman named Marion Dougherty. She gave the casting profession the credibility it now has because she had extraordinarily good taste, she knew talent and she always cared about the whole project. The power she brought to her position remains: the taste with which she personally wielded that power does not. Or not necessarily. There are some great casting directors out there. There are some dolts, too.

Breakdowns make it possible for any fool to come along and say: What about so and so for such and such a part? What about my client? What about *me*? Today, many actors have (illegal) access to the Breakdowns. They read them and call their agents and ask if they could be submitted for some part they are perfect for or, if not quite perfect they could still do it in a heartbeat – if they were only given the chance. As if the agent hadn't already thought of them and submitted them.

Don't go quarterbacking your agent. I could wring a client's neck when he calls me about something on Breakdowns. You think you're right for a role? Why on earth wouldn't your agent think the same thing and submit you for it? Maybe you aren't really right for the role. The actor hasn't read the script (the agent should have) so he can't really see the character in the context of the whole story – and context can make all the difference in who is or is not right for a role. If I don't submit an actor who is right for something, what am I doing being his agent? I should be fired. Let me do my damn job. Are you really going to trust your agent with deciding *context*? Well, yeah. It's called trust. Today, many managers make those untrusting calls to the agents. Did you submit our Tracy for that new series regular on "Girls"? Yes, I suggested her last week when I was having lunch with the casting director. How come you didn't know about it then? I thought you were a manager!

IMDb Pro is a great website that will tell you who represents who, who works where, what projects are in development, what projects are close to being green lit or have been green lit. It gives you an overview of what is going on and therefore makes you feel a part of something that you may not actually yet *be* a part of. The very feeling of belonging is valuable so I think it's worthwhile. (It costs about a hundred bucks a year.) If you are not represented and you see a movie being made from a book you love, put yourself on tape doing a scene from the book and send it to the casting director. If there's a cool director involved, send a copy to him or her, too. Vera Farmiga got "The Departed" by putting herself on tape. Jesse Eisenberg got "The Social Network" the same way. They were not unknowns but they saw something they wanted and they went for it. Emma Stone *was* an unknown when she sent in an audition tape of her callback for "Easy A" (that tape is all over the internet, so you can watch it yourself and see how it's done).

Also see "Internet Resources for Actors" on page 356.

Social Media — Keep it Simple

Social media is highly touted as a means to advance one's career. And if you already have a career, that may be so. But to establish a career? Probably not.

You have about as much chance of going viral on YouTube as you do of winning the lottery. A few people do, sure. But only if they've got a really original idea with really great execution, or somewhat of a following in another form of media already. Still, it seems important to have a YouTube page, as that's often the easiest way to share necessary videos of yourself. If you're uploading a performance to your *Backstage* profile, or sending one of those self-taped auditions we are about to talk about, dealing with emailing or downloading large video files can be a pain both for yourself and the recipient (and, if it's too big of a pain for the recipient, they may not bother to open your video at all). YouTube is user-friendly, and you can make a video "private," so that only you and people you send the link to have access to it. That way, you don't have to worry about your 50-cent PC's video being compatible when the casting director downloads it on her shiny new Macbook. In short, learn how to use YouTube for business, but don't expect to get famous off it.

A few years ago you didn't dare show your head without a personal website. These days people sometimes find personal websites static, dead. You can't interact with them and people expect to interact. You can control what's there – 'Just landed a show in the fringe festival!' – but you will get better and faster results on Facebook. If you have done anything at all significant in the business, IMDb and IBDb and Playbill.com will have taken note of you and they will keep your credits current.

If you haven't done anything, neither Facebook nor Twitter will get you that first job. If you don't have a body of work – or even one piece of work – to promote, then what do you need with social media? Do you want to post a selfie of your hot bod on Instagram? Well, that's a different kind of show business.

Actors in LA have been known to get jobs over other actors because they have more followers on Twitter. That is not true in New York. But it may be next year. Or it may stop being true in Los Angeles.

Facebook is a terrific way of keeping your friends informed of what you are up to. Twitter is a terrific way of keeping anyone who's interested informed of what you are up to. Since Facebook forces you to confirm any connections, you have the power there to control your audience, and if I were you, I'd control it. Twitter is a different story – anyone who knows your name can follow you (unless you have implemented strict privacy controls, which is also possible). A few plays in New York may help you grow your number of followers to five or six hundred. Consider Twitter your practice for being in the public eye – tailor your posts accordingly. One guest lead on "CSI" could get you ten thousand followers overnight. Though if you have done a guest lead on "CSI," you are probably past needing this book.

Most young actors I know are active on Facebook for strictly professional reasons. If you do hit some sort of measurable success, either don't use Facebook for personal reasons, or keep your profile private. Do you want to post a picture of your mom and dad and your little sister backstage in your first Broadway dressing room? Do you really want people knowing what your mom and dad and your little sister look like? Not to imply that there are a lot of freaks out there ... but there are.

Facebook is great for telling people when you have gotten a job. It's not helpful *finding* jobs – except when it is. A young actor I know received an invitation via the net to receive breakdowns for two weeks for free after which he would have to pay. He saw nothing that he felt he would die if he didn't do. Except there was a Columbia grad school movie, for no pay, about a soldier recently returned from Iraq and this young actor had wanted to play a soldier ever since his first G.I. Joe. There was an actual casting director attached to the project. A fairly well known one. (Some of these Columbia kids have money to spread around – not that they give it to actors.) He didn't know anyone else connected with the project who was listed on the breakdown but he found the director on Facebook. He sent her a note telling her how passionate he was about playing a soldier and he sent her a tape of himself doing a monologue which he imagined might be similar to what was going on with the soldier in this student film. She wrote the young actor back how much she loved what he'd sent her; their final callbacks were the next day and he should come. She emailed him sides. He got the job: the film went to the South By Southwest Film Festival, won Best Short. The young actor won Best Actor and he got himself an agent. He didn't make a dime from the whole experience and, in fact, spent more than his savings to go to the SXSW Film Festival but I think we can say that his use of Facebook was helpful to his career. He tells me that celebrities mostly tweet but, for now, he's sticking with Facebook. (And Twitter sometimes.)

Keep it simple when it comes to social media. There are solid arguments for up-and-coming actors to keep a well-polished Facebook, Twitter, and maybe – *maybe* – an Instagram. That, plus your *Backstage* profile, is enough to keep up. There's no need to also spend hours updating your public YouTube page, SoundCloud, Snapchat, personal website, Vine, or whatever else will be having its moment by the time this book goes into circulation. It's just a waste of your energy. Why does any actor have a LinkedIn page? Has anyone ever gotten cast from LinkedIn? Nobody needs to see your extensive waitressing resume to cast you in a student film.

Awards – Get Over It, Sweetheart

Well, it's always awards season out there. You are fascinated by them. The media makes fascination unavoidable. Oscars, Emmys, Tonys, Golden Globes, SAG Awards, MTV Awards – the list is long. Awards are an extension of the marketing department of the entertainment industry. They have to do with the business. And perhaps with your Aunt Minnie who has never missed a red carpet.

Awards exist to sell products, and only incidentally to promote talent. Cary Grant never got an Oscar for Best Actor. He got an Honorary Oscar because The Academy was so embarrassed he never got a real one, they gave him a token of the industry's affection and hoped it would be enough. By that point, Cary Grant was not worried about how to break into show business. Leonardo DiCaprio finally has his Oscar but I have to say that his often-cited lack of one didn't seem to slow his career path even a little. You can still take comfort in fellow Oscar-less stars Annette Bening, Edward Norton or Sigourney Weaver. Or Johnny Depp or Samuel L. Jackson. Even Ralph Fiennes emerged from "Schindler's List" without an Oscar in sight. Catch my drift yet?

It's a very compelling fantasy: you win an award and overnight you are catapulted to the front ranks of American Actors. You will soon be hobnobbing with Meryl and Jack and Stephen and Francis and Scott and David and you will never have to worry about paying your rent again, ever. Four words for you: Get over it, sweetheart.

Awards are nice. I mean, they are. But they will not necessarily get you to where you want to go. If you are massively recognized and rewarded for something which doesn't make anybody a serious amount of money, you will probably have to be content to live on the prestige of your award and find other sources to pay your rent. A recent Tony winner for Best Supporting Actress (in a role for which she made near scale) will be following up that triumph by starring in a play at a not-for-profit theatre which will pay her less than half what she made for her supporting role on Broadway.

There is a nefarious urban legend trotted out from time to time that the Oscar for Best Supporting Actress comes with some kind of curse. People who would perpetrate this myth point out that the film careers of a large number of actresses came to a crashing halt after winning for Supporting Actress: Marisa Tomei, Mira Sorvino, Brenda Fricker, Jennifer Hudson, Mercedes Ruehl, Kim Bassinger. That is indeed a large number.

Personally, I suspect there are a number of other factors at work in the stalling of those careers that had nothing to do with a curse. And likely different in each case. Angelina Jolie was largely derided for going from the Academy Award for her supporting role in "Girl, Interrupted" to her monster starring role in "Lara Croft: Tomb Raider." Whereas Philip Seymour Hoffman was lauded for following "Capote" with "Mission Impossible III." But that's just plain old-fashioned sexism, not some curse. I urge you not to dwell too much on awards. Let the pundits have their fun. You concentrate on being brilliant.

Diversity

Can we talk about diversity for a second? These days it's actually pretty hard not to talk about diversity, especially in regards to awards. Recently, many high-profile celebrities have spoken out against, or even boycotted, the Oscars because of the lack of diversity. Didn't I just tell you not to think about awards because they're overrated? This is still worth talking about, anyway.

Years ago, there was an episode of a successful ninety-minute television show which the powers that be decided that for one episode, they would have a completely black guest cast. Every single person – who was not a series regular – would be someone of color. It was not a political statement. It was a stunt. It was meant to increase ratings. And be fun. And increase ratings. Well, the level of the acting on that episode, shall we say, left something to be desired. I watched it at Clarence Williams III's house. He wasn't in the guest cast. He was, that night, in addition to being a television star, a television viewer. The level of the talent we were watching on screen was at the very least disheartening. No one in our small group remarked on that, however. Then at 10:58 as the credits were rolling on the television screen, Terrence's phone rang. It was a black celebrity whose first words were, "Man, we're terrible. We gotta get us some good actors."

Over the years, I have represented a fairly large number of sublime African American actors. Cleavon Little was already famous when I came into his life. Cleavant Derricks is a wonder we don't hear too much about these days. Viola Davis took far too long to be recognized as the monumental talent she is. Idris Elba was sent to me by a British agent who said, "Don't be under the illusion that he's a star or anything. But he is useful." (Of course, the Brits are so busy looking down on each other, it's tough to see where the racism begins and the classism ends.) Terrence Howard had such a chip on his shoulder, it was hard to tell if anyone would ever get past that and just give him a job. I don't think I ever led Rosalind Chao to a role.

In my classes where there are now routinely several African American students (used to be none, then one or two, now a few to several), it is those kids who are the most fun to watch. It is those kids who just automatically know how to go deeper, to touch the pain, to find the funny. But make no mistake, the schools are still populated overwhelmingly by white students. I think if there were more African American teachers (there are woefully few) the schools might be turning out more and more exciting African American actors – who will still be competing for a finite (but growing) number of jobs. If this sounds like reverse racism, then I guess it may be but it doesn't pay off in more work for those talented students, I will tell you that much. In fact, I think the business has begrudgingly made the room it has made for people of color simply because there are so many of them who are so good and they need a showcase for their gifts if all the guys in offices are going to make any money off them.

Unfortunately, I don't think the same can be said of Asian actors. I can promise you that a sure way to heartbreak is to represent a gifted Asian or Asian American actor. There is almost no work. And color blind casting? Forget about it. I don't think much more than lip service was paid that concept when it was first introduced but at least it opened the door. I will say that. It started the conversation. A conversation which, if you ask me, has only just begun. For years, I have been asking students to imagine that they are agents and to create a Dream Client List. It is astounding to me the number of young people who can come up with a roster of actors they want to represent without one person of color on the list! Even back when I started at the management company, we had two African American clients (out of 35). One got a television series in very short order and one worked all the time in the theatre. I can't say I was paying a lot of attention to who was black and who was white. They all needed a job, and that was my charge.

What it comes down to is this: The entertainment industry, like many other industries in our nation, is run by rich white men. And it has been run by rich white men since the industry was first born. If it were just regular white men, it would be hard enough to squeeze some diversity in there. But throw a couple billion dollars into the mix and it's near impossible to break down those walls. In short, there's no instant fix to the diversity problem in Hollywood or on Broadway. There's no rule some union can pass that will make it all better. What it takes is people like you – the next generation of professionals – slowly but surely chipping away at that wall until it crumbles. So what are you waiting for? Go do it. Make your talent known. Make someone make a place for you.

Sentimental Value Doesn't Make Any Cents

There are some awards that have great sentimental value inside the theatre community, but they won't pay for your bus fare home from the reception. The Theatre World Awards, for instance, is a family-style ceremony where great actors of our time attend year after year. The Theatre World Awards, for debut New York performances, is often the first award anyone ever receives. But don't confuse genuine warm sentiment and praise from your peers with actual financial impact on your career. There is none.

Philip Seymour Hoffman's Academy award for *Capote*, which skyrocketed him to forever-fame and finally serious money, probably did a lot to bring attention to his career in the eyes of the public who may not have been aware of him until then. Everyone in the business already knew perfectly well who he was. Plus everyone in and out of the business who knew him at all was dying for Phil to be recognized and rewarded because they loved him. By that point, he had been around for fifteen years and there was a very long line of people who wanted to see him recognized for the genius he was. When you have been around for fifteen years without major recognition (i.e., a serious payday) maybe you will have some justification for pinning your hopes on an award. Although it was never really about the money for Phil. He really personified doing it for love. What other motivation could possibly explain *Synecdoche, New York*?

I represented a brilliant actor named Owen Teale who won the TONY for Best Actor in a play. As his contract with the play was coming to an end, I was shopping him around like a madman all over LA. No one was rising to the bait. "He won a damn TONY!" was my inelegant rebuttal to the army of those who refused to see him. Finally someone with an ounce of compassion said to me, "Philip, nobody out here gives a crap about the TONYs." And, you know, they really don't.

With that in mind, let's examine how you can get them to give a crap about you.

Self-Taping And Self-Starting

Self-taping is, if for no other reason than what it did for Vera Farmiga and Jesse Eisenberg and Emma Stone, an option to be reckoned with. They took the initiative – what's stopping you?

Technology changes hourly and what is true today will certainly not be true in a month. As little as a year ago, people used to self-tape with a flip cam and today they don't even make flip cams anymore. A process that used to take hours on a flip cam can now be accomplished in minutes on an iPad or an iPhone. Now you can even do live self-taping via Skype. That's how Jennifer Lawrence got her role in *Silver Linings Playbook*, which in turn got her an Oscar. The lord above – and maybe Steven Spielberg – knows what will be the method of choice a year or five from now.

But the *idea* of self-taping is here to stay. So what is it? It's very simple. You put yourself on tape with some sides from the script. Either (ideally) at your agent's request or (and there is much to be said for this) at the urging of your own inner voice which tells you how right you are for this part because, somehow or other, you get hold of the sides and, man, you know you can kill with this part.

The pros are, you can do it as many times as you need to do it to be satisfied with what you have done. The cons are that if you are close to what they are looking for but need a piece of direction to get closer, there is no one from the production in your living room to give you that piece of direction.

Still, safe to say, get an iPad or an iPhone and get yourself conversant with some serious on-camera technique. Marcia DeBonis and Amy Christopher are excellent at helping actors chart their course on film. There are others.

Just technically – tape against as neutral a backdrop as you can find. A brick wall looks like a prison, or a high school (is there a difference?). Paintings on the wall can be unnecessarily intriguing. Find something simple and unadorned. Wear something that is vaguely, not aggressively, right for the role. The wardrobe shouldn't be more interesting than you. Start with a full body shot and zoom into your head and shoulders. While the camera is doing that, introduce yourself and say what you'll be doing.

"Hi, I'm Phil Carlson. I'm going to be reading for Professor Higgins."

Remember they will be judging you starting at "Hi." Do not let this intimidate you. Simply be aware. Let their scrutiny relax you. Let it turn you on. Make sure the person who is reading with you (off-camera) is a good actor and of the appropriate sex. Make sure they don't act up a storm – this is *your* audition. Why does it matter that they be a good actor? Because if they are not, it will look amateurish. We just don't want them to be *too* good. When you are done, you can say thank you. You can say something you'd like to say. Don't be cute. Be adorable. What's the difference? Oh, come on.

Vera Farmiga and Jesse Eisenberg and the young gentleman who contacted that director via Facebook all have one thing in common: they took their careers into their own hands, when it was appropriate and when their instincts led them to do so. What did I say before? No one works better for you than you. And if you are going to work for you, you are going to need to devise yourself a road map.

For next time, let's put it all together. Bring in that map – an organized career plan. Take out your binoculars. Look way down that winding road. A five year plan, if you will. You do not have to rigidly adhere to what you propose for yourself. If, in your second year in the business, you have your sights set on landing a guest role on a television series and you are offered a nine month tour of the world doing two Shakespeare plays in Rep (sounds like The Bridge Company to me), you will, of course, take the world tour. On the other hand, if you are set to understudy on Broadway and you get the chance to test for a pilot which shoots in LA and the Broadway producers will not let you out of your contract, you will, naturally, give notice on the play immediately. This does not make you a superficial person always chasing after the easy buck. (First of all, there is nothing easy about shooting a pilot.) No, it means that the Broadway producers are bullies who need to recognize that other people have priorities, too, and that's why they have outs on theatrical contracts. So develop a plan.

Steps must be taken. What steps shall they be? In what direction? Planning month by month how you will attack your first five years is one approach. But you may also break down your assignments, tactics, and goals by year. Let me give you an idea:

Year 1

Get a killer 8x10.

Find an apartment. Make sure it has a sublet clause. (You may get a job out of town.)

Find a job with flexible hours. Do not tell your agent that a time is bad for you when you are given an audition. *Never* tell your agent that a time is bad when you get a callback.

Find a professional acting class.

Locate at least three reputable coaches you like and trust.

Identify all small theatre companies in New York that are relatively new. (Bushwick Starr, Strange Men & Co., Transport Group, etc.)

See at least one play at each of those companies.

Meet the Artistic Director or the General Manager (if they have one) or whoever is the appropriate person at each theatre you felt did good work.

Identify all small theatre companies that have been around a while. (Pearl, Cherry Lane, The York, Abingdon, etc.) See at least one show at each theatre, find out who casts for them, meet and audition for that person.

Identify all LORT houses in NYC (Lincoln Center, Roundabout, Manhattan Theatre Club, The Public Theatre, Playwrights Horizons, Second Stage, there's a bunch of them).

Find out when they hold open auditions (which they have to do – as per the union, see their plays, write their casting directors, always offer to be a reader).

Get Up To Date Theatricals (agents, casting directors, theatres).

Get a *Backstage* account and set up your online profile. You can put your resume on there, your headshot, reels, vocal recordings, and more. Try to audition for *everything* that you are right for. Every week.

See everything off-Broadway. (Offer to usher.)

Second-act Broadway shows. (Not the cakewalk it used to be but doable sometimes). If you're willing to shell out a little change, hang on to your college student ID – box offices will believe that for at least another 2 to 3 years, and you'll be able to get student rush tickets.

Identify all LORT houses across the country. Find out who their New York casting directors are. Meet them. Find out their seasons. Get an audition for anything you are right for. Work at one of them. (Oh, you can't promise? You'd better!)

Work on a monologue every day. Get a new one every two months.

Audition for every tiny theatre you can find. Do everything you are cast in, even if there are maniacs in charge. (You think maniacs are not in charge on Broadway or in studio movies?)

Do NYU and Columbia (and anywhere else) student films. Make sure you get a copy of the finished film.

Year 2

Identify the New York heads of casting at all the Networks. Meet at least someone in their department.

Identify every independent casting director who casts for TV in New York and meet them or meet someone in their office.

Do at least one TV show. (Do it!)

Year 3

Identify every casting director in New York who does movies and meet them or someone in their office.

Do at least one movie.

Get cast in a good theatre in town.

Year 4

Do a pilot.

Do a Broadway show.

Year 5

Win an OBIE.

Do a great part in an independent film.

Do a studio film.

Got it? Great.

If the above seems to set too slow a pace for you, pick up the pace. If adding personal goals makes it more real for you, do that. Your personal life needs to be on a growth curve too. I had a student once who had "Fall in love with someone nice, funny, creative and pretty" on his list. That same student put down "Spend my first Christmas and New Years in the city." In his second year he had "Go home for Christmas." I asked him why each of those choices were important to him, especially as I didn't understand the order. I mean, go back home your first year away from home, right? Wrong. He replied that in his first year on his own, it was important to him to set down roots, establish that he was a grownup and New York was now his home. In his second year, because of what he imagined would be the demands of his career, he could never be absolutely certain he would be able to go home for Christmas again and he wanted to make this commitment to his family. This actor could *see* his career – and I promise you, he will have one.

Are we all lit? Let's get a career. See you next week!

Lloyd Richards, director, teacher, icon:

" ... I've done really what I wanted to do. Some things could have been better. There were all kinds of constraints – of time, of money and of space – but not the constraints of thought, imagination, or artistry. I've been able to follow through on impulse."

WORKSHOP EIGHT:
Next Stop – Your Career

You were asked to map out a plan for your first five years as an actor. This usually brings delightful surprises – both to me and to you — in uncovering how one goes about actually becoming a part of the profession. If only because it has never occurred to many people in your situation that you will have to actually *do* something. And as usual in our travels, we will discover that it doesn't matter so much what you do as it matters that you do *something*. Steps must be taken. What steps shall they be? Planning month by month how you will attack your first five years is not necessary, though I had a student do so once. But a single sentence such as "I will be king of the world," also done once, isn't going to cut it either.

Now that you've eavesdropped on all of our workshops, I would like to invite you, the reader, to create your own. The important part of this exercise is not so much what you say you will do, but that you will discover the need – and indeed the joy – of having a list of things you can actually *do* to help your career.

I firmly believe that all the points I touched on in the sample are essential for your first five years. You may disagree. You may have other choices, other plans. I had an acting teacher (very old school) who told us all that we had to visit every serious tourist attraction in New York. Why? Because he felt it was necessary to know what made a city the city it was and what made an epoch an epoch in order to act in anything that might be characterized as a period play. By which he meant anything taking place more than ten years ago. Well, that sounds a bit ... extreme. But he believed it with all his heart and soul. And he taught Sidney Poitier and Barbara Loden, so we know he was a good acting teacher. He also insisted we learn a foreign language. And a musical instrument. One of us actually did, and he founded a theatre company which still exists today. Worked for him.

I would ask you now to put down the book, pick up a pad of yellow legal-sized paper (it doesn't have to be yellow) and chart out your first five years in show business.

Did anyone actually do it? You did? I will love you forever. I will give you a free lifetime pass to Grant's tomb. But for those of you who did not do as I so respectfully asked you to do, why don't we hear one last time from Ms. Harris and learn what her plan of attack might be. Miss Harris? I know you would prefer not to but I insist.

Ms. Harris: Well, first of all, I would do everything Mr. Carlson suggests. In addition, my mother's best friend is a big deal real estate agent in town so I thought I could ask her if she could help me find an affordable apartment. I'd be prepared to have a roommate for the first year. After that, no.

I've been looking through my friend's headshots and researching online. I found three photographers whose work I like and who are affordable. I'm going to meet with each of them.

I'm going to make an appointment with a personal shopper at Barney's, Bergdorf's, and Bloomingdales. Obviously, I can't afford a personal shopper, but I figure if I look and act enough like I could, they will all give me a meeting and, I hope, some clues about how they think I should dress.

I'm going to find out who does Rita Wilson's hair, since we have kind of the same texture and hers always looks great. I'll splurge for one haircut at that salon and absorb as many tips and tricks from the stylist as I can. Maybe I'll do that on the way to getting my headshots taken. Then I'll be able to go somewhere cheap every other time, and tell them exactly what I want done.

I'm going to subscribe to New York Theatre Workshop. I think my parents would pay for that. Then I'll go to all their opening nights. I will meet their casting director or die trying.

I'll also get a year's subscription to *Backstage*. And IMDbPro. I know I'm racking up a long bill here, but I can split those subscriptions with some friends.

Lastly, I know a Pilates studio where lots of actors go. Some famous ones.

Mr. Zawadski: Where is it?

Ms. Harris: Wouldn't you like to know?

Ms. Harris, I am enjoying your presentation and somehow imagine that you will be working as an actor before too long. As you know, I am not a fan of your headshot. Are you getting a new one?

Ms. Harris: Not until I settle on a hairstyle.

This young woman says everything right. I would watch out for her. Especially if I were another young woman. Thank you, Ms. Harris, for what you have told us of your plans. Since you have already demonstrated to us your ability to be assertive when you improvised being an agent and just this moment your ability to make strong and clever choices for yourself, I feel compelled to point out to you that this continued mask of demureness does not serve you. Time after time you wait for an invitation to show yourself. Such false modesty does not serve you. Ambivalence will not intrigue the people you need on your side. It will turn them off. You are a fascinating young woman. Let me see you.

I am going to stop you here, stop all of you, in fact, for if you have truly thought about and done this exercise, you have derived from it all there is to derive. You now have to put your plans into action.

Above all, and I cannot say this enough: Go to the theatre. Go to movies. Watch television. Learn the tone of each show that shoots in New York. Know the name of every casting director of every show that shoots in New York. Find roles you might be able to understudy (and actually get cast in when the play is done at the regional theatres). Know everything that is going on. *Feel* like you are a part of this business. What would make you feel more like a part of this business? Yeah, I know, a job. Well, get one.

Unions

Any lingering questions? No, I haven't said anything about joining the unions. When you get a union job, you will join the union. In thirty-two years of representing actors, I was never once asked if a client was a member of the union. I realize that before you have an agent you have to be a union member to gain admittance to some auditions. If it's so all-fired important to you, crash the audition. How? You're an actor, are you not?

There are two actors' unions: SAG-AFTRA (formerly SAG, The Screen Actors' Guild, and AFTRA, The American Federation of Radio and Television Artists, that have now merged) and AEA (Actors' Equity Association).

The SAG half of SAG-AFTRA has province over film, and AFTRA deals with taped and live television. Some television series used to be shot under the aegis of SAG and some (even though they were on film and not tape) were under AFTRA. SAG's terms were much more favorable to actors; thus, their membership resisted merging the two. Now that they have joined, a period of adjustment has ensued.

The unions have always felt that agents have no business producing projects which would put them in a conflict of interest situation with their clients, some of whom might be right for a project and others of whom might not. Who is to say? Certainly not the agent – who might go and hire an actor from another agency. That wouldn't be fair, would it? Fair? In show business? Why not just make the whole idea illegal? So they did. Managers – since they answer to no union – were allowed to produce and agents were not.

Joining SAG-AFTRA will set you back $3,000 initially and $201 annually. AEA is $1100 and $118 annually. You will become eligible for health care under SAG-AFTRA once your income as an actor in that union reaches $15,100. Should you make it to being a senior citizen and still be an actor, $600 a year will get you all the health care you need – which they will simply deduct from your pension. AEA's health care kicks in after eleven weeks of employment. This will qualify you for six months of health care for which you will still pay $100 a quarter. It's a good deal. The trick is getting those initial eleven weeks of employment.

I have to say I feel that the unions and their rules and their machinations and their doings are a matter of complete disinterest to me. In fact, I did a three-picture deal for a client with a business affairs attorney who was chagrined beyond words to have given me a million and a half for the third picture for an actor who he discovered had yet to join SAG. (That was sweet.)

There are some theatre auditions which require a union card to get into. Film and television auditions, which are almost impossible to get without an agent, require no such proof of worthiness.

There are theatres – and even schools – which offer acting courses or apprenticeships, the completion of which will give the beginning actor a certain number of points which will get them closer to being eligible to join Equity. I would remind you, though, that this means you would pay $1100 to join a union that allows you to become eligible to audition for parts that an agent can send you on for free (or that you could just get into with a little ingenuity and determination). Every year or so someone lands a plum role from an open call and so the legend of it being worthwhile to audition at some cattle call which required a union card to get into is kept alive. Shanice Williams was cast as Dorothy in the live television production of "The Wiz" from an open call which required *no* union card. (That's why Bernie Telsey's office is such a good casting office.)

If you want to be an actor, and possibly even a star, I suggest you keep auditioning for everything you are conceivably right for and pound on every agent's door until you find one who wants to work for you.

As a final note, thanks to the Taft-Hartley act, you're allowed to work on one union job without having to join the union overseeing that job. This means one role on a television show or in a movie. If we are talking about a play, you can work on that play for up to a month before you will be required to join AEA.

I Wish You Smooth Sailing

To quote the shrink at the end of *Portnoy's Complaint*, "Now vee may perhaps to begin. Yes?" What are the training and the prototypes and the head shots and the gym trips all *for* if not for the chance to finally get to act? I have tried to demystify the process. When young actors first move to New York they very naturally make mistakes. I have tried to point out that mistakes are a part of it all. No mistake is irrevocable and, in fact, the more mistakes you make, the more you are likely to learn. You are the final arbiter of all things having to do with you. It is OK to be a beginner. A beginner is someone who has begun. Do so, please.

At the beginning of your career and always, your own ambition is your best friend in the world. And necessary to your ultimate success.

You have to *use* that ambition. It is not enough to just *have* it. At the opening night party for your best friend's play, you have to go up to the director and tell him how much you liked the play and how much you hope to work with him some day. Some day not too far from now. Don't say what you don't believe but know enough to know what to believe. You have to tell the casting director at the audition that when she found Ed Norton for "Primal Fear" it was the single greatest piece of casting in the history of movies. You are in awe. So be a little bit in awe. That casting director is proud of having found Ed Norton (and she should be). Why not give her a compliment? Sooner or later, someone will find you. What I am saying is, why not sooner?

I'm not saying be a suck-up. Does it sound like that's what I'm saying? I am saying know what the people you are meeting have done. If you are auditioning for Sam Gold, tell him that "Look Back in Anger" shook you to your bones. That's not sucking-up. It shook me to *my* bones. Tell David Fincher you saw "The Social Network" five times. I saw it six. Doing proper research on people you meet is using your ambition in a good and helpful way. Since you have no idea what the people you will be meeting are actually looking for, learn how to convince yourself, really convince yourself, that they are looking for you. If they didn't hope you were right for this part, they wouldn't be seeing you. Do not talk about it. Do not tell them how much you have thought about what you would do with this part. There is a certain kind of actor, usually an intelligent one, who feels the need to explain why they are right for a role. Do not explain. Just be right for the role.

I am not suggesting that there is a conspiracy to keep actors from expressing opinions. However, when an actor comes along who has the wordless conviction that he is the answer to your casting problem, that actor stands a very, very fair chance of being heard. And hired.

So you've had your showcase and you didn't get an agent. What do you do now? You get to work.

INTERNET RESOURCES FOR ACTORS

CASTING NOTICES

Playbill.com

Playbill has a section called "Playbill Jobs" which has casting calls for actors, both union and non-union, as well as other theater industry jobs for designers, directors, choreographers, and offices. A few recruiting agencies have caught on to this, and will also post non-arts industry jobs that are actor-friendly and support the sometimes spontaneous schedule changes that come with a career as a performer. It's basically your one-stop site for everything.

Backstage.com

Backstage.com is the online evolution of the old fashioned Backstage Magazine, and has become the number one spot for performing jobs. Here, you have the ability to make a profile with your headshot, resume, reels and recordings. Not only can you search through casting calls, but casting directors can search for actors that meet their needs and reach out to you directly.

ActorsAccess.com

Actors' Access is another Backstage-type site where you can create a profile and apply to casting notices.

ActorsEquity.org

Actors' Equity is, of course, the union that many stage and screen actors belong to. Their website posts casting notices for Equity actors only.

Mandy.com

Mandy.com is a casting website exclusively for film and TV roles and projects.

Lastly, check out the digital boards on local **university film department websites** for student films.

INFORMATION AND EDUCATION

IMDB.com

IMDB is the best place to research industry professionals, get film and television history, and see what your favorite actors and directors are up to next.

EverythingActingPodcast.com

Everything Acting is a podcast in which each episode includes casting directors, producers, actors, directors, and more talking about the actors' journey whether in film, theater, or TV. You can always listen to the most recent episode on their website, or hear all the episodes by purchasing their App.

The New York Public Library

The Library's app has access to audio of Shakespeare and other texts.

Rehearsal 2

This app is the answer to all actors who lose their scripts. You can easily upload scripts to the app, then highlight and leave comments on them in the form of text, photos, or videos. There's also "Blackout" mode, in which the app will black out all of your lines to help you learn them. Or, you can audio record your scenes to listen to them instead. It does require a fee to use, and you can download the app at RehearsalTheApp.com.

PAY-TO-PLAY

This is an app that allows you to buy acting classes and workshops from a number of different venues all in one place, including:

One on One NYC

Paul Michael's the Network

Actor's Connection

Actor's Insite

MailChimp

You can make a free account on MailChimp and add the email address of any industry contacts you make, then keep them up to date on what you're doing by sending out professional e-blasts.

AFFORDABLE THEATER TICKETS

TodayTix

You need to download the app on your phone to use TodayTix, which offers discounted tickets to performances the day of or within the next few days.

Goldstar.com

Goldstar has cheap tickets to Broadway, off-Broadway, and Regional theater shows.

TDF.org

The Theater Development Fund offers discount tickets to all union members, or you can head to the TKTS booth in Times Square for discount day-of tickets.

BroadwayForBrokePeople.com

This site has instructions on how to get rush or lottery tickets (usually $20-$40) for every show playing on Broadway.

ESSENTIAL FILM PERFORMANCES FOR ACTORS

"The Life of Emile Zola"
Muni is great, Schildkraut is greater.

"Alexander Nevsky" and "Ivan the Terrible" Parts 1 & 2
These silent Russian classics all starring Nikolai Cherkasov are a staggering lesson in size, in going as far as you can, in sheer passion.

"The Passion of Joan of Arc" directed by Carl Dreyer.
Falconetti, directed by Bergman's mentor Dryer, is every inch a match for Cherkasov in   power. Just magnificent.

"The Spy Who Came in for the Cold" with Oskar Werner.
Anything with Oskar Werner. Does anyone *listen* as humanly as he? Not even Tracy.
(See him with Simone Signoret in "Ship of Fools.")

"Inherit the Wind"
Speaking of Spencer Tracy. Check out Frederic March while you're at it.

"On the Waterfront"
Brando. Brando. Brando. Also everybody else.

"A Streetcar Named Desire"
Ditto Brando. Ditto everybody else.

"Midnight Cowboy"
Voigt is superb and Dustin Hoffman just goes into the stratosphere. Everybody else is first rate. You forget how strong actors used to be.

"Scent of a Woman"
    Philip Seymour Hoffman becomes a star.

"La Strada"
    Gulietta Masina and Anthony Quinn are the first and last
    word in greatness.

While in Italy, watch Anna Magnani stroll in "Mamma Roma"
    and run in "Open City."

"Sunday Bloody Sunday"
    Glenda Jackson and Peter Finch rule. And Peggy Ashcroft
    gives a five minute performance you will remember forever
    and she does nothing.

"The Duelists"
    Yes, that's Albert Finney inside all that makeup. Anything
    with Finney.

"The Entertainer"
    Well, it was Olivier's favorite.

"The Man Who Played God"
    Bette Davis's big break. Anything with Bette Davis is
    essential but this has the added benefit of George Arliss
    or, as he came to be billed, *Mr.* George Arliss.

"Summertime"
    And, yes, Katherine Hepburn could act and here she does
    so wonderfully.

"Tender Mercies"
    How does Robert Duval *do* it?

"Hamlet" with Christopher Plummer
> This can be found though it may take some doing.

"Sweet Bird of Youth"
> Geraldine Page is a cabaret, old chum.

"The Whisperer"
> Dame May Whitty. Ah. Great acting.

"The Private Life of Henry VIII"
> Was Charles Laughton ever less than completely memorable?

"The Young Lions"
> Here you get Montgomery Clift *and* Brando.

"The Ugly American"
> My personal Brando favorite.

"Topper"
> No one was ever funnier than Roland Young. OK, maybe Edward Everett Horton. Definitely Margaret Rutherford. Oh, and Alastair Sim.

"The Champ" with Jackie Cooper
> One of the all time best acting performances.

"East of Eden"
> James Dean was a god of sorts. And let Lois Smith break your heart while you're at it. And everybody else.

"North by Northwest"
> Cary Grant simply grabs the screen and never lets go. What a lesson he is.

"The Charge of the Light Brigade"
> The remake directed by Tony Richardson. Gielgud is masterful. So is everyone else.

Four phone conversations that define the art form: Dianne Weist on the phone at the top of "A Guide to Recognizing Your Saints;" Colin Firth on the phone at the top of "A Single Man;" Liza Minnelli (yes, Liza Minnelli) in a phone booth in "The Sterile Cuckoo" (it was the first scene she shot on her first day on a film.) And you'll never forget Al Pacino in "Dog Day Afternoon."

"The Liberation of L. B. Jones"
> Not nearly enough people know of the genius of Roscoe Lee Browne.

"To Kill a Mockingbird"
> For Gregory Peck, etc., and a look at what a director (Robert Mulligan) and producer (Alan J. Pakula) could elicit from kids. Not to mention it's Duvall's first movie.

"Klute"
> Jane Fonda under the direction of Alan J. Pakula. Keep your eyes open for Jean Stapleton, perfect in a one-scene cameo. It only takes a moment.

"Lincoln" with Daniel Day Lewis
> Daniel Day Lewis lived in a log cabin for months to prepare for the role. The least you can do is watch the film. Bathe in "There Will Be Blood" while you're at it.

"Foxcatcher"

> We've mentioned actors who aren't funny getting cast in comedies. But what about actors who *are* known for being funny? How do they get their footing in dramas? If you haven't seen "The Office" (though I don't know how you could have avoided seeing "The Office" at this point), watch an episode before you watch *Foxcatcher.* Steve Carell will show you how it's done.

Liv Ullman and Erland Josephson together in "Scenes from a Marriage."

The ensemble work in Mike Leigh's films.

Michael Fassbender in "Hunger."

Penelope Cruz in "Volver."

Julie Christie in "Away From Her."

Felicity Huffman in "Transamerica."

Kevin Corrigan in "Goodfellas," yes, but check out "Big Fan."
> Why is this guy not major? His talent is.

Bradley Cooper in "American Sniper." This Hollywood movie star is a great actor.

> And so on.

ACKNOWLEDGMENTS

J. Michael Miller who is godfather to this book.

Glenn Young, a publisher and editor with an elegant mind and a gentleman with a gracious heart. And Danielle DeMatteo, Glenn's stealth-like and tireless assistant.

I would also like to express gratitude to the following supporters, readers and generally helpful people:

Judy Dennis

Ron Van Lieu

Ray Dooley

Mark Jenkins

Jed Diamond

Mark Schlegel

Sarah Fargo

James Francis Ginty

Alex Birnie

Jonny Orsini

Jason Ralph

Steven Hart

Susan Ginsburg

Julia Lord

Beth Dixon

Kevin O'Rourke

Beth Teitelman

Photo credit: Lear Levin

PHILIP CARLSON represented actors for over thirty years. He was sustained during that entire time by the most glorious woman who ever lived, his wife Leslie Revsin. He currently lives in New York City with his plants and some quite nice art.

PHIL has taught at NYU and at SUNY Purchase and is currently on the faculty of The Atlantic Acting School. He has taught, and lectured at ACT Theatre School in San Francisco, The Juilliard School, Vassar College, The University of Washington, Emerson College, Dean College, Fordham University, The University of Tennessee and Hamilton College.

He was the New York head of talent at three of the most prestigious agencies in the business